HANS KÜNG – His Work and His Way

Dr Hermann Häring, born in 1937, is Academic Counsellor at the Institute for Ecumenical Research at the University of Tübingen. He gained his doctorate in theology with a thesis on "Church and Kerygma: The image of the Church in the Bultmann School", and has just published an advanced thesis on "The power of evil: The Augustinian Heritage".

Dr Karl-Josef Kuschel, born in 1948, is Scientific Adviser at the Institute for Ecumenical Research at the University of Tübingen. He gained his doctorate in theology with a study on "Jesus in Contemporary German Literature", and is now working on an advanced thesis on "The Pre-existence of Christ".

HANS KÜNG
His Work and His Way

Edited by HERMANN HÄRING and
KARL-JOSEF KUSCHEL
Bibliography by MARGRET GENTNER

Translated by Robert Nowell

Collins
FOUNT PAPERBACKS

First published as HANS KÜNG – Weg und Werk, by
R. Piper & Co. Verlag, Munich, 1978
First published in English by
Fount Paperbacks, London, 1979
© R. Piper & Co. Verlag, München 1978
© English translation
William Collins Sons & Co Ltd, Glasgow, 1979

Made and printed in Great Britain by
William Collins Sons & Co Ltd, Glasgow

Contents

Passages marked ** were not translated by Robert Nowell.

Foreword: Who is Hans Küng?

The aim of this book is to help people to get better acquainted with one of the most controversial figures of the post-conciliar Church: the Swiss Catholic theologian Hans Küng. Educated in Rome under Pius XII in the strictest traditions of Counter-Reformation Catholicism, under John XXIII he shared in shaping the revolution brought about by Vatican II, and under Paul VI he increasingly became one of the leaders of what can perhaps best be described as His Holiness's loyal opposition. Without wishing to, he represents for many people something like a one-man embodiment of democracy within the Church. His writings are read both inside and outside the Catholic Church. Nevertheless, though many people know *of* him, only a few know him. There are many stereotypes in circulation about him, both positive and negative, but only a few know what he is really thinking and what he really wants. There is hardly a theologian of the post-war era who has affected public opinion so strongly while at the same time polarizing it to the extent that Hans Küng has through his conflict with the official Catholic Church. His public statements challenge others to make their position clear, whether for or against, both at home and abroad. And there is hardly any other modern theologian who is the recipient both of such enthusiastic approval and aggressive rejection at virtually the same time.

The aim of this book is to sketch a portrait of this theologian, to outline the basic characteristics both of his work and of the man himself, and to indicate what has been constant and what has changed in his development. For many people in the Church and throughout the world, Hans Küng may be a contradictory figure – too critical for some, not critical enough for others; too Catholic still for some, by others long since regarded as no longer Catholic; for some too religious, for others too crudely outspoken. Yet he is at one and the same time a theologian and a scholar, a pastoral worker and a writer, a preacher and a professor, a priest and a controversialist, a Catholic and an ecumenist. How does all this fit together? How does he see himself? Who has he been influenced by? What people has he met? What has left its lasting stamp on him?

Through the media of essays, an interview and documentation, this book hopes to provide neither more nor less than an introduction: an introduction to a body of work that, thanks to the abundance of publications, both brief and lengthy, becomes increasingly difficult even for theologians to grasp, and that at first sight appears marked by a bewildering diversity. It contains scholarly analyses alongside devotional writings, polemical writings alongside meditations, popular theological works alongside those that can be thought of as "heavy", appeals to public opinion alongside sermons delivered in church. What is the connecting thread that runs through all this? What are the themes of his teaching, writing and actions?

The book consists of four parts. The aim of the chronological summary is to enable the reader quickly and easily to grasp the pattern of Hans Küng's life and work. It is set out on facing pages, with data about his life and work on the left-hand page, and on the right-hand one key events in the history of the Church and the world at that time, plus the basic elements in Hans Küng's conflict with the official Church. The sharp contrast between the two pages in various places was not intended but is unavoidable. The essays have been selected in order to provide an introduction to Hans Küng's major writings, and they have been chosen purely from this point of view: it was not intended to compile a volume which not only discusses his theology but also includes the various kinds of criticism that he has encountered. Collections of this kind are already available in German in *The Church* (edited by H. Häring and J. Nolte), and in *Infallible? An Enquiry* (edited by Hans Küng). Nor is it the intention of this volume to document the effect of Hans Küng's work and the reactions to it. The sole function of these essays is to introduce the book in question to a reader unfamiliar with it and to give a critical account of its contents, so as to encourage the reader to go on to read the work for him- or herself. The purpose of the interview is to give Hans Küng himself the opportunity to speak on questions connected with his development, on the background to his work, and on how he sees himself both as a theologian and as a member of the Church. Finally, there is a bibliography which for the first time provides a complete documentation of all Hans Küng's publications on the most diverse subjects and which will surely become an invaluable source for future work on Hans Küng and his theology. An appendix provides a statement of the first fourteen years of work of the University of Tübingen's Institute for Ecumenical Research, of which Hans Küng is director. This reports on the Institute's objectives, activity and achievements.

In this way the purpose of this book is to make a provisional assessment in a year during which Hans Küng can look back on thirty years' work in theology and the Church. And we are sure the reader will not mind if there is also a very personal element involved in this, since this book is also meant to be a small token of gratitude from pupils to their master, from staff to their "boss", an expression of thanks from those who for many years have in a spirit of critical loyalty joined with him in treading the often difficult path of the renewal of theology and the Church, and who have shared with him in both success and disappointment. Not the least of the aims of this book is that it is also meant to be a modest present for Hans Küng on his fiftieth birthday.

Tübingen
19 March 1978

Hermann Häring
Karl-Josef Kuschel

A. Chronological Summary 1928-1978

CHRONOLOGICAL SUMMARY

(Books are listed under their English titles at the date of their first publication in German, even though the English translation may have appeared some time later. Books listed with the title in German and an English translation in brackets have not yet appeared in English.)

1928 Born at Sursee, in the canton of Lucerne, Switzerland, 19 March.

1948 Matura (school-leaving certificate) at the cantonal *Gymnasium* in Lucerne. Enters the Germanicum college in Rome.

1948–1951 Study of philosophy at the Gregorian.

Strict training according to the pattern of a Tridentine seminary – the model for which was the Germanicum founded by Ignatius of Loyola and run by the Jesuits. Intensive education in the spirit of neo-Thomism.

Influential teachers: René Arnou (natural theology), Alois Naber (history of philosophy), Gustav A. Wetter (dialectical materialism). Tutors at the Germanicum: Emerich Coreth, Walter Kern.

Throughout his entire time in Rome strongly influenced in the fields of philosophy, theology and spirituality by the then spiritual director of the Germanicum, Fr Wilhelm Klein.

1951 Licentiate of philosophy (dissertation on the atheist humanism of Jean-Paul Sartre, supervised by Alois Naber).

1951–1955 Study of theology at the Gregorian.

Influential teachers: Sebastian Tromp and Timotheus Zapelena (fundamental theology), Juan Alfaro and Maurizio Flick (dogmatics), Franz Hürth (moral theology), Gustav Gundlach (social teaching), Stanislas Lyonnet (Pontifical Biblical Institute). Along with the Jesuit Augustin Bea and Robert Leiber, Pius XII's private secretary, and others who frequented the Germanicum, Tromp, Hürth and Gundlach were among the Pope's most influential advisers. Influenced by meeting Joseph Lortz (the Catholic historian of the

1928 Pius XI's encyclical *Mortalium animos* directed against the ecumenical movement.

1939 Election of Eugenio Pacelli as Pope Pius XII (1939–58).

1948 First plenary assembly of the World Council of Churches held at Amsterdam.

1949 Visitation of the Germanicum by Fr Augustin Bea, S.J., rector of the Pontifical Biblical Institute and Pius XII's confessor, and later to become a cardinal and first president of the Secretariat for Christian Unity.

1950 Holy Year, proclaimed by Pius XII.

Proclamation of the Assumption as a dogma.

Encyclical *Humani generis* directed against theological errors.

Dismissal of French Jesuit theologians (H. de Lubac, H. Bouillard and others).

Later Karl Rahner too subjected to special censorship.

1953 Suppression of the worker priests in France and further steps taken against theologians.

Closure of the seminary of the *Mission de France*.

Dismissal of the leading French Dominican theologians (M.-D. Chenu, Yves Congar).

Reformation), Hans Urs von Balthasar, Yves Congar and various French theologians.

Began studying Karl Barth.

1954   Ordination and first Mass at St Peter's, Rome, 10 and 11 October.

1955   Licentiate of theology (dissertation on Karl Barth's doctrine of justification, supervised by M. Flick).

1955–1957   Study at Paris, at the Institut Catholique and the Sorbonne. Influential teachers: in philosophy Maurice de Gandillac, Henri Gouhier, Jean Wahl; in theology Henri Bouillard, Louis Bouyer, Guy de Broglie.

Meets Karl Barth for the first time. Visits Amsterdam, Berlin, Madrid, London, for periods of study in these cities.

Starts work on Hegel's understanding of the incarnation (in due course to take shape as *Menschwerdung Gottes*).

1957   Gains doctorate of theology, Paris, 21 February. Dissertation supervised by Louis Bouyer on *Justification: La doctrine de Karl Barth et une réflexion Catholique* (*Justification: The Doctrine of Karl Barth and a Catholic Reflection*).

Simultaneous publication in book-form in German by Hans Urs von Balthasar at the Johannes-Verlag, Einsiedeln, with a warmly welcoming letter from Karl Barth himself.

First conversation with Mgr Jan Willebrands, later to become secretary, and then to succeed Cardinal Bea as president, of the Unity Secretariat. Invited to join the International Catholic Conference for Ecumenical Questions he was running – the seed from which the Unity Secretariat grew.

1957–1959   Engaged in pastoral work as assistant priest at the Hofkirche, Lucerne.

Invited to lecture on *Justification* at Regensburg.

Close links with Otto Karrer.

In the Autumn of 1957 took part for the first time in the work of the Association of German-speaking Dogmatic and Fundamental Theologians, meeting at Innsbruck.

On the advice of Heinrich Fries, Karl Rahner and Hermann Volk decided to enter for the *Habilitation* (the qualifying examination for a university post) in Germany.

1954 Second plenary assembly of the World Council of Churches held at Evanston, USA.
Marian Year proclaimed by Pius XII.

1957 Opening of the file on Küng (reference 399/57/i) by the department of the Index at the Holy Office in Rome. But the threat of the book on *Justification* falling foul of Roman theology and the Roman authorities does not come to anything.

1958 Election of Angelo Roncalli as Pope John XXIII (1958–63).

1959 At Karl Barth's suggestion lectured at Basle University on "*Ecclesia semper reformanda*".

1959–1960 Research assistant for dogmatic theology under Professor Hermann Volk (now Bishop of Mainz and a cardinal) at the Catholic Faculty of Theology at the University of Münster, Westphalia.

Spiritual director of the College of St Thomas More (student hostel).

1959 First conversations on the Council and reunion with Cardinals Julius Döpfner and G. B. Montini.

Strong objections raised by Professor Volk and Cardinal Döpfner against the publication of *The Council and Reunion*. Support from Mgr Josef Höfer, counsellor at the German Embassy to the Vatican.

1960 *The Council and Reunion* published with introductory message from Cardinal Franziskus König, Archbishop of Vienna.

Completion of the first draft of the work on Hegel's Christology, *Menschwerdung Gottes* (*The Incarnation*). Appointed to succeed Heinrich Fries as Professor of Fundamental Theology at the University of Tübingen.

Inaugural lecture: "Towards a theology of ecumenical councils".

1960–1962 During the period of preparation for the Council numerous lectures in Germany, Austria, Switzerland, Holland and England on "Is the Council being held too soon?" and "What do Christians expect from the Council?".

Became involved in serious discussion with the Protestant school of historical and critical exegesis (particularly with Ernst Käsemann in Tübingen) and with the Protestant school of systematic theology (particularly with Karl Barth's disciple Hermann Diem in Tübingen), and also with Edmund Schlink.

Article on early Catholicism in the New Testament as a problem in controversial theology.

1962 *Structures of the Church* published. Despite the strong objections he raised, Karl Rahner included it in his series *Quaestiones disputatae*.

1959   Announcement (25 January) by John XXIII of the Second Vatican Council.

1961   The encyclical *Mater et magistra* on social questions. Third plenary assembly of the World Council of Churches at New Delhi.

1962–1965   Second Vatican Council

1962   First session, 11 October to 8 December.

That the World May Believe: Letters to Young People published.

1960–1964 Lectures in fundamental theology from the summer semester of 1960 to the winter semester of 1963–4: "The Question of Human Existence"; "Christ and our Faith"; "The Teaching of the Church"; "Hegel's View of the Incarnation"; "Faith and Knowledge"; "The Question of Christ in the Contemporary World".

Seminars: "The Ecclesiology of Barth's *Church Dogmatics* and the Encyclical *Mystici corporis*"; "Questions about the Council and the Church"; "The Responses to Hegel's Christology"; "The Discussion about the Historical Jesus"; "The Ecclesiology of Calvin's *Institutes*"; "Questions of Ecclesiology Today".

1962 First session of the Council.

Appointed an official theological adviser (*peritus*) by Pope John XXIII; gave numerous lectures to groups of bishops from various parts of the world and to the international press on the council's programme, nature and reality, on liturgical and doctrinal reform, on ecumenical questions, on the relationship between the primacy and the episcopate, etc.

1963 March and April: first lecture tour lasting six weeks and covering the entire United States and England. Lecture on "The Church and Freedom" made particularly strong impression on audiences.

Turned down offer of post at Münster, stayed at Tübingen and accepted newly founded chair of Dogmatic and Ecumenical Theology as well as directorship of newly established Institute for Ecumenical Research.

Collected Council lectures published as *The Living Church*.

Second session of the Council: following an insufficiently thorough revision by that commission of the schema on the Church, turned down the opportunity of working on the Council's doctrinal commission headed by Cardinal Ottaviani.

Started work on *The Church*.

Co-founder (along with Paul Brand, Franz Böckle, Yves Congar, Johann Baptist Metz, Karl Rahner, Edward

1963   Banned from lecturing by the Catholic University of America, Washington, D.C., awarded honorary LL.D. by the Catholic University of St Louis, Missouri, and received by President Kennedy.

Pope John XXIII's encyclical on peace, *Pacem in terris*.

Deaths of John XXIII and John F Kennedy; election of G. B. Montini as Pope Paul VI (1963–78).

Second session of the Council: 29 September to 4 December.

The Holy Office started proceedings against *Structures of the Church*.

Hearing in Rome presided over by Cardinal Bea, in the presence of the Bishops of Basle and Rottenburg.

Schillebeeckx and others) of the international theological
review *Concilium*.
1964–1970 Summer semester of 1964 to the winter semester of 1969–70: normal lectures on dogmatic theology
("The Doctrine of Grace and Justification"; "Ecclesiology";
"The Doctrine of the Sacraments").
Special lectures on: "Ministry in the Church as a Problem
of Controversial Theology"; "Truthfulness in the Church
and in Theology"; "The Difficulties raised by the Church's
Infallibility".
Seminars and ecumenical classes: "The Discussion of Justi-
fication"; "Vatican II's Constitution on the Church";
"Vatican II's Constitution on Revelation"; "Ecumenical
Endeavours in Sixteenth-Century Catholic Theology"; "The
Doctrine of Justification in Luther and at Trent" (with
H. A. Oberman); "The Arnoldshain Theses on the Euchar-
ist"; "The Changing Image of the Priest"; "Luther's *De
captivitate babylonica Ecclesiae*"; "Presence and Dialogue –
Contemporary Reflections on the Missionary Encounter
with Christian Churches" (with P. Beyerhaus); "New
Interpretations of Christology"; "Contemporary Questions
in Christology" (with J. Moltmann); "The Discussion of
Hans Küng's *The Church*".
1964 12 February: lecture on "The Church and Freedom"
to mark the opening of the Institute for Ecumenical
Research.
Co-editor with Y. Congar and D. O'Hanlon of a selection
of important *Council Speeches of Vatican II*.
Third session of the Council: lecture on "Truthfulness in the
Church".
Disappointed by the way the Council is going. Returned to
Tübingen earlier than planned. Negative judgement on the
third session in article "The Council – End or Beginning?".
As part of the preparation for the Eucharistic Congress in
Bombay lecture on "The Church and the Religions of the
World". Further lectures in India and America (175th
anniversary of Georgetown University, Washington).
Started series of "Theological Meditations":
Freedom in the World: Sir Thomas More.

1964 Proceedings against *Structures of the Church* halted,
thanks mainly to the influence of Cardinal Bea.

Third session of the Council: 14 September to 21 November.
Eucharistic Congress in Bombay (December).

The Theologian and the Church (Georgetown University lecture).

The Church and Freedom (lecture given on first US tour).

1965 Fourth session of the Council: mainly occupied with work on *The Church*.

Lecture and article "What has the Council achieved?".

Christianity as a Minority (Bombay lecture).

Lectures in Holland and England on "The Church and Truthfulness".

1966 Took part in theological symposium in June at Montreal, Canada, with Harvey Cox and Martin E. Marty.

October: second US lecture tour, on "The Church and Truthfulness".

1967 February: article (under pseudonym "Helveticus") attacking threat to freedom of election of new Bishop of Basle.

July: public protest against Paul VI's encyclical on celibacy (and private debate with Cardinal Döpfner in Munich).

God and Suffering (in the series "Theological Meditations").

With J. Ratzinger starts the series "Ecumenical Studies".

The Church.

Lectures in Germany, Switzerland, Holland, France, Portugal, and the Near East (centenary of the American University, Beirut) on "Truthfulness", "The Church and Freedom", and "Luther's Doctrine of Justification".

1968 February to April: Visiting Professor at Union Theological Seminary, New York. Lectures on "The Sacraments" and on "Truthfulness in the Church".

August: critical reaction to *Humanae vitae* on Swiss television and in the international press.

Truthfulness: The Future of the Church.

December: speech at the memorial service for Karl Barth.

1965 Fourth session of the Council: 14 September to 8 December.
Warning from Cardinal Ottaviani at the Holy Office because of negative judgement on the Council and lecture on truthfulness in the Church.
Received in private audience by Paul VI.
1966 11 October: honorary doctorate of divinity from Pacific School of Religion, Berkeley, California.

1967 Paul VI's encyclicals *Sacerdotalis caelibatus* on celibacy and *Populorum progressio* on social questions.
According to a decree of the Holy Office (now renamed the Congregation for the Doctrine of the Faith) issued in Christmas week a stop should be put to publication and translation of *The Church* until a discussion has been held in Rome. The book however continues to be published and is translated into several languages.

1968 Murder of Martin Luther King.
May: abruptly summoned to a discussion at the Vatican, but invitation had to be declined owing to previous engagements. The start of lengthy negotiations about suitable conditions for such a discussion and about putting an end to the Roman proceedings.
Paul VI's encyclical *Humanae vitae*.
Death of Karl Barth.
Statement issued originally by 38 theologians and ultimately signed by 1300 on freedom for theology.
Fourth plenary assembly of the World Council of Churches, Uppsala.

1969 Summer semester: Visiting Professor at the Evangelical Faculty of Theology at Basle University.
Lecture on the sacraments and public discussions with Max Geiger and Heinrich Ott.
June: lecture in Milan; press conference to mark the publication of the Italian edition of *The Church* (in connection with which discussion with the papal theologian Carlo Colombo).
1970 February: *Menschwerdung Gottes* (*The Incarnation*, subtitled "An Introduction to Hegel's Theological Thought as Prolegomena to a Future Christology").
March–April: lectures in USA, Scotland and England on infallibility and on the sacraments.
May: statement on mixed marriages provokes first public censure by the German bishops' conference.
June: co-operated in founding the association of university ecumenical institutes in Germany. Start of work on the first project, reform and recognition of ministries.
18 July: *Infallible? An Enquiry* (Italian edition appeared a week earlier) sparked off a major debate both in Germany and abroad.
August: *Was ist Kirche?* (condensed version of *The Church*).
September: lecture on "What is the Christian Message?" (at Brussels, together with Karl Rahner and Raymond Brown).

1970–1978 Summer semester of 1970 to the winter semester of 1977–78: normal lectures on dogmatic theology ("The Doctrine of God"; "Christology"; "The Doctrine of Grace and Justification"; "The Doctrine of the Sacraments"). Special lectures: "Theological Questions Concerned with the Proclamation of the Word"; "Introduction to Christianity"; "Following Christ"; "Prayer, Meditation, Worship".

1970   January: honorary doctorate in the humane sciences from Loyola University of Chicago.
April: Roman *motu proprio* on mixed marriages.
German bishops' conference's statement criticizing Küng's statement on mixed marriages but at the same time revision of existing practice.

18 July: centenary of the definition of infallibility by Vatican I.

September: international theological congress in Brussels on "The Future of the Church", organized by *Concilium*.
October: Rahner's criticism of thesis on infallibility.
November: public discussion of infallibility at Frankfurt with H. Bacht, G. Denzler, H. Fries, W. Kasper, K. Lehmann, N. Lohfink, R. Pesch, K. Rahner, R. Schnackenburg, O. Semmelroth, H. Volk and others.

Seminars: "What is the Christian message?"; "New Books on Jesus"; "Questions on Baptism and Infant Baptism"; "The Discussion about Infallibility" (with the participation of H. Fries, K. Lehmann, K. Rahner, and J. Ratzinger); "Prayer"; "The Apostles' Creed"; "The Decisively Christian Aspect in Contemporary Ethics"; "Ernst Bloch's understanding of God"; "The Neo-Marxist and Neo-Positivist Critique of Religion"; "The Prob.em of Natural Theology in Karl Barth's *Church Dogmatics*" (together with E. Jüngel); "Theology and Science" (together with L. Oeing-Hanhoff); "How Should We Talk About Justification To-day?".

1971 January: article: "To Get to the Heart of the Matter: Answer to Karl Rahner".

Replies to the German and Italian bishops' conferences on infallibility.

Why Priests?

Freiheit des Christen ("The Freedom of the Christian", collected theological meditations).

July–December: visit to Soviet Union; lectures in India, Indonesia, Australia, New Zealand, and USA on "What Must Remain in the Church" and "What is Ecclesiastical Ministry?".

1972 Lectures in Switzerland, Germany (including East Germany) and Italy on "What Must Remain in the Church". Summer semester: seminar on infallibility at Tübingen with Karl Rahner and the other most important opponents.

1973 Statement in the Swiss press in favour of scrapping the clauses in the constitution imposing restrictions on the Catholic Church.

1971 Hearing on *Infallible?* before Bishop H. Volk of Mainz, Bishop F. Wetter of Speyer and Professors J. Ratzinger and H. Schlier of the German doctrinal commission, Stuttgart, 9 January.

Statement by German bishops' conference against *Infallible?* (8 February).

Statement by the Italian doctrinal commission against *Infallible?* (21 February).

Collection of essays by various theologians, edited by Karl Rahner, criticizing *Infallible?*.

June: honorary doctorate of divinity from Glasgow University.

August: declaration of solidarity with Hans Küng by 300 Catholic and Protestant theologians of the German-speaking and English-speaking world.

1972 Public discussions on infallibility in Berne (January) with the Catholic/Old Catholic commission and in Paris (May) with Y. Congar, B. Dupuy, H. Geffré, A. Jaubert, J. Ladrière, C. Langlois, H. Legrand, R. Rémond and others.

March: publication by 33 theologians of the statement "Against Resignation in the Church".

Memorandum by university ecumenical institutes in Germany on "Reform and the Mutual Recognition of Ministries".

1973 Bare majority (55 per cent) in Swiss referendum for deleting clauses in the constitution imposing restrictions on the Catholic Church.

Fehlbar? Eine Bilanz ("Fallible? An Assessment", collection of essays by various hands on *Infallible?*).
Numerous statements in the press and on television against the Roman statement *Mysterium Ecclesiae*.
What must remain in the Church.
1974 Various statements against the continuation of proceedings in Rome.
On Being A Christian.
Lecture to Catholic Academy in Munich on "What is it that is Distinctively Christian?".
1975 Lectures in Finland on "Twenty Theses on being a Christian" and "Ecclesiastical Ministry".
June: German Evangelical *Kirchentag* in Frankfurt: discussion with Heinz Zahrnt.
Symposium with Ernst Bloch to mark his ninetieth birthday together with Jürgen Moltmann and H. Fahrenbach.
Zwanzig Thesen zum Christsein ("Twenty Theses on being a Christian").

1976 *Was ist Firmung?* ("What is Confirmation?").
Brother or Lord? A Jew and a Christian talk together about Jesus.
Gottesdienst – warum? ("Why Worship?").
April: press conference in Rome for the Italian edition of *On Being A Christian.*
Article answering volume of essays by German theologians criticizing *On Being A Christian* published in *Frankfurter Allgemeine Zeitung* (22 May).
"Feminism: A New Reformation" in the *New York Times* (23 May).
November: lectures in the USA on "Theses on being a Christian"; press conference in New York for American edition of *On Being A Christian.*
1977 Lectures in Dublin, London, Madrid, Copenhagen, Oslo, Washington.
German paperback edition of *The Church.*

Mysterium Ecclesiae, the Doctrinal Congregation's statement on the Church and infallibility, published (5 July) with
a press conference at the Vatican.
1974 Continuation of proceedings against *The Church* and
Infallible? Petition against this in Switzerland, with 20,000
signatures.
Swiss bishops visit Rome in connection with the Küng case.
Efforts at mediation by Cardinal Döpfner and others.
1975 January: meeting in Lucerne on Christology of the
association of dogmatic and fundamental theologians of the
German-speaking world.
Conclusion of proceedings against *The Church* and *Infallible?*, with statements by the Doctrinal Congregation in
Rome and the German bishops' conference, together with
the latter's first statement against *On Being A Christian*
(20 February).
May: *Concilium* congress in Munich (23 May) on the situation of Christendom.
Ludwig Thoma medal for civil courage in public affairs
awarded by the city of Munich (11 July).
1976 April: private and confidential talks with the prefect
and secretary of the Doctrinal Congregation in Rome,
Cardinal Šeper and Archbishop Hamer; details of talks
confided to Cardinal Döpfner in letter made public by
German bishops' conference press office in November 1977.
24 July: death of Cardinal Döpfner.
Cardinal Josef Höffner, Archbishop of Cologne, becomes
President of German bishops' conference.

1977 Discussion with the German doctrinal commission
about *On Being A Christian* (Stuttgart, 22 January), with
Cardinals J. Höffner (Cologne) and H. Volk (Mainz),

8 October: lecture on "Science and Religion" to mark the quincentenary of Tübingen University, published, together with the speech delivered by the German President, Walter Scheel, under the title *Heute noch an Gott glauben?* ("Is Belief in God Still Possible Today?").

1978 *Existiert Gott? Antwort auf die Gottesfrage der Neuzeit* ("Does God Exist?").
Condensed version of *On Being A Christian.*
Lectures in Holland and USA.

Bishop G. Moser (Rottenburg), and Professors K. Lehmann and O. Semmelroth.

Second statement by the German bishops' conference critical of *On Being A Christian* (3 March).

Congress of theologians organized by *Concilium* and the Catholic Theological Society of America, held at Notre Dame, Indiana (29 May to 1 June), on the theme: "Vatican III: The Work that Needs to be Done".

Third statement by the German bishops' conference critical of *On Being A Christian*, issued together with its selection of documentation (17 November).

1978 Volume of documentation edited by Walter Jens with the title: *Um nichts als die Wahrheit. Deutsche Bischofskonferenz contra Hans Küng.*

B. Studies and Reactions

I: The Central Issue of the Reformation

JUSTIFICATION: The Doctrine of Karl Barth and a
Catholic Reflection (1957)

KARL BARTH
A Letter to the Author[1]

Dear Hans Küng

You have asked me to put in writing something about
that book of yours – more than once a subject of conversation between us. Why not? And if you really want to in-
corporate this note of mine into your book, then something
novel, something unique, will have come about in theological literature; and why shouldn't this happen, too?
Startling things have taken place lately in this area of study –
in what used to be called the "Theology of Controversy".
And as I reflect on these recent developments, I must confess that your book, dealing with my view of justification, is
so especially startling that it would hardly add to the shock
if I made a personal appearance in it with a few lines of my
own.

First, let me make three comments on the content of your
book:

1. I here gladly, gratefully, and publicly testify not only
that you have adequately covered all significant aspects of
justification treated in the ten volumes of my *Church Dogmatics* published so far, and that you have fully and accurately reproduced my views as I myself understand them;
but also that you have brought all this beautifully into focus
through your brief yet precise presentation of details and
your numerous, apposite pointers from the particular to the
larger context. Furthermore, your readers may rest assured –
until such time as they themselves might get to my books –
that you have me say what I actually do say and that I mean
it in the way you have me say it.

2. The positive conclusion of your critique is this: What

I say about justification – making allowances for certain doubtful yet not unacceptable turns of phrase – does objectively concur on all points with the correctly understood teaching of the Roman Catholic Church.* You can imagine my considerable amazement at this bit of news; and I suppose that many Roman Catholic readers will at first be no less amazed – at least until they come to realize what a cloud of witnesses you have produced in support of your position. All I can say is this: If what you have presented in Part Two of this book is actually the teaching of the Roman Catholic Church, then I must certainly admit that my view of justification agrees with the Roman Catholic view; if only for the reason that the Roman Catholic teaching would then be most strikingly in accord with mine! Of course, the problem is whether what you have presented here really represents the teaching of your Church. This you will have to take up and sort out with biblical, historical, and dogmatic experts among your co-religionists. I don't have to assure you that I am keenly interested in discovering what reception your book will find among them. For my part, I can only acknowledge and reflect upon the fact that you have presented considerable evidence in support of this sort of understanding and interpretation of the teaching of your Church.

3. The negative conclusion of your critique is this: Due to my erroneous (because unhistorical) evaluation of the infallible definitions and declarations collected in Denzinger and of the statements of the Church's magisterium in general, I have been guilty of a persistent misunderstanding and, consequently, of a persistent injustice regarding the teaching of your Church, especially that of the Fathers of Trent. *Quid dicemus ad haec?* If the things you cite from Scripture, from older and more recent Roman Catholic theology, from Denzinger and hence from the Tridentine texts, do actually represent the teaching of your Church and are establishable as such (perhaps this single book of yours will be enough to create a consensus!), then, having twice gone to the Church of Santa Maria Maggiore in Trent to

---

* Translator's note: The term "Roman Catholic" is Barth's own usage.

commune with the *genius loci*, I may very well have to hasten there a third time to make a contrite confession – "Fathers, I have sinned". But taking the statements of that Sixth Session as we now have them before us – statements correctly or incorrectly formulated for reasons then considered compelling – don't you agree that I should be permitted to plead mitigating circumstances due to the considerable difficulty I had trying to discover in that text what you have found to be true Catholic teaching? Imagine! So unexpected a view of freedom, of grace, of juridico-real justification and its realization and foundation in Christ's death, of the formulae *simul justus et peccator* and *sola fide*, and so on! How do you explain the fact that all this could remain hidden so long, and from so many, both outside and inside the Church? And now, in self-defence, may I just whisper a question (a very confidential question, but one not liable to detract from your book in the mind of any serious reader): Did you yourself discover all this before you so carefully read my *Church Dogmatics* or was it during or after your reading?

And now I come at last to the most important point, that is, to tell you what great pleasure I have derived from your book.

This is, first of all, simply because of the open-minded and resolute way you seem to have addressed yourself at the Germanicum in Rome to Roman Catholic exegesis and to the history of dogma and theology, and then proceeded, like an undaunted son of Switzerland, to study my books as well and to come to grips with the theological phenomenon you encountered in them. Then, too, I admire and applaud the skill and sound German of your argument. Regardless of the problems touched on above, and regardless of the reception and success your book may have, it is a very noteworthy achievement; and the work you have done will not be wasted so far as your priestly and scholarly future is concerned. Moreover, I do not hesitate to tell you that, so far as your whole attitude is concerned, I feel that I may regard you as a true Israelite, in whom there is no guile.

So, then, like Noah I look forth from the window of my

ark and salute your book as another clear omen that the
flood tide of those days when Catholic and Protestant
theologians would talk only against one another polemically
or with one another in a spirit of noncommittal pacifism,
but preferably not at all – that flood tide is, if not entirely
abated, at least definitely receding. "Divided in faith?" It is
true, as you yourself know and insist, that the problem seen
from either side is beset with such difficulties, that the hour,
humanly speaking, would seem still a long way off when
both sides no longer would be forced to admit that, yes,
unfortunately, we are divided in faith. The idea that I might
be a crypto-Catholic or you a crypto-Protestant – let us
hope that neither of these foolish notions will occur to any
of your readers. Yet it is true, isn't it, that today a few on
both sides, you and I among them, are coming to realize that,
while we are divided in faith, we are divided within the same
faith – the same, because and insofar as we and you can
believe in the self-same Lord. Those who begin to see this
may and must talk to one another, but with a new approach;
they should proceed from points on which they are united
to discuss what separates them; and discuss what separates
them with an eye to what unites them. And how else can
this happen, as you say so well in your Introduction, but by
our holding up to each other the mirror of the Gospel of
Jesus Christ? – not forgetting that on both sides the "converts" will be those who turn to examine their own coun-
tenance ever more carefully in that mirror. And what will
be the effect of such a mutual use of this mirror, at least
initially, but that people will try, as you have tried in your
book, to view one another in the best possible light? These
are small and perhaps even problematical steps forward,
but in any event better than none at all. Involved as you are
with a subject so crucial as justification, you have taken a
rather sizeable step; how feasible a step remains to be seen.
When and if this step proves to have been well taken, many
others will have to follow. Do not content yourself with the
fine beginning you have made in this important search. It
will certainly take quite an effort, once (as we hope) the
central area has been cleared, to make somewhat plausible

to us matters like Transubstantiation, the Sacrifice of the Mass, Mary, and the infallible papacy, and the other things with which we are confronted – pardon me, I could not resist picking up Denzinger again – in the Tridentine profession of faith. But these are for the future to worry about. Significant and sufficiently rewarding for the day is this, that the view in both directions (in this division within the self-same faith between people who believe otherwise but in no Other!) will open up and brighten up again. For this, we on both sides can give thanks. For the rest – *Veni Creator Spiritus!*

Now, then, may God bless you.

Cordially yours,
KARL BARTH

Basle
31 January 1957

TRIBUTE TO KARL BARTH[2]
Hans Küng at Basle

If I am permitted to speak as a Catholic theologian at the funeral of this great Protestant theologian, it is not only because I have been allowed for the last fifteen years to regard Karl Barth as my fatherly friend and constant spiritual companion, but also because Catholic theology itself should have a chance to speak at this grave. And I thank you for allowing this. Sorrowing with you today are countless Catholics theologians and laymen, everywhere on earth where the word of Karl Barth has encountered them in so many languages.

There was a time which needed the *doctor utriusque iuris*, the doctor of both laws. Our time urgently needs the *doctor utriusque theologiae*, the doctor of both theologies, Protestant and Catholic. And if anyone in our century has offered an outstanding example of this, it was Karl Barth.

This may be surprising when we consider that hardly one important theologian of our century has attacked the Catholic Church and Catholic theology as positively, as

angrily, and as defiantly as has Karl Barth – in his *Church
Dogmatics* as surely as at the General Assembly of the
World Council of Churches in Amsterdam. Yes, he chal-
lenged us Catholics to the right no less than neo-Protestant
opponents to the left. And he opposed us not always in the
tones of Mozart, of whom he asserted somewhat sadly in
Church Dogmatics, notwithstanding his love, that he apparently was not an especially diligent Christian and moreover he was even Catholic. But his challenge was set forth
for all its polemic with that quality which he so praised in
Mozart – a great, passionate, free objectivity. And the subject for which he wished to obtain a hearing – a wide hearing
– was the Christian message.

With the Gospel as his starting point, he believed it necessary to speak so sharply, he believed it necessary to *protest*
against us. And he seemed to many of us to be the Protestant
theologian *par excellence*. But actually he protested not only
when he was *against* something but when he was *for* something – something for which it was worth protesting even
today and perhaps today even more so: for the wholly other
living God whom a shallow Protestant and Catholic theology
thinks it can completely capture within its human system;
for the continuingly relevant word of God in Scripture which
even in the Church can be heard only with difficulty because
of the merely pious and clever but all too human word,
spoken and written; for the one Jesus Christ, whom people
in the Church again and again are gladly willing to use for the
support of another political or spiritual leader or even simply
mankind itself; for the community of believing men which
again and again in the history of the Church is threatened
either as an institution itself become powerful or as a
fanaticism, arrogant and powerful.

With his positive protest, his great evangelical intentions,
which must be maintained throughout, no matter what one's
position regarding the Barthian system, Karl Barth has
again made Protestant theology itself an earnest, evangelical
discussion partner for us Catholics. And with this protest
he has at the same time awakened many of us Catholics.
His prophetic word, also in the *Dogmatics*, was heard in our

Church too, and he himself was surprised how well heard it was. Karl Barth, precisely as a fundamentally evangelical theologian in his influence even on the Catholic Church – very indirect and yet very effective (and to say this is no exaggeration) – has become one of the spiritual fathers of the Catholic renewal in connection with the Second Vatican Council, a renewal which in most recent years often permitted him to ask with mixed feelings of sadness and joy whether the Spirit of God was not as much alive in the Catholic Church as in his own.

But up to the end he did not think much of "Catholicization", that all too superficial self-adjustment, just as he also did not want his Catholic friends to "Protestantize". He warned against a repetition of Protestant mistakes in the post-conciliar era. He expected others to have the same attitude he had, namely, not to get right off when one's own ship was in storm and peril, but to get to work with trust in God's word, standing fast in one's own church but with a view toward the other.

He already had this open view. With it he had made it easier for us Catholic theologians to understand him and, through him, Protestant theology. And as he united a human, humorous gentleness with a relentless power of discernment, so he had also, with all his uncompromising Protestant emphasis, a theological breadth which allowed him to become a doctor of our theology also. It is this radical Protestant theologian who exhibits, despite differences, especially two characteristics which demonstrate Protestant-Catholic breadth above a narrow Protestantism.

For Karl Barth the *whole* Church was important, and this means first of all in its temporal dimension, even the Church of the past. He had long since opposed a historical view and a theological attitude which, in an unhistorical tie with the early Church, regards the interval between the early Church and the Reformation as an ecclesiastical vacuum. The foreword to Volume I of *Church Dogmatics*, despite its clearcut rejection of the Catholic *analogia entis*, argues vigorously against those for whom church history begins with the year 1517 and who, as he says, based on the fairy tale of "sterile

Scholasticism" and the catchwords of "the Greek thought of the Fathers of the Church", stop thinking precisely where the interesting problems begin. He wanted it to be permissible to refer to Anselm and Thomas "without any signs of disgust". Thus, Karl Barth, at once critical and understanding, stood in the Church of two thousand years, which in no century was absent from the world, joined with the great theologians whom he, constantly examining, still recognized as his fathers and brothers in the faith. He thereby acquired not only a Catholic breadth but also a Protestant substance. And precisely because he did not forsake continuity, but took his stand with the Church and theology of the past, his criticism became so unignorable for us and so urgent.

For Karl Barth the *whole* Church was important, and that means then also in a spatial dimension: *the Church of the whole world*. Standing convinced in the Reformed tradition, and never rejecting Calvin as his particular church father, despite reservations, he had nothing in his theology and attitude of sectarian Protestantism as such. His theology was neither provincial nor, even worse, nationalistic. He did not think much of the introversion of boxed-in congregations, established churches, or even complacent confessional churches and alliances. Filled with the Pauline "care for all the churches", he realized in theory and practice a progressively universal outlook. And because he endeavoured to think broadly, he was also widely listened to. He was universal in thought, and thus was able to bring about everywhere an evangelical emphasis. Thus he widely became – and this is perhaps the most beautiful thing we can say about him – a sign of our common faith. And precisely as such he was better able than anyone else to make the Reformation faith understandable to us, and this includes even the crucial and divisive question of the Reformation 450 years ago, namely, the justification of the sinner by faith alone, a question over which division is no longer necessary today.

Many years ago we were discussing, as we did so often, the pope and the Petrine office in the Church. And as he did not then agree with me, I said smilingly: "Well, all right. I grant you good faith!" Thereupon he became serious and said: "So you allow me good faith. I have never conceded myself good faith. And when once the day comes when I have to appear before my Lord, then I will not come with my deeds, with the volumes of my *Dogmatics* in the basket upon my back. All the angels there would have to laugh. But then I shall also not say, 'I have always meant well; I had good faith.' No, then I will only say one thing: 'Lord, be merciful to me a poor sinner!' "

That is the common belief of Christendom. And our comforting hope is that Karl Barth will be given that for which he prayed.

Notes
1. Karl Barth (1886–1968), professor successively at Münster (1925), Bonn (1930), and Basle (1935), was one of the outstanding Protestant theologians of this century.
Taken from Hans Küng, *Justification: The Doctrine of Karl Barth and a Catholic Reflection* (New York 1964, London 1965), pp. xvii–xx.
2. This translation by James Biechler first appeared in the *Journal of Ecumenical Studies*, Vol. 6, No. 2 (1969), pp. 233–6, and is used by kind permission of Temple University.

II: Reform and Reunion

THE COUNCIL AND REUNION:
Renewal as a call to Unity (1960)

Elmer O'Brien
The Council and Reunion
Reflections on a Recent Book[1]

Unforgivably, I am unable at the moment to recall what small master of the telling phrase it might have been. But some such one, tongue more or less in cheek and hand firmly to aching head, once remarked that the German theological mentality was the deep-down-divingest, under-water-stayingest, mud-up-bringingest ever accorded to man by a beneficent Providence. Anyone much given to the reading of German theologians can only, ruefully, agree.

Now, however, there happens along Dr Küng. He is the major theological talent to appear in this decade. He is a German of the Germans as only a native-born Swiss, it would seem, ever properly manages to be. He dives deep. Yet in the book before us he thinks as clearly as a Frenchman and (even in Miss Hastings' excellent English version) speaks with the directness of an American.

This, I would suggest, is suitable cause for rejoicing. Amid all the books that might conceivably be occasioned by the forthcoming General Council there was an indisputable need for one which, with penetration, clarity, and forthrightness, would address itself explicitly to the Council's problems and prospects. Dr Küng, so untraditionally endowed, has provided it.

At first glance its contents would appear to belie its title. There is much about the Council and reformation of the Church. There seems precious little about the Council and reunion of the churches. Yet, truly, the whole book is about reunion and it is so – given the nature of the projected Council – in the sole way possible. For Second Vatican is expected by the Pope to be an aid to reunion through its renovation and reformation of the Church. Whatever, then, the author says about reformation has direct bearing upon the question of reunion.

He says, it so happens, uncommonly strong things about reformation. [i] The atmosphere fortunately is much changed since last a theologian wrote so seriously and at such length of the need for reform in the Church. One recalls the brief, stormy history of Père Congar's *Vraie et fausse réforme dans l'Eglise*, which appeared in 1950 and disappeared shortly thereafter. And one recalls the address, in 1960, of the Pope to the clergy of his diocese when, speaking of the Council, he said, "We do not wish to put anyone in history on trial. We shall not seek to establish who was right and who was wrong. Responsibility is divided. We only want to say, 'Let us come together. Let us make an end to our divisions'." This new air nimbly and sweetly recommends itself unto the gentle senses of such as Dr Küng. He says very strong things about Church reformation. But he is able to say them calmly and with balance and with no sudden constrictions of his pen hand at the thought of being misunderstood.

Wherever there are men, there is failure. Where there is failure, there is the need of improving, of reforming. Reformation is a permanent necessity in the Church because the Church is made up of men. It is as obvious as that. A *divine-human* mystery, the Church is situated within the dimensions of space and time, her *divine* institutions and constitutions necessarily working themselves out, on the *human* side, in a variety of forms. Therefore,

it is clear that we cannot simply speak of "irreformable

(i) After the first chapter he normally uses the word "renewal" rather than "reformation". I am aware that "reformation", when applied to the Church, can induce a distinct and quite understandable *malaise* in most Catholic minds. If I continue to use it here, it is not for the pedantic reason that it is a perfectly good, Catholic word which had a large and noble history before ever it was adopted for narrow and sectarian purposes. My reason is practical: "renewal" is a term altogether too wishy-washy properly to express the bold intent of the coming Council.

areas" of the Church, as though there were two storeys of
a building, one on top of the other, or which one was
reformable and the other irreformable; as though it were
possible to separate off the irreformable essence of the
Church's institutions, as established by God, from the
concrete working-out of them and the living structure
given to them by men in the history of the Church. It is
rather that the essence is embedded in the human working-
out in history somewhat as the plan, and the permanent
principles of architecture and engineering, enter into the
actual concrete building. Every part of the building, even
the innermost room of it, or the most important or the
most valuable, is, basically, liable to need a renewing and
can therefore be reformed and renewed. Only, the plan
as expressed in any particular part of the building, and
the laws of construction, as they apply to it, must not be
set aside; no part of the building must become simply
something else, or collapse altogether. Every institution,
even the holiest (the celebration of the Eucharist, or the
preaching of the Gospel), every aspect of organization
(even the primacy of Rome, or the episcopal government
of the Church) can, through the historical process of for-
mation and deformation, come to need renewal, and must
then be reformed and renewed; only, the basic irreformable pattern given by God through Christ must not be set
aside. Indeed, the holier the institution, the worse the
damage, and the more urgent the renewal . . .[ii]

There are no irreformable areas of the Church because the
divine and immutable is nowhere except embedded in the
human and mutable. And how very human it is that the
human and mutable has shown itself sometimes so immutable in the Church's history. Dr Küng compiles no catalogue of such sad ironies, but he does mention one or two
by way of doctrinal illustration. For example:

Despite the steady branching out of the Church, we can

(ii) *op. cit.*, pp. 77–8.

hardly avoid observing that there has been at the same time a progressive narrowing. While the Church, like St Paul, became Greek to the Greeks and barbarian to the barbarians, it has not been Arab to the Arabs, Negro to the Negroes, Indian to the Indians nor Chinese to the Chinese. The Church of Christ, taken as a whole, has remained a European–American affair. [iii]

This sort of thing, and with it the necessity for reformation, one finds in the Church because the infallible Church is made up of fallible men. It is also, the author goes on to point out, made up of sinful men. [iv] The Church is holy, but not wholly so. Nor will she be until the end of time, thinks Dr Küng, making his own the view of Augustine and Thomas. [v] The various degrees of her hierarchic structure are threatened not only by the quite human deformations of the historical process in which she is situated but also by the personal sins of those who occupy them as priests, teachers, shepherds.

The Church needs, not only one to form her in the first place, but always, because she is deformed, a *reformer*. And this is Christ himself. This is why, throughout everything that we must not shirk saying, in painful compassion and sorrowfully recognizing our co-responsibility, about the shadow-side of the Church, yet we can always firmly believe, in glad and unshakable faith, not in a sinful Church but in the holy Church. For Christ himself, through his Holy Spirit, ensures that the bright, invincible light of the Church's true nature will always in the end

(iii) *op. cit.*, p. 23.

(iv) *op. cit.*, pp. 34–50.

(v) But not, curiously, that of Pope John, who in his address to the diocesan presidents of Italian Catholic Action said, "When we have carried out this strenuous task, eliminated everything which could at the human level hinder our rapid progress, then we shall point to the Church in all her splendour, 'without spot or wrinkle', and say to all those who are separated from us, Orthodox, Protestants, and the rest: 'Look, brothers, this is the Church of Christ . . .' " Quoted, without comment, in Küng, *op. cit.*, p. 6.

break through the darkness of her un-nature. But not without the co-operation of all of us as responsible members of her.[vi]

"But not without the co-operation of all . . ." Such certainly is the realistic view of Pope John; that is why he takes every possible opportunity to speak to every sort of group of the reform purposes of the Council. Dr Küng suggests four levels upon which this universal co-operation can and should be had: suffering, prayer, criticism, action. Suffering because of the failures and sins in the Church as she now is, as one becomes painfully and honestly aware of how one is forever revealing oneself as an unreformed member of the Church which is to be reformed. Prayer for deliverance from evil, that not our own but God's will be done, for it is possible "to have some definite, all-too-human mental image of reunion, and then pray, consciously or unconsciously, that reunion may happen like that. We shall, on the contrary, pray that reunion may happen as and when *God* wills."[vii] Criticism, because as "a Church of *men*, sinful men, the Church, though of divine foundation, *needs* criticizing; as the Church of *God*, she is, more than any other institution, *worth* criticizing."[viii] Action, not for revolution (which is without piety towards the past) nor for restoration (which often is only the revival of the outworn) nor for a mere interior change of heart (which outward conditions, if left unchanged, can render ineffective) nor for a mere exterior reform of abuses (which, because times have changed, would leave the institution or regulation pure but ineffective), but for a creative reform of the state of the Church.[ix] "The

(vi) *op. cit.*, pp. 49–50.
(vii) *op. cit.*, p. 60.
(viii) *op. cit.*, pp. 61–2. The Christmas pastoral of the Dutch Hierarchy in 1960 made the same point (*Le Sens du Concile*, Paris: Desclée de Brouwer, 1961). Recent instances of such constructive criticism are the symposia, "What Lay People Want in the Church" (*The Sign*, October, 1961, pp. 11–15) and *Umfrage zum Konzil* (Freiburg: Herder, 1961), which was conducted by the Vienna periodical, "Wort und Wahrheit".
(ix) *op. cit.*, pp. 70–84.

ancient basilica is not to be torn down and rebuilt, but nor
is it merely to be scrubbed down, patched up and dusted off;
it is to be, in accordance with the ancient plan of its founder,
but for the needs of this new age, *renewed*. Such is Catholic
reform."[x]

Arrived at this point, readers of Dr Küng's book would
be pardoned for concluding that the Council's problems are
too many and too vast ("There are no irreformable areas of
the Church") and its prospects accordingly, as an aid to
reunion, meagre indeed. Therefore to help toward one's seeing the work of the Council in something like proper pro-
portion the author devotes the largest section of his volume
(pp. 87–214) to a "brief survey" of the history of the Church
as a history of reform. It would be idle to essay here a
necessarily briefer survey of his brief survey. Attention will
simply be called to certain of the more fascinating points
which come to the fore in the course of his engaging recital:
why the Church rejected the Protestant Reformation (pp.
102–8); how Trent, intended as a Council of reform,
ended up being merely one of restoration (pp. 108–20); the
question of reform of doctrine (pp. 161–77).

After having done so much, Dr Küng would be something less than human were he not tempted, before he had
done, to do the Council's work for it. Tempted, he yields
briefly. In a final, short chapter he indicates what it might
do about restoring full value to the episcopal office, setting
down the invariable minimum that is to be manifested in
every Catholic Mass-liturgy, creating a Breviary specifically
for secular priests, rethinking the law of clerical celibacy,
revising (or abolishing) the Index, establishing the significance of the laity in the Church by a declaration of principle, etc., etc. Many a one, I should think, will in the long
winter nights ahead play at being the Council within the
quiet conclave of his skull. Few will be as good at it, or get
so much obvious enjoyment from it, as Hans Küng.

"Will there be reunion?" he asks in conclusion. His final
words are truly the last word that can be said in the matter:

(x) *op. cit.*, p. 85.

"We base nothing upon our own strength; our unshakable
hope is in the Holy Spirit: Send forth Thy Spirit and Thou
shalt renew the face of the earth!"

HANS KÜNG
Looking Back[2]

What tremendous strides the Catholic Church has made in
six short years! In 1960, the publishing of this book was
deemed a considerable risk, against which I was warned by a
number of wise and well-meaning friends. Today, five years
later, as I look back over the course of developments, I am
filled with joy and gratitude.

On Sunday, 18 January, 1959, at the beginning of the
World Prayer Octave for Christian Unity, the author
preached a sermon at the Hofkirche of Lucerne, Switzerland,
on the reunion of separated Christians. On Monday,
19 January, he lectured at the University of Basle on a subject suggested by Karl Barth. (He had said, with a pleased
smile, that it would be most interesting to hear a Catholic
speaking on the theme of *Ecclesia semper reformanda* – the
constant renewal of the Church!) That lecture contained all
the basic theses, findings, and arguments, indeed the entire
outline of this book. It caused a Protestant student of theology to ask during the discussion that followed, whether
my view of the Catholic Church was not too optimistic. The
answer then was that for three months we had had a new
Pope who already had taken some unusually good steps and
that these were certainly not to be his last.

On the following Sunday, 25 January, at the Feast of St
Paul's Conversion and the conclusion of the World Prayer
Octave, an astounded world learned that an Ecumenical
Council was to be called to prepare the way for the reunion
of the separated Christians. John XXIII had opened a new
era of hope for the Catholic Church and for all Christians.
It was no longer difficult to expand the lecture given at Basle
into a book.

I owe an inexpressible debt of gratitude to John XXIII, a

true "man of God" to so many inside and outside the Catholic Church, Christians and non-Christians, men of the West and men of the East. More than almost any Pope before him, he gave new meaning to the Gospel of Jesus Christ as he applied disarming kindness, understanding goodness, and courageous determination to unusual actions which imbued the Catholic Church with new life, endowed all Christians with a new will to understanding, and gave the world new hope. It is due to him that this book had a future.

The Archbishop of Vienna, Dr Francis Cardinal König, not only read the galley proofs under unusually trying circumstances while bedridden after a serious accident on the way to the funeral of Cardinal Stepinac, but also wrote an introduction. A similar introduction was later done for the French edition by Achille Cardinal Liénart. To both of these distinguished prelates I owe thanks for the fact that this book met with so little opposition and so much understanding. Before publication the manuscript was read by many, of whom only three shall be mentioned here because I owe them special, decisive thanks: my teacher at the University of Münster, now Bishop of Mainz, Dr Hermann Volk; my great and fatherly friend, Karl Barth, through whom I received the grace of access to Evangelical theology; and one whom I really should have mentioned first, Father Dr Wilhelm Klein, S.J., the hidden great inspiration and spiritual director of the Pontificum Collegium Germanicum. By his prayer and advice, he not only prevented my course of studies at Rome from becoming a failure, but also, by wise inspiration and supporting love, made it fruitful. Our new generation of theologians stands on the shoulders of others to whom we can never be grateful enough for stimulating us during our years of study: Hans Urs von Balthasar, Otto Karrer and Karl Rahner, Louis Bouyer, Yves Congar and Henri de Lubac, whose friendship and help I received as a young man without earning it, are mentioned here as representatives of a great many. Misunderstood, attacked, and persecuted, they have for decades, with indomitable and exemplary courage, worked untiringly for that breakthrough without which the Second Vatican Council could never have accomplished what it has in spite of every trial.

In the meantime, this book has reached around the world and been published in German, French, English, American, Dutch, Spanish, Polish, Portuguese, Japanese, and Italian editions. The developments of the Second Vatican Council have stamped it as "prophetic". In regard to both renewal of the Church and reunion of separated Christians, the progress made in the face of foreseeable disappointment has been greater than anyone would have dared to dream five years ago. It may therefore be of interest to the reader, as well as to the author, to observe how this book has accurately sketched not only the basic attitudes and directions of the Council, but also how its predicted "concrete possibilities" have successively been realized in spite of all difficulties. The Decree on Ecumenism is, perhaps more than anything else, an indication of the great strides the Catholic Church has taken in the years just past, and a demonstration of how statements which sounded dangerous then have since become, as it were, self-evident propositions affirmed by the Council in moral unanimity.

However, the Council is not an end but merely a beginning: its theoretical conclusions call for practical consequences. The progress within Catholicism must be brought to ecumenical fruition. The temporary, tactical solutions are but road signs toward radically basic solutions. This is the real meaning of it all: the Council is not an end but a beginning. Much has been achieved; much more remains to be done, not only in Rome but in every land, diocese, and parish, among Catholic, Orthodox, and Protestant Christians. More than ever it is now up to the individual. He must not delay, nor must he grow weary; he must do whatever he can do by fearless, determined, active engagement in his personal task – no matter how humble or influential his station in life – to bring about the full realization of the goal envisioned in the subtitle of this book – a subtitle suggested by Karl Barth: "Renewal As a Call to Unity".

Thus, this book may continue to be of service as an already proven signpost and guide for informed participation

and partnership in our blessed striving along those path-
ways which were opened by Vatican Council II for the
Church, Christendom, and the World.

*Tübingen, on the sixth anniversary
of the calling of Vatican II*

Notes

1. Elmer O'Brien, S.J., theologian, born 1911, professor at
Fordham Graduate School 1952–3 and 1954–8, and at Con-
cordia University, Montreal, 1962–73.
Taken from *The Month*, January 1962, pp. 15–49, and used
by kind permission of the Editor.
2. Taken from the Image Book edition of *The Council and
Reunion*, New York 1965, pp. 5–8, and used by kind permission of Image Books.

III: Questions of Structure

STRUCTURES OF THE CHURCH (1962)

OTTO KARRER
Conciliar Structures[1]

The distinguishing marks of Küng's work are the posing of questions that are relevant today, thorough research (making full use of all the available material), and the presentation of the results of his labours in fresh and lively language. The announcement of the Council was not merely the occasion for him to express Catholic concerns and expectations in his well-known book on the subject but it also stimulated him to undertake a piece of theological research on a larger scale. The starting point of this was the question how it came about that after the First Vatican Council a Council was something that for the most part people just did not take into consideration any longer. Did it not arise from the very one-sided ideas people developed of the Church's structure? However, the aim of this new work is not to describe the structure of the Church as a whole, but "merely" to offer some ecclesiological indications as to how the problems he points out can be settled. The aim of what follows is to provide a brief sketch of the book's contents with only a few additional comments.

Chapters 1 to 3: The Church is "the ecumenical council by divine convocation", whereas the ecumenical council is the representation of the Church convoked by men. But how the council is convoked, presided over, and composed and how its acts are approved can take very different forms. According to the current code of canon law (canon 222) it must be summoned and presided over and its decrees confirmed by the Pope; but that this is not a theologically binding statement is shown by the historical fact that the early ecumenical councils were convoked "by the grace of God and of the emperor", and corresponding to this was the influence the emperor was able to exert on the council itself. Of the general councils that took place in the Middle Ages following the schism between West and East, that of Florence brought the bishops of both the Western and the Eastern Churches together (on an equal footing) without, of course, its being able to win acceptance in the East. The other general councils – of the Lateran, of Lyons, of Constance, and of Trent – are regarded by us as ecumenical, although they were not able to speak in the name of the separated Eastern Churches as well as of the Western Church, with the result that their binding character is disputed by the Eastern Churches. There is no dogmatically binding list of ecumenical councils.

Chapters 4–6: The credible representation of the Church by the council is entailed by the need for the credible representation of the marks of the Church.

(1) The *one* Church is credibly represented by the council if the unity of the council fathers springs from an inner unity of faith and life and consequently finds expression in unanimous decisions freely arrived at. Hence councils strive to achieve the greatest possible unanimity in their decisions by trying to establish by means of debates and votes the outlines of the understanding and awareness the Church at that time has of itself. The First Vatican Council, despite the protests of the minority, contented itself with aiming at a simple majority in its voting and was finally able to achieve moral unanimity by abstentions or by subsequent agreement. Since in this case unreasonable methods were used, Catholic (as well as Protestant) historians and theologians ask themselves whether the unanimity that was finally attained was not reached at the expense of credibility in practice (not to be confused with validity) and whether if things had been handled with more understanding it might not have been possible to avoid the Old Catholic schism.

Involved in the credible representation of the one Church by the council is the participation of both the ministerial priesthood and the universal priesthood of all believers. From the Council of the Apostles, right up to 1870, this was

realized to a considerable degree, even if for the most part
the right to vote was reserved to the bishops. In the Middle
Ages secular elites were represented alongside the emperors,
while there was considerable lay representation (with the
right to vote) at the Council of Constance which brought the
great Western schism to an end. Even at the Council of
Trent the ambassadors of the princes were able to exert influence on the proceedings, and one of the council presidents
was a layman. Since the First Vatican Council the representation of the laity has fallen behind that of earlier councils. In making important decisions the Apostles asked the
representatives of the people for their view; but this fundamental relationship was, in the clerical Church of the Middle
Ages, shifted out of alignment to the extent that the laity no
longer felt themselves to be responsible. For the present
council lay people have been able to send in their suggestions
and wishes, and those involved in providing press, radio and
television coverage have been drawn into the council's work,
while in addition a new lay presence comes from the participation of observers and guests from outside the Roman
Catholic Church. The question of the extent to which the
validity of a council depends on the agreement of the people
is in the Latin Church answered differently from the response
given by recent theology in the Eastern Church. We regard
the council as valid from the formal conclusion of the assembly, though of course its effectiveness depends on the
attitude of the whole body of the Church, whereas the
Orthodox make its validity dependent on acceptance by the
people.

(2) The *holy* Church is first of all represented in the holding of a council by the opening service of worship, while
before each public session the Pope leads the fathers in
praying the *Adsumus*, a humble prayer by the fallible and
sinful people taking part for the assistance of the spirit of
God. The book of the gospels on the altar shows that what
this assembly is concerned about is the sanctification of the
Church and the interests of the kingdom of God.

(3) The *catholic* Church – the Church of the different
peoples and cultures – is credibly represented by means of

unity in what is essential and variety and diversity in the forms in which this is expressed (in theology, rites, patterns of worship, etc.). In historical reality this ideal diversity suffers not a few limitations, and the greatest damage to its credibility in the eyes of the surrounding world is the unbrotherly rivalry between the particular values cultivated by the separated confessions, values which only become completely meaningful and carry their full power of conviction in member Churches of the one Catholic Church that are ecumenically "united, not absorbed". This is the hope for the future – in the long run, humanly speaking.

(4) The *apostolic* Church would, according to Luther, be sufficiently guaranteed by word and sacrament on the basis of holy scripture (with the dogmatic statements of the early ecumenical councils). As far as the Catholic Church is concerned the episcopal office transmitted by ordination together with the Petrine office belongs to the Church's apostolic character. It is thus an office which does not simply depend on delegation by the people forming the community but on an "apostolic call that bestows the spirit" in the sign of sacramental ordination. Its meaning is not domination and self-glorification but service for the reign of God in the spirit of Christ, for the maintenance and spreading of the apostolic faith. According to the official confessional documents the preaching office of the Reformation does admittedly include the sacramental and pastoral ministries, and in Lutheranism the office of bishop was to begin with maintained; but "the predominantly unapostolic behaviour of the Catholic bishops" was an essential reason for the fact that the Reformation was ultimately carried through at the expense of the apostolic office. The confessional documents of the Reformation do indeed emphasize an ecclesiastical office due to institution by Christ, and thus "of divine right", and (according to E. Schlink) it is in fact this that is meant by the *rite vocatus* of the Augsburg Confession; but the sacramental transmission of the charisms of office was "completely overlooked" by Luther. It is here that the real difficulty and the initial cause of separation must lie. For the rest a theological rapprochement seems to be taking shape.

According to E. Schlink's outstanding study of apostolic
succession there is by divine right a "pastoral office" which
admits of variations reflecting the Church's history, while
according to the Council of Trent there is of divine right "a
hierarchy which is instituted by divine ordinance and which
consists of bishops, presbyters and ministers" (DS 1776).
If the Tridentine phrase "instituted by divine ordinance" is
related to the "hierarchy" in general (as is suggested by the
text and by the interpretation in practice of Church history),
then "hierarchy" in the language of Trent is the same as
"pastoral office". According to Karl Rahner "no Catholic
theologian is prevented from regarding the distinction of
bishop, priest and deacon as made by the Church itself as a
free but irreversible decision" – irreversible once it had imposed itself, probably for practical rather than for strictly
dogmatic reasons. Because a *decision* of this kind is lacking
on the Protestant side, what prevails there is a feeling of
unease about the Church's constitution, whereas Catholic
theology of both East and West has consistently valued the
office of bishop as the backbone of the Church's structure.

Recent exegesis has had a stimulating effect. According to
R. Bultmann the Church order of the pastoral epistles is
"clearly Catholic". E. Käsemann has established that, orig-
inating in the Jewish Christian tradition (the primitive apostolic tradition), ordination gradually prevailed over the
Pauline charismatic structure, in a necessary tightening up
against the gnostic heresies. In Acts Luke "was the first to
propagate the early Catholic theory of tradition and legitimacy". The canon of scripture should be understood as a
dogmatic decree of the early Church; it gave scope and
persistence to early Catholicism (Acts and the pastoral
epistles) as it did to Judaeo-Christian and Pauline Christianity. Hence "in the fact of its existence" the canon of the
New Testament is "no longer the word of God". To the
question "why not?" Käsemann answers: because the core
of the Gospel, belief in justification, has been given a contrasting programme in the office of order. Catholic theology
finds this kind of procedure inadmissible, since it clearly
rests on a preconception which, according to Küng's valid

criticism, in no way warrants the exclusion of an alternative preconception – that all the writings contained in the canon are inspired. And is the doctrine of justification really the central theme of Christ's message? Are Christ's summons to surrender to God's reign over us and to follow him by becoming his disciples, the Sermon on the Mount and the great commandment, the fellowship of the Apostles in his spirit, the glory of God – are all these to be rejected from the New Testament as contrasting themes? Moreover, if H. Schlier is right, this exclusion should be concerned not just with the pastoral epistles but also with a document as early as 1 Corinthians, in which it is not just the charismatic principle that is stressed but also the principle of order, so that the spirit of prophecy is from the start linked to the apostolic witness that has been handed down with regard to the Lord's Supper and the Resurrection (1 Cor. 11:23ff and 15:3ff) and to the principle of order (1 Cor. 16:2ff and the whole of chapter 14). It follows from all this that the special responsibility of the institutional charism of office belongs just as much to the nature or essence of the Church as the non-institutional or spontaneous charisms (cf. Eph. 2:20).

What H. Schelkle says about the difference between the Catholic and Protestant view is well put: "Catholic theology will evaluate the evidence of early Catholicism differently from Protestant theology; it will accept the New Testament in its totality while confirming the existence of a genuine and valid development." From the very beginning the Church cannot exist at all other than historically. And history means development – in the preservation of the kerygma of the formative apostolic period. In view of this, Catholic dogmatic theology, informed by the findings of exegesis, will for example in contrast to exegetical radicalism refrain from reading out of 2 Peter 1:21 a fundamental rejection of non-institutional charismatic gifts but will rather find the distinction between genuine and licentious prophecy well-founded and for the rest agree with Küng in regarding everything in the New Testament not as having the same value and importance but as having equal rights, indeed according to how close a text in fact is to the Gospel of Jesus

Christ, who in all the writings of the New Testament is somehow "the core of the Gospel".

In a further section Küng discusses the question of apostolic succession. Here the ecumenical dialogue is enriched by an extremely significant contribution from E. Schlink. According to him there is agreement on the following. Charism and office belong together. Commissioning to office took place in the Palestinian communities through the laying on of hands with prayer, and it is something that must be taken into consideration even when it is not explicitly mentioned. But from the exegetical point of view it cannot be elevated into a condition *sine qua non*; for there seems also to have taken place the process of spontaneous vocation to office without formal commissioning or ordination. But naturally as the formative stages of the Church's history receded into the past the institutional process of commissioning took on an increasing significance – as a means of preserving the apostolic message. The tripartite division of bishop, presbyter and deacon cannot be presupposed as the only valid arrangement; yet succession by ordination in the Church's pastoral office is desirable and is something to be striven for where it is lacking. Thus far Schlink. The dogmatic statements of Nicaea and Trent on the episcopate are in themselves, like every dogma, capable of being supplemented, but succession by ordination has in its favour the entire tradition of fifteen centuries against which mere exegetical possibilities or conjectures can hardly prevail. Provided something that may be feasible in an emergency is not elevated into a permanent principle, then here in the case of Schlink the highest degree of ecumenical unity has been reached on an important issue.

In chapter 7 on the Petrine office in Church and council a significant finding of the history of dogma is thrown open for discussion: all the theoretical and practical difficulties of ecclesiastical office boil down to the credible representation of the Petrine office. First the Vatican concepts *summepiscopus* and *potestas ordinaria*, *immediata*, *plena* are dealt with. The Pope cannot act against the entire Church. A possible link between Pope and Church is discussed with the application of recent research. Studies on the Council of Constance show that it involved an ecclesiologically significant polarity opposite to the First Vatican Council. If canon law ascribes *suprema potestas* both to ecumenical councils and to the Pope, this means that the papacy and the episcopate, being related to each other, form *one* subject or agent of leadership; the papacy only exists "embedded" in the entirety of the Church (Dutch bishops' pastoral letter). From one point of view the two centres of power are on the same footing, from another they are not; Peter (the Petrine office) has the task of strengthening the brethren and in an emergency intervening over the head of a particular bishop. But from the other point of view the fullness of the Pope's pastoral authority is not unlimited: just as Paul as an Apostle could withstand Peter, and just as Bernard of Clairvaux and Catherine of Siena could admonish the Pope, bishops like Irenaeus or Cyprian acted on the basis of their co-responsibility for the Church in admonishing the Petrine office and in extreme cases of emergency (e.g. when faced with violence, mental illness, heresy, grave scandal) the episcopate has a function of control over the Pope up to the point of deposition (in a declarative sense). This has not been a unique case in history: the Council of Constance did so legitimately in a particular emergency. Papal freedom from error is not of an objective nature but is related to the content of an abstract *ex cathedra* definition. *Ex sese* indicates the function of the supreme office of arbitration in the Church. In a historical context Y. Congar explains congregationalist counter-tendencies as a reaction to a one-sidedly juridical emphasis on its own prerogatives by the papacy. Not a few papal prerogatives are of human right, and Western juridical patterns of thought can learn something from the symbolic way of thinking of the Eastern Church – to their mutual advantage.

In "Remarks on the Problematic Aspects" Protestant theology poses the question whether it is in any way possible for a human being to be free from error. It is only by the spirit of God that the Church is maintained in the right faith. The Evangelical judgement is that the postulate of infallibility is the sign of a lack of faith in the spirit of God, which is at work through and despite human frailty and fallibility. Küng rightly remarks that on the basis of Vatican I it is difficult to approach this way of looking at things. All he has wanted to do is to present the problem for discussion, and it will "still require the efforts of many theologians". Perhaps some additional comments can be made here – with every awareness that they are open to being supplemented and amended by more competent people: (1) "Freedom from error" (along with truth not in the philosophical sense but in the biblical sense of sharing through grace in Christ's trustworthiness and of the apostolic kerygma) is not predicated of a person or persons but of some definite act done by this person or persons in connection with the entirety of the Church. (2) A presupposition in this is that the representatives of the Church of Christ are not guided by self-awareness and self-glorification but humbly beg the spirit of the Lord for protection from error (in the attitude of the conciliar prayer *Adsumus*). (3) A further presupposition is that the representatives of the Church of Christ are not for reasons of intellectual and human convenience aiming to add to the truth of Christ in a quantitative sense, but want to encourage in people s hearts surrender to the reign of God and in awareness of their responsibility for Christian unity can see no other way to protect those who belong to the Church from serious error.

The distinction between faith and formulations of faith is theologically significant. In keeping with this dogmatic improvements are always possible. There is progress in our knowledge of the faith, though only in its congruence with revelation. It would be a disastrous error to regard a numerical increase in dogmatic formulae without more ado as a qualitative improvement. Fundamentally definitions are in intention of a doxological and at the same time defensive character. But to the extent that a formula is polemical and defensive and is "aimed" at one-sided distortions it can easily overlook a justified concern. An ecumenical task of theology on both sides is to remind itself that no dogma exhausts the mystery and that for this reason the content of truth in the other's error is to be looked at seriously, just as on the other hand the danger of one-sidedness in one's own truth has to be seen. Truth and error are absolute opposites – in the abstract. It is easy to stress this opposition, but, said an important Roman theologian, it is a "Catholic Hegelianism of ideas". In actual reality the opposition is for the *most* part not pure and absolute: there is a kernel of truth in the error – and vice versa. In keeping with this Küng concludes that it is in the acknowledgement of shared truth that encounter takes place and that the Church is established as "the pillar and bulwark of the truth".

Note
1. Otto Karrer (1888–1976), theologian, lived in Lucerne and made significant contributions to Catholic theology through his work in the biblical, ecumenical and pastoral fields.
Taken from *Schweizerische Kirchenzeitung* No. 5 (1962).

IV: The Nature of the Church

THE CHURCH (1967)

HANS URS VON BALTHASAR
The Task Imposed by our Heritage[1]

Hans Küng's book *The Church* is without doubt his most powerful work to date, and most of his earlier works now look like preparatory studies for it. It is a book which, although marked by passionate feeling, is superlative and well-knit in its construction, lucid in its analysis and written in a vigorous, clear, sometimes sweeping, rhetorical style. It deliberately offers an ecumenical doctrine of the Church by the end of which every Catholic scandal in the eyes of Protestants has basically been done away with. It builds on and incorporates the work of both Karl Barth (especially as far as ecclesiology is concerned) and Rudolf Bultmann (especially with regard to Christology), something that definitely needed to be done, just as much as the liberation of the old Catholic ecclesiology of the schoolmen from a heap of obsolete things piled up all askew, the inventions of that "evasive logic" (Przywara) of neoscholasticism that often did not dare look difficulties in the eye but escaped from the dilemma with tortuous distinctions.[i] Küng does a great job of mucking out, like a Hercules in the Augean stables or a Cyclops using boulders as stones for building; behind the book lies a great mass of painstaking detailed work, which has been absorbed in a clear and polished result. With regard to many of the subjects that are raised one says with a sigh of relief: "At last things are being called by their proper name." To list only a few: the sections on "The

(i) In many books Küng has extolled the virtue of Christian "truthfulness"; what he means by this can be seen from those passages where he eliminates Catholic "evasions" (e.g. pp. 281-3, 322-4).

Church and the Jews" (pp. 132ff), on "The Church and the heretics" (pp. 241ff), on the meaning and limitations of excommunication (pp. 256–7), on all forms of triumphalism in the Church, the clericalization of the Church, the perversion even in the case of the papacy of the "primacy of service" into a "rigid, impatient and aggressive authoritarianism" (p. 465), etc. Throughout the attempt is made to come to grips with the exegetical difficulties (there is an excellent passage on "the twelve" and the "apostolate", pp. 344ff) – to such an extent, admittedly, that in efforts to take the wind out of the sails of even the most radical views some of the substance that cannot be abandoned seems to have been surrendered. It should also be noted that it is only with one side, with Protestantism, that the dialogue is conducted; Küng has little appreciation for the particular virtues of the Eastern Church. [ii] And of course it would be petty and out of place in a book as full of passion as this to demand that in every case formulations should be balanced precisely down to the last detail. What matters primarily is the design that is to be sketched out.

If in what follows we register some hesitations regarding this design, this should in no way diminish admiration for an extraordinary achievement. but should rather prompt the reader to make his or her own considered reflections about the consequences for the work of construction and consolidation that follows (which of course involves one at once in the Church's practice and discipline) and about how abrupt the break is with past tradition. For it is clear that if in practice one accepts the idea of *sola scriptura* (tradition is the *norma normata* [p. 16] in such a way that what cannot be *directly* deduced from scripture must without fail be dropped), then everything that is shown to be merely the conclusion from scriptural premises already seems questionable. In this Küng demonstrates a lively understanding of the variety of perspectives in which the mystery of the

(ii) "The much-vaunted continuity of the Eastern tradition with the New Testament does not stand the test of critical investigation at important points" (pp. 278–9). Neoplatonism was victorious there.

Church is seen as early as the New Testament itself (pp. 16ff); he wants these differing viewpoints to be neither dissociated nor to suffer from premature harmonization (p. 18). And he puts forward what in our view is a very exact threefold criterion for the New Testament writings themselves according to which their importance for the interpretation of the core of revelation can and should be investigated: chronology (1 Corinthians is *earlier* than Ephesians), authenticity (1 Corinthians is *genuine*, Titus probably not), and relevance (1 Corinthians is closer to the matter of the Gospel of Jesus himself than James) (p. 19). But in applying these criteria certain things appear which do not emerge from Küng's work: Galatians (2:20) is earlier than Romans, and it is from this that one must interpret what "faith" means in Paul's writings. 2 Corinthians – a genuine major epistle on the apostolate and obedience – is never valued by Küng according to its real significance. But the problem emerges to its fullest extent if, going along with the radical critique of the gospels, one begins to dissect the core of the message of Christ itself layer by layer, so that hardly anything is left of the original layer, and a testimony as early and as authentic as the verse from Galatians referred to above (2:20): "The life I now live in the flesh I live by faith in the Son of God, who loved me and gave himself for me", is itself reduced to an "objectively" late piece of interpretation of the "Jesus event".

Hence in what follows three considerations that affect the foundations of Küng's doctrine of the Church need setting out together with their consequences.

(1) It is clear that the form of every New Testament ecclesiology is determined by the Christology on which it is based. As far as Küng is concerned what Jesus proclaimed can (after all post-Easter additions have been removed) be summed up under five headings (pp. 47ff): the final and absolute reign of God at the end of time is as an event near at hand; it is a powerful, sovereign act of God himself; it is a purely religious (non-political) reign; it is the saving event for sinners; and it demands of men and women a radical decision for God, not by withdrawal from the world but by

conversion as faith in the message of salvation. With Bultmann the expectation that the end was near (as a secondary
factor) is interpreted in terms of the primacy factor of the
absolute decision for the (present and future) reign of God
(p. 61). That the pre-Easter Jesus founded a Church is denied
by Küng (p. 72). The Church emerges only after the experience of the resurrection of him who had been crucified: it is
a "post-Easter phenomenon" (p. 73); "it was not any particular words of Jesus, nor ultimately his teachings, but his
person as the hidden Messiah and as the risen Christ, which
historically speaking constitutes the roots of the Church"
(p. 76). These statements need not be disputed here. But if
A. Vögtle is right in his opinion (summarized in small print
on pp. 76–7)[iii] that as a result of his rejection by his people
Jesus came to understand himself as the representative
suffering servant of God and his cross as an "atoning death"
(cf. the words of institution at the Last Supper), and if in
connection with this we talk of imitating Jesus up to and
including his cross (something which Küng overlooks almost
entirely), then this goes considerably beyond the five points
cited above and to a quite considerable extent establishes
the relationship between teacher and disciples, between the
Church's one foundation and the Church itself.

Meanwhile the post-Easter proclamation by the Church –
of course with continual reference to the sign of salvation
which God has raised up in Jesus's cross and resurrection –
is now governed and limited by these five points of Jesus's
proclamation of the kingdom, among which his own person
(and even more his suffering) is not objectively included.[iv]
Inasmuch as the aim here is to limit the proclamation of the

(iii) That Küng rejects Vögtle's interpretation as too far-reaching seems
to emerge clearly from the statement on p. 365: "It was only the deep
impression made by Jesus's life and death, as showing a unique obedience and a devotion to God and man, that caused the community to
describe Jesus's death in terms of cultic images of sacrifice (only one of
many kinds of imagery used to describe the event of Christ)."
(iv) "The five perspectives of the preaching of the reign of God through
Jesus . . . thus become ecclesiological imperatives" (p. 97). Without a
doubt this is true, but it is not the whole truth.

Gospel to testimony to an act of pure grace by God in Christ and to demand a radical decision for God, this is absolutely right. But is it true that the Church can "only testify" (p. 98), that "the one and only essential commission which the Church has been given with regard to the world" is this, "to be a witness to the world" (p. 487)? This latter point is then given special emphasis for the benefit of those who hold office in the Church: while the Church is always in danger of turning itself into a mediator, Christ is the only mediator and "all the others are no more and no less than the witnesses and ambassadors of this one mediator" (p. 369). This is a proposition that has been emphatically defended by Karl Barth. But it hardly seems to do justice to something testified to by the gospels, the involvement of the disciples in Jesus's life before Easter, up to and including his eucharist and passion (however wretched this involvement may then have appeared), and thus to the real connection between Jesus and his Church (which certainly only understood itself as such after Easter). If it is said that the Apostle is "not just a witness . . . but someone who has been sent and authorized by the Lord himself" (p. 352) to "exercise discipline in the Churches" (ibid.) and to "command the obedience of the community" (p. 353), this statement is however (a) limited to the apostles and (b) not brought into connection with Christ's obedience unto death on the cross, just as the passion in its concrete significance nowhere comes into view despite its determining so decisively the life of Paul ("I have been crucified with Christ", Gal. 2:20) and through him that of the community.

The pre-Pauline hymn on Christ obedient unto death, to which Paul added the phrase "even death on a cross" (Phil. 2:6–11), is not, despite all Protestant efforts, something to be cut loose from the ecclesiological context. All this kind of thing has been emphasized more strongly by Barth than by Küng. Connected with this is the fact that the Church's character as a mystery (with which the constitution on the Church makes its beginning in chapter 1) recedes very much into the background in favour of the theology of the "people of God" (in the second chapter of Vatican II's constitution), and in the process the doctrine of the "people of God" is more heavily overburdened than it was by the Council in its New Testament application. (v) The phrase "people of God" is primarily an Old Testament term which is hardly used by the New Testament apart from citations of Old Testament passages; (vi) it remains an appellation which today has a very topical and polemical application as against a purely "hierarchical" conception of the Church (pp. 125ff), but which already has a somewhat anachronistic effect in an age when nationalisms and national characteristics belong to the past or ought gradually to form part of it. "People" is an "image" just as much as "body" or "bride" or "temple" or "vineyard"; and in the same way important analogies can be drawn from the "democratic" outlook – all Christians on an equal footing, all offices *only* ministries – provided their analogical character is not overlooked. From all this the two further considerations are derived.

(2) Starting from the concept of "people" it is natural to go on to let the "functions" of the individual be articulated from the whole, as "charisms" (ministerial graces) in the community of the faithful; and "each Christian has *his* charism" (p. 187). Corresponding to this are the statements: "All Church offices can be subsumed under the charism" (p. 187) (vii) and "the charismatic structure of the Church . . . includes but goes far beyond the hierarchical structure of the Church" (p. 188). In this it is clearly stressed that it is God alone who by his vocation bestows charisms and not the Church that autonomously distributes them: it remains "under the reign of the Spirit" (p. 173). But what, then, is office in the Church and where does it come from? In dealing with this question of Küng's, difficult enough for anyone to answer, let us try not always to oversimplify by combining quite clear ideas: there are the Pauline communities, charis-

(v) As far as the Council is concerned this has been emphasized particularly by, among many others, Henri de Lubac, e.g. in his *Paradoxe et Mystère de l'Église* (Paris 1967).
(vi) Küng's citations from the New Testament on pp. 121–2 need careful examination to see what they actually prove.
(vii) Cf. p. 420: "office and charism" would be an unreal alternative

matically structured, the model of which is Corinth, and in
these to begin with there is nothing of a presidential office
to be seen, this being something that is first sketched in by
the Lucan Acts of the Apostles and by the late pastoral
epistles;[viii] there is on the other hand the community of
Jerusalem, which was organized on much more officially
structured lines, and which took over, among other things,
from contemporary Judaism the rites of transmission of
office (ordination through the laying on of hands). But since
both forms of ministry "presuppose the original witness and
the original commission of the apostles" (p. 420) and must
be in agreement with this, there are "common features"
shared by these two forms of Church order, and "finally
these common features are the reason why the Church of
the present does not have to make an exclusive choice
between two alternatives" (p. 422). To put it another way:
it is not the bishops but "the whole Church" that is the
successor of the Apostles (p. 355). It is the whole Church
which baptizes, "which bears the authority to forgive sins"
(p. 332), is "empowered . . . to celebrate the Lord's Supper"
(ibid.). But inasmuch as the whole Church must be obedient
to the Lord (p. 357) it must order itself according to the
pattern of Christ and his Apostles and must perform its
ministerial services in such a way that in the mutual[ix] sub-
ordination of members to each other charisms and offices
are exercised in a Christ-like and apostle-like way. The
necessary conclusion, with of course reference to the original
model, is the Church's articulation of itself in its offices, the

(viii) Evidence like that of 1 Thess. 5:12 ff. and 1 Clement 44 seems to
me to be undervalued.

(ix) "Authority in the community is derived not from the holding of a
certain rank . . . but from the performance of a ministry in the Spirit.
The obedience of all is due to God, Christ, the Spirit; only a limited,
and never a unilateral, obedience is due to other men in the community. The consequence of the obedience of all to God, Christ and
the Spirit is voluntary and *mutual* submission, . . . voluntary obedience
to the different charisms of others" (p. 401, author's italics). This is an
ideal picture that can probably only be realized in heaven, not however
in this real Church composed as it is, as Küng continually stresses, of
sinners.

distribution and criticism of which pertains to the entire Church community (the possibility of deposing all office-holders up to and including the Pope is dealt with on pp. 452–3). This and nothing else is the "constructional formula" which must not be contravened (p. 341), while everything else, including the Church structure brought forward by Vatican II, represents "the historical forms of ecclesiastical office as conditioned by changing circumstances" (p. 420). One of the consequences of this set of ideas would be that, just as every lay man and woman can baptize in an emergency and can probably also give absolution in an emergency (pp. 379–80), a layman or laywoman could on the basis of a charism bestowed on him or her "by the freedom of the spirit of God" approach the altar in order to celebrate an "emergency eucharist" (p. 443). "These", Küng remarks, "are at least debatable questions", which the author of this review does not presume to settle but on which the Church itself will have to judge whether or not in this case it reaches the responsible understanding of itself in the face of God's word that is needed.

A further point needs to be discussed under the heading of charisms. When the "chief difficulties" for the Protestants with regard to the Catholic Church are being dealt with, "the primacy and infallibility of the Pope (and in the latter connection [sic] the recent Marian dogmas)" are mentioned (p. 311). The papacy is explicitly discussed, but Mariology on the other hand – though it is the object of two thousand years' reflection by the Church on manifest scriptural data, and moreover the object of the important concluding chapter of Vatican II's constitution on the Church – is passed over with noticeable silence apart from a mention of Mary's assent which, like the assent and the faith of every individual Christian, is a presupposition for the Church to be possible (p. 129). But not a word on the Church's insight, grasped continuously since the second century, that this personal assent by Mary has in a completely unique sense the quality of founding the Church, that it is both the Church's archetype or original and its model for imitation, that the relationship of the son of God to his mother remains of the highest

ecclesiological relevance. This complex of ideas that for
Catholic ecclesiology cannot be surrendered must either be
destroyed along with much else or (as the Council has done)
be integrated in a new way; dead silence serves no one in
this case, and it is not true (as Karl Barth once held) that
dogmas can in this way simply become superannuated and
obsolete. It would moreover not have been difficult to inte-
grate the great charisms of the Church's history into the
theory of charisms as they have been bestowed by the Holy
Spirit, instead of passing over these too in almost complete
silence – there is a mention of Francis of Assisi in one
passage[x] – although seen as a whole they constitute the
major evangelical impulses of the Church's history in contrast to its dark sides (which are so strongly emphasized).
Admittedly, Küng makes no secret of his antipathy towards
all monastic existence, which seems to him to be marked by
a flight from the world and by particularism[xi] and which
also marks an institutionalization of the charisms. The
charism of celibacy, too, should not in his view be made a
general prescription of canon law (p. 437). From the general
principle that it is not incumbent upon the Christian to make
atonement, since Christ has done that sufficiently for all, it
follows that he or she should occupy himself or herself as a
"sacrifice of thanks and praise" in the service of his or her
neighbour (pp. 369–70), and on the basis of this the Lord's
Supper can no longer be regarded as a sacrifice of the Church
(p. 215).

(3) The final consideration is concerned with whether the
Church's character as a mystery finds sufficient expression
in this theology. Küng emphasizes very forcefully that it is
his aim to talk about "the Church as it is" which is composed of sinful human beings (p. 34), which never in history
mirrors its essence "perfectly and exhaustively" (p. 6), which
does not hover above its members as a Platonic idea, not
even as far as its holiness is concerned (and this in turn is a

(x) "What would have become of the Church if Francis of Assisi had
never been?" (p. 434).
(xi) An attitude to be detected when he argues that Jesus cannot have
singled out the Apostles (pp. 52 and 72).

purely eschatological concept [p. 327], as is true if you drop Mariology), which does not possess any "institutional sanctity" in the sense of "a sacred 'it' " (p. 325), but only a "completely personal sanctity" depending on the forgiving and sanctifying action of a personal God and on the acceptance of this gracious gift of God in the personal act of faith. "There must be no hypostatization of the Church", it can "never be merely a super-entity poised above real human beings and their real decision" (p. 129). Now, all this is stated in polemical terms, and is also good Barthian stuff; nevertheless this Church which "grows from below" and is "definitely the work of man" (p. 93, cf. p. 33) is not formed "by the free association of individuals" but "is more than the sum of its members" (p. 86) inasmuch as it is the community summoned together by God.

In the analysis of the idea of the "body of Christ" (pp. 203–60) an isolated *opus operatum* concept of the sacraments (i.e. baptism and eucharist) is admittedly criticized,[xii] but there is then need for reflection on being given "a share in the death and resurrection of Christ" through baptism (Rom. 6:3–11) and on the "share in Christ's unique sacrifice on the cross" in the eucharist (pp. 208, 215). In this all abstract interpretation of "being in Christ" and of "sanctifying grace" is avoided; instead Küng prefers to talk of a "legal concept" and "competence" (p. 206) or of a personal "presence" of the Lord (p. 217), of "encounter with a person" (p. 221). He is right in saying that the "organic images" (head and body, vine and branches, etc.) must always be corrected by the personal ones (such as husband and wife), and that on this basis no essential identification of Christ and the Church can be made (p. 239). But is not the contrasted line of thought necessary if one does not want to end up in an anthropomorphic personalism for which God is simply man's "other", which in intellectual terms would be just the other side of the road? I leave the question open, in

(xii) "The concept of sacrament needs further examination which is outside the scope of this book" (p. 379, n. 12), but it must have been developed in outline in working out an ecclesiology.

the same way as so many other vitally interesting questions raised by Küng's book must also be left open.

One concluding wish: that the series of "ecumenical studies" planned by Küng and Ratzinger (announced on the last page) will present not only Protestants who have shaped our image of the Church (Luther, Calvin, confessional writings of the Reformation, the Anglicans, Wesley, Schleiermacher, Bonhoeffer, and the Bultmann school are announced – and the only Catholic to balance these would have to be Bellarmine) but also standard and representative Catholics, and of these the most central would probably be the saints: Augustine (but he needs a fresh presentation), but also the Victorines, Hildegard, Catherine of Siena, Fénelon, etc. From such figures one would discover the source from which Catholic piety is fed: from the living out of the mystery of following and imitating Christ, in a reverential but burning love of the person, both divine and human, of the redeemer, as we see it aflame in Paul and in the entire New Testament; something for which hardly any room still seems to be left in the historical and critical Christology of our age.

HUGH MONTEFIORE
A New Classic on the Church[2]

I had only to glance at the book to see it was good. By page 100 I realized it was very good. By page 250 I knew it was a classic. By page 500, although panting somewhat, I stood firm in my conviction. When you do get to the end, you feel as though you have successfully completed an Oxfam walk. You certainly need your second wind before page 388, where you are somewhat daunted to read in small type, with reference to Küng's earlier work *Structures of the Church*, that "Chapters VI–VIII of that book (pp. 95–352) must be presupposed here."

Why am I so sure it's a classic? In the first place, it so happens that there's a vacancy in the subject. It's extraordinary, after all the upsurge of ecclesiastical concern that accompanied "biblical theology", that until now no one has produced an English classic about the church. (If you read again Thornton's *Common Life in the Body of Christ* you'll find it dated.) Secondly, Küng is a rare bird, a systematic theologian without an axe to grind. And so he writes with sensitivity, simplicity, orderliness and immense learning: a very remarkable foursome. Thirdly, Küng has mastered biblical exegesis. His aim is to "awaken a living consciousness of the word of God as witnessed in Scripture". It's strange, but when Roman Catholic scholars turn their attention to the Bible, they often seem to me to make better exegetes than Protestants. Fourthly, this book is *not merely radical and reformatory: it's revolutionary*. Once people take the Bible seriously and intelligently, there's no knowing what can result. Küng is guided by a profound biblical spirituality. Fifthly, *the book breathes throughout a real ecumenism*. Again and again the non-Roman will say at least an *Amen* if not an *Alleluiah* and he will turn back with amazement to that *Nihil obstat* sticking out obstinately on the title page.

Hans Küng is Professor of Fundamental Theology at the Catholic Faculty of Theology at Tübingen. He became well known from his radical writings at the time of Vatican II. His influence on the ecumenical movement has been vast. How "far out" is he as a Roman Catholic? I wish I knew whether his influence on his own church has been or will be proportionately great; for here's the rub.

Within this systematic study many fundamental matters get discussed, for example, the relation of the Church to the Jews, to "enthusiasts", to heretics, and to those "*extra ecclesiam*". Küng's method is to find scriptural principles by which to attack each problem. The selection of such principles may however involve an unacknowledged subjectivity. Take for example heresy. Küng acknowledges that there is always truth in heresy, and asserts the good faith of heretics as well as the bad record of the Church. He propounds the basic principle that "love must be the rule even in matters of faith". Excellent; but I doubt whether this is in fact the basic principle about heresy in the Bible itself.

Küng begins by distinguishing the reality of the Church

from its vocation, and he sets the Church and the Kingdom of God in splendid perspective. Turning to the Church's fundamental structure, he expounds it as the People of God (but why the "new" people of God, an unbiblical addition?), as the Creation of the Spirit and as the Body of Christ. Turning next to what he calls the "dimensions" of the Church, he discusses what it means to be one, catholic, holy and apostolic, incidentally turning upside down conventional meanings. ("Apostolic succession" means the whole Church confronted with the witness of the apostles and continuing their apostolic mission and obedience!) The last section of the book is devoted to the "Offices of the Church" (with an excellent discussion of the ministry in the apostolic and sub-apostolic age); and only the final chapter is concerned with the Petrine power and the Petrine ministry. As Küng properly observes, "readers who begin at this point are making a mistake".

Nonetheless the last section is important. The English edition (which, apart from misprints, has been well translated) is dedicated to the Archbishop of Canterbury. "This will record my humble hope that there lies within the pages of this book a theological basis for a *rapprochement* between the churches of Rome and Canterbury." (I wish that Küng had seen fit to notice Dr Ramsey's own *Gospel and the Catholic Church*, a harbinger in this country at least of a more biblical ecclesiology.) Here is Küng's vision of what might happen:

> The Church of England for its part would be given the guarantee that it could retain in its entirety its present autochthonous and autonomous church order under the Primate of Canterbury (not merely, therefore, like the Eastern "rites" in communion with Rome): and on the other hand the Church of England would recognize a pastoral primacy of the Petrine ministry as the supreme court of appeal, mediating and settling disputes between the churches.

Does "pastoral primacy" include settling disputes such as

the pill, I wonder? If so, matters would have to move far and fast before Küng's entrancing vision could become sober reality.

How does Küng hope that these two churches may be reconciled? On the subject of Papal Infallibility and the Marian dogmas practically nothing is said, and the reader is referred to *Structures of the Church*. (I cannot help noting that the Blessed Virgin Mary, far from being the "Mother of the Church", is not so much as mentioned in either index or text. This suggests the distance which separates Küng from many of his Roman Catholic contemporaries.) So far as Papal Jurisdiction is concerned, the Pope is urged to undertake a voluntary renunciation of spiritual power, without which both the reunion of Christendom and the renewal of the Church are seen to be impossible.

> Can we hope that the offensive aspects of the definitions of Vatican I might become as immaterial as, for example, the *dictatus papae* . . ., if the successors of John XXIII, voluntarily renouncing their spiritual power, were to commit themselves to serving the Church along these lines? The voluntary laying aside of the tiara, the emblem of papal dominion, by Pope Paul VI, and other measures of reform in the same direction show that this hope is not entirely without foundation.

Küng is not over-sanguine – his hope is "not entirely without foundation". Would not a voluntary renunciation *in perpetuo* of truths and functions believed to have been infallibly defined, come perilously near to their repudiation? Küng himself can face this, but can the whole Church to which he belongs? "The decisions of the Council of Trent (*or of other councils*) cannot be regarded as binding definitions where they concern questions which are being put differently today in the light of completely different problems" (italics mine).

At this point I cannot help thinking of Charles Davis's *A Question of Conscience*. Küng is quoted on the blurb thus: "Precisely because *The Church* was not written in an attempt to justify any continuing allegiance to the Church, it may all

the better perform this service." Küng in his way is just as
concerned with the credibility of the Church as Davis, just
as aware of the difference between scriptural testimony and
current practice. Davis believes that certain papal dogmas
are wrong and should be openly denounced: and so he left
the Church. Küng believes that certain papal functions are
unbiblical and should be voluntarily renounced, and so he
speaks from within the Church. Davis believes that the Pope's
equivocation over contraception, and the continuance of
curial politics, symbolize hopeless structural obstacles in the
way of the Church's renewal. Küng sets no bounds to the
renewal of the Church when confronted by the word of God
as witnessed in Scripture.

You pay your money and take your choice. Historically
speaking, there can be no doubt that the odds on Küng's
vision turning into reality must be very long indeed. But
then for a Christian, the odds are always very long. It's part
of the gamble.

Notes
1. Hans Urs von Balthasar, theologian, born 1905, lives in
Basle, and is one of the leading Catholic theologians of his
generation.
Taken from *Civitas* 23 (1967–8), pp. 450–4.
2. Hugh Montefiore, Anglican Bishop of Birmingham since
1978, born 1920, a convert from Judaism while still at
school. Fellow of Gonville and Caius, Cambridge, 1954–63,
vicar of Great St Mary's, Cambridge, 1963–70, suffragan
Bishop of Kingston-upon-Thames, 1970–7.
Taken from *New Christian*, 13 June 1968, and used by kind
permission of the author.

V: The Dispute about Infallibility

INFALLIBLE? An Enquiry (1970)

JOHN L. MCKENZIE
Hans Küng on Infallibility: This Tiger is not Discreet[1]

The centennial of the proclamation of the dogma of papal infallibility has been celebrated by Hans Küng in his own private and personal way: He has published this book attacking the dogma.

Bishop Francis Simons of Indore, India, anticipated the centennial with his own slender volume attacking infallibility in 1968. Granted that the bishop is not a professional theologian; granted also that his book employed remarkably fundamentalist theological method and argument to attack a very fundamentalist thesis. The fact remains that I expected the book to receive more attention than it did receive.

But when the Herr Professor of the Catholic Faculty of Tübingen works on infallibility, it is another story; the Herr Professor happens to be the most articulate and prolific Catholic theologian of continental Europe (and this may indeed limit him more than he deserves). That he should receive more and closer attention may be something more than the snobbishness of the intellectual world, although this is one's first impression.

He has been dignified by an almost instant response from Karl Rahner (of which more below); the German bishops' conference has found that the book fails to uphold some fundamental elements; and *L'Osservatore Romano* surprises us by coming in late with no more than a report that the bishops have issued "a clear and severe judgement". This, Küng has responded, is exactly what it is not, and he appears to be correct. The recent Roman statements on the abandonment of such things as condemnation, censure and prohibition have been put to a test very early after their publication; it looks as if they were prepared in anticipation of this response.

Küng's book is another spin-off from *Humanae vitae*, and he begins with a fairly full discussion of the encyclical and of reasons why it cannot be a truthful statement of moral teaching. One may wonder, as this writer did, whether the problem of the encyclical has to lead to an examination of the infallible teaching office, an examination which is certain to exacerbate controversy. Küng explains his own motivation clearly by a reconstruction of the thinking behind the encyclical.

He believes it was the conviction of the Pope and the curia that the teaching on birth control had been so frequently and so clearly stated that they regarded it as already established infallibly on that basis which theologians call "the ordinary teaching office". In their minds the encyclical said nothing new and could not say anything new. I do not know whether this analysis is correct, and my own analysis has been slightly different; but I cannot claim to be as close to the boiler room as Küng has been.

I said in a small symposium (*Erosion of Authority*, edited by Clyde Manschreck, Abingdon Press, 1970) that in my own candidly conjectural interpretation the Pope and the curia never expected the encyclical to be taken seriously. It had to be said in order to protect the image of pontifical teaching, especially since most of this teaching has been stated in this century; and the preservation of this image was more important, in the long range view of the Church, than moral clarity and peace of conscience among the faithful.

The memory of Pius XI and Pius XII had been vindicated; the encyclical would be praised, accepted and quickly forgotten. It had not been necessary to reverse the Galileo verdict, and neither should it be necessary to reverse *Casti Connubii*. Such reversals are left to history, not to the Roman curia.

I am quite aware that this interpretation may appear to presume a high degree of cynicism in the Roman authorities, and this imputation is not necessarily implied. Such thinking can appear cynical only to those who do not know the depth of the sincerity with which the Roman curia identifies the good of the Roman Catholic Church with the image of the papacy. At the same time, the Roman curia has proved its capacity for cynicism; and those who make decisions of common concern must expect the decisions to be examined by those who are concerned.

I have had occasion to touch infallibility in two books which I have published since 1965, and I looked back to see what I had done. I found no tiger lurking in the pages; I did not touch infallibility, I skirted it. I had some half-formed ideas at the time, which I shall employ this occasion to set forth with a little more fullness below. Küng has made it unnecessary to do another full scale survey of the theological material. At least I am not the man to fault Küng for bringing into the open a problem with which I, judged on my own writings, had some extensive poorly concealed dissatisfaction.

I was what Rahner says Küng was not, *vorsichtig*, which is not so much prudent or foresighted as circumspect. Well, you hardly ever meet a circumspect tiger. *Vorsicht* in a theologian is that quality by which he knows when to say nothing that has not been said so often it is safe to repeat it.

Küng's examination of Vatican Council I reveals nothing that all theologians have not known – namely, that the biblical and traditional evidence for infallibility is scanty, and that the personal desires of Pius IX had much to do with the declaration. The main thrust of Küng's attack, however, is found in his argument that an infallibility of propositions is impossible. Once again the basis of the argument is not novel; "propositional revelation" has been in bad odour in recent theology for the past 20 years. The argument is epistemological rather than theological, and I doubt very much that it will convince those who habitually think in neo-scholastic patterns. The definition of "truth" is a philosophical dispute which the White Queen almost always wins.

I would myself lay more stress on the essential contingency

of language, which makes it impossible to present an eternally meaningful proposition, although in the neo-scholastic sense of the word it may be eternally true. I have in mind such things as the ancient Trinitarian and Christological formulae, which speak in no way to the contemporary understanding of personality, or transubstantiation, which is meaningless in so far as it is taken to imply an Aristotelian theory of the constitution of matter. Yet it was the ancient understanding of personality and the Aristotelian theory of matter which were in the minds of the authors of these formulae.

An infallible declaration, even in the most conservative theology, has never been construed to mean that it was impossible to say any more on the subject, that new knowledge and new understanding were perpetually excluded. Defenders of infallibility rather easily fall into this trap. The principle is also valid for the declaration of infallibility, and this makes it possible for Küng to proceed to his next step. I may add as illustrations the more recent dogmas of the Immaculate Conception and the Assumption, which I confess as what the Catholic Church believes and teaches; I have not the slightest idea of what either dogma means, and therefore they create no problem for me.

Should it be a problem for me that I believe something which I find meaningless? I do not see why; many Catholics believe what they misunderstand or do not understand. It is a defined article of faith that the bodies of the just in the resurrection will not be spheroid; I happen to know why this was declared, but I have never attempted to make this eternal verity the object of contemplation, I have never used it in preaching and I cannot say that it has enriched my Christian life. It may be an early example of magisterial overkill, which is certainly part not only of Küng's problem, but of the problem of the Church. In the usual sense of the term, this dogma is meaningless.

DOCTRINAL BLOOPERS
Most Catholics think their basic dogma is the divinity of Christ. Ask them to define it, and they will say it means of

course that Christ is God. Translate that statement into Greek and say it to St Paul, and he will throw you out of the Church. Surely if there is an eternal verity here, there is some difficulty in formulating it.

Küng has given less space than it needs to the exposition of error in the exercise of the teaching office. I say less because even theological students sometimes cherish illusions about the actual state of inerrancy in the Church. In fact the teaching authority of the Church has made about as many mistakes on the average as any agency which has ever engaged in teaching. Since *Humanae vitae* several theologians have prepared lists of doctrinal bloopers of the Holy See. Most of them are obscure, of course; Rome buries its bodies rather well. I would not say that all are trivial, and many of them deal with morality.

My own question – one of those half-formed ideas – is: What name do you give to an infallible teaching authority which makes mistakes? The first word that comes to mind is "fallible". The correct theological answer at this point would be to enumerate the restrictions under which the infallible authority is exercised. The next question is how I know whether these restrictions are observed in the case before me, or whether the teacher knows when they are observed. I fear my colleagues do not realize that their answer sounds very much like a statement that the teaching authority is infallible except when it makes mistakes. Since I can claim that much infallibility, I can live with it; but it seems that the doctrine might be one of those which I termed meaningless. Infallibility, I submit, is like virginity in that you cannot have some of it sometimes. In baseball, errorless play means that each chance is handled correctly; but perhaps baseball has higher ideals of performance than theology.

The central question, as Küng calls it, does not lie for me where he puts it, although there is room enough in this can of worms for everyone to have his own central question. The central question for a theologian of good intentions who would like to find meaning in what he believes is that the Roman interpretation of infallibility claims so much that it becomes irrational and unreal, and if the claim is modified as I suggested above, it becomes meaningless.

TWO UNHAPPY EXTREMES

Now Küng has tried to locate the doctrine between two unhappy extremes; I am not sure he has found the right place, or that his colleagues will agree with him; but the question has to be raised some time, and this may be the hour.

I believe, on this reading both of his book and of Rahner's criticism, that Küng has restated a dogma rather than denied it; he has certainly denied the prevailing interpretation, which may not be *vorsichtig* but is certainly honest and may be accurate. The prevailing interpretation needs something; maybe what it needs is help, but maybe it is reinterpretation.

Küng more or less collapses infallibility into another quality of the Church called indefectibility. This quality does not mean only that the Church will not cease to exist, but that it will never lose its identity. Now Küng asserts that error in doctrine manifestly does not destroy the identity of the Church. Infallibility of propositions is unnecessary to safeguard its identity. The history of error in Catholic doctrine is enough to show that error in doctrine does not destroy identity; if it did, identity would be long gone.

What the Church is secured against is that kind or degree of error which would mean that it no longer proclaimed the Gospel. Granted that this is much less definite than the prevailing interpretation, it also does not run into the rocks of reality. It makes clearer the responsibility of the teachers to assure themselves of the truth of their teaching and to exercise a personal restraint on their authority, which as yet no one is trying to take away from them nor to put under restraints other than the conscience of the Church. I think this conscience affirms that doctrine is not a private game preserve in which only popes, bishops and Lateran theologians may hunt.

Küng, I believe, moves in the right direction, and much more must be said. I take him seriously when he says equivalently that he wishes to open a discussion rather than to close it – one of the qualities which makes him a more attractive person than curial theologians.

I have a couple of not too well related remarks to add – more of those half-formed ideas.

One is that infallibility means at least this: The Church and only the Church knows what it believes, just as only I know what I believe. The Church may not at this moment see its own mind clearly, as I may not see mine; it may not find the right expression for what it believes, it may find a better expression later, it may learn something which illuminates the dark corners of its faith. But ultimately if I wish to know what I must believe only the Church can tell me what it believes. My main interest is not whether the faith of the Church is infallible in all details; as a professional theologian I know that it has never been. My main interest is whether it is the faith of the Church. I am not looking for any other faith, and I believe that this Church, with its spots and wrinkles, proclaims the faith that saves.

I said the Church; and therefore I think that *ex cathedra* must be clearly understood to mean that the Pope speaks only *in* the Church, never *to* the Church. It must be the faith of the Church and not his own which he proclaims if he is to speak with authority. If it be not blasphemy to say it, the Church is bigger than the Roman See.

PREJUDICED REMARK

Küng quotes a remark made in the pontifical commission on birth control; I have seen it quoted elsewhere, but never directly attributed to anyone by name. The remark was that acceptance of the majority view would say to the world that the Holy Spirit had been with Lambeth in 1930 and not with Rome in 1931, and that the Holy Spirit has been with the Protestants ever since.

It is easy to dismiss this incredibly narrow and prejudiced remark, and to take it as evidence that the interest of such men was not primarily either with sound moral doctrine or with the consciences of Catholics. I ask those who disclaim it to realize the ecumenical implications of the disclaimer. If one accepts the language of this speaker one must recognize that he is entirely right; to disclaim the remark is to disclaim the language. Those who think that *Humanae vitae* is in error are not thereby implying that the Holy Spirit is either at Lambeth or at Rome; they clearly imply that the Lambeth synod spoke the truth where Pius XI did not, but let us leave the Holy Spirit out of it.

In a divided Christianity one may feel the Spirit in other places than Rome. I suppose the Holy Spirit was vacationing in Frascati while they burned Giordano Bruno. It is time for Rome, Lambeth, Wittenberg and Geneva to recognize that they all make it difficult for the Holy Spirit to get anything done.

This furnishes a somewhat tenuous bridge to my next (and otherwise unrelated) observation. It is hard to find the words for what I have in mind, but I take off from Thomas Aquinas, who said that action follows being. The Church *is* something before the Church *does* something, and what it does comes from what it is. Teaching is an activity of the Church, not the reality of the Church. It has never occurred even to Roman theologians to claim impeccability for the Church; the facts will not allow it. Neither will the facts allow infallibility, except in so limited a range that the claim loses meaning. Yet is not the sinfulness of the Church as much a defect in its reality as error is a defect in the teaching office?

I think it can be said safely that the member of the Church should encounter the living and present reality of Jesus in the Church. No one can encounter the whole Church all at once, but only the Church where he is. Let us drop the abstractions and think of real persons; cannot the sinfulness of the Church where one experiences it prevent the individual from faith because he cannot recognize Jesus in the Church?

Let us take a safely remote example, Alexander VI; how easily would one encounter the living presence of Jesus in the papacy of Alexander? Ah yes, the apologist will say, but his doctrine was pure. Who cares? Infallibility so conceived makes it possible to say that it is not important whether the Church is holy as long as its doctrine is pure. Allow me to say that it is important; that the Church in the New Testament is recognized as the people of God not because it is

infallible but because it loves. One may ask in how many
bishops, priests and laity the living presence of Jesus is so
obscured that the Church becomes incredible.

The indefectibility of the Church means that the living
presence of Jesus is always manifested in the Church, but not
always and everywhere with equal clarity. It must not be
forgotten that the Church proclaims by her reality as much
as by the teaching office – or rather proclaims more. We
have to believe that a sinful Church can and does proclaim
by her reality, because that is the only kind of Church we
have.

Karl Rahner responded to Küng's book in *Stimmen der
Zeit* (December, 1970), and the first part of a two-part response from Küng appeared in the next issue. I must record
my own impression that Rahner's critique does not exhibit
the depth and strength which we are accustomed to expect
in Rahner's writings.

He meets Küng's use of *Humanae vitae* by denying that
the doctrine on birth control is a dogma. The only official
or semi-official interpretation of this aspect known to me is
the statement of Mgr Fausto Vallainc, the Vatican press
secretary, that the encyclical is not infallible. I understand
that the monsignor has since been promoted out of Rome;
no connection is hinted. Rahner here as elsewhere in his
writings never clearly affirms the teaching of *Humanae vitae*.
I deduce that he thinks that infallibility can be maintained
even if *Humanae vitae* is wrong. I have stated above my own
difficulties with this position. Much depends here on whether
Küng's interpretation of Vatican thinking about the ordinary teaching office is correct.

RAHNER "EVASIVE"
Rahner goes on to reject Küng's epistemological argument
and to assert that surely some infallible propositions are
possible. I am sorry, but I find this simply evasive; and it
does not justify Rahner's extremely harsh declaration that
his discussion with Küng is not an intra-Catholic discussion.
It was not entirely kind of Küng either to remind Rahner
that one who has so often felt the scourge of curial tongues,

and was even forbidden to publish, cannot gracefully make this kind of imputation concerning another theologian.

Küng's answer is largely an expansion of his argument concerning *Humanae vitae*, and he does adduce some additional material. He also is able to quote the early Rahner against the late Rahner; the early Rahner had a more flexible idea of infallibility than he shows in this article, and Küng not too delicately implies that he departs no more from Vatican I than Rahner has already done. Since I have only the first of two parts, a full discussion of Küng's response is not now possible.

In *Stimmen der Zeit* of February 1971, Küng presents an extended criticism of Rahner's theological methods. This is far too large a question for treatment here; but I should mention that he finds that Rahner is not historical and critical, and calls his method "Denzinger-theology". Denzinger is a famous handbook of quotations from pope, bishops and councils. Küng means that Rahner has a theology of authoritative quotations, divorced from their historical context, their contemporary interpretation and their limitations.

It was, of course, inevitable that a controversy on such a sensitive theme should sooner or later be lowered in tone. I was edified at the tone of the response of the German bishops; even *L'Osservatore* stayed above the level which it knows so well. I am sorry that it was Rahner who lowered the tone. One has the feeling that it was a request performance, but it is his name at the head of the article. Many of us would be happy with a withdrawal and a replacement by another critique more worthy of the author.

WALTHER VON LÖWENICH
Is Küng still a Catholic? The View of a Protestant Theologian[2]

Looking back once on his ninety-five theses on indulgences, Martin Luther remarked that all he had done was to bell the cat: he had simply had the courage to say out loud what innumerable others were thinking in silence. In doing so Luther in 1517 did not in any way see himself as other than a loyal son of the Catholic Church. All this could well be called to mind when one observes the disputes that have broken out around the book *Infallible? An Enquiry* by the well-known Catholic Tübingen theologian Hans Küng.

From the start Küng's published writings have caused a sensation, and rightly so. In his first work, in 1957, he provided an interpretation of the Tridentine doctrine of justification that meant it could no longer be seen as a cause of division between the churches. Various critical utterances concerning the Second Vatican Council brought him an admonition from Rome. In his large-scale book *The Church*, which appeared in 1967, he developed an understanding of the Church which consistently took the biblical message as its starting point and at the same time included historical reality in its purview in an open and, when necessary, critical spirit. The practical consequences he drew from this appeared in the book *Truthfulness: The Future of the Church*, which appeared in 1968. His most recent major work to appear, *Infallible?*, does not provide anything fundamentally new to go beyond what is contained in its predecessors. But it has now in reality done something that in Küng's view others have neglected to do: it has taken the bull by the horns. Hence the tornado it has aroused.

In the event, no Catholic theologian has for a long time expressed himself so unequivocally and unambiguously on a subject that for the past hundred years has been regarded as taboo. What the theology of the Roman schools understands by the infallibility of the Church and of the Pope has been disputed by Küng in a manner that cannot be ignored. Nevertheless he asserts that he is a convinced Catholic theologian. He thinks that in his basic views he is of one mind with other leading contemporary Catholic theologians. He expresses the highest appreciation for Paul VI's integrity. The Council was a magnificent success. But in Küng's view there is now every chance of gambling away all the opportunities that have been opened up. His strong criticism springs from love for the Church. It is not responsible for the unrest that has arisen: all it does is give expression to what already exists and can no longer be passed over in silence.

It is thus easy to understand the extent to which Küng was taken aback when Karl Rahner, his ally for so many years, published an article critical of him in the journal *Stimmen der Zeit* without discussing the matter with him beforehand. His own answer appeared in the January and February issues of 1971, and a concluding statement by Rahner appeared in the March issue. Rahner commits himself to "indisputable propositions" that have their origin in an ultimate fundamental decision. If Küng should no longer adhere to these, then dialogue with him can only be on the same basis as with a "liberal Protestant" or even a "sceptical philosopher". Meanwhile the German bishops' conference published a declaration signed by Cardinal Döpfner on the Küng case. This has met with a varied response from the press.

The reason for the difference in the response is that this episcopal declaration cannot be seen as taking a precise stand on Küng's clearly defined enquiry about the possibility of "infallible" propositions. Küng rightly pointed out that the word "infallible" did not appear in the entire document. He thus regards a further constructive discussion as possible.

Admittedly this declaration includes statements which may be formulated in more reticent terms but which can only be understood as "Roman" in the traditional sense. The Church can lay down propositions "with an ultimate binding force" ("dogmas"). A dogma derives its binding force not from its "agreement with the normative source" (in other words, presumably, with the biblical message) but through the charism of truth that has been bestowed on the Church. The power and authority to make such "ultimately binding" statements belongs to ecumenical councils but also to the Bishop of Rome as successor of St Peter and head of the college of bishops. The bishops explicitly acknowledge the statements of the First and Second Vatican Councils. The five guiding principles laid down by the bishops avoid any actual condemnation. All they do is to describe where in their view the line is to be drawn between what is "Catholic" and what is no longer so.

Has Küng stepped over this line? The Protestant asked to make his own judgement of this question will have to refrain from an unequivocal yes or no, and this not primarily for tactical considerations but predominantly for reasons arising out of the nature of what is at issue. In his book, for which he declined to seek an *imprimatur*, Küng takes as his starting point the crisis of authority which has been occasioned by Paul VI's well-known encyclical on birth control, *Humanae vitae*, along with other papal statements of recent years. Paul VI was unable to decide other than he did because, despite the impression made on him by expert opinion in the contrary sense, he felt in his conscience bound to the Church's doctrinal consensus. The prevention of births was condemned as immoral in the Church's tradition, most recently by Pius XI in 1930. A prohibition of this kind does not need to be the subject of an explicit definition in order to count in practice as infallible. Paul VI could not admit that there had been a mistake in the Church's teaching. In this view of the binding nature of the Church's doctrinal tradition he was supported by the prevailing theology of the Roman schools. The only alternative that remains is to call this entire theory of infallibility into question.

That is what Küng has done. Vatican I was able to provide neither a biblical nor a historical basis for the theory of infallibility. It simply presupposed it. The same charge must also be brought against Vatican II. Over against this Küng asserts that there are no infallible propositions at all. Absolute infallibility belongs to God alone. Neither the Bible nor a council nor such a thing as the Church's teaching authority can lay down "infallible" propositions. All propositions must be understood in their relationship to an actual situation. All propositions fail to measure up to the truth of God. They are not fundamentally protected from error. Insistence on infallible propositions arises from the rationalism of neo-scholasticism and at Vatican I sprang from fear, in other words from lack of faith.

But no more than the faith is the Church dependent on

"infallible" propositions. It lived for centuries without an "infallible" juridical doctrinal principle. It has been given the promise that it will remain preserved in God's truth despite and through all error. The truth of God, however, cannot be identified with "infallible" propositions. For this reason Küng would prefer to talk of "indefectibility" or "persistence in the truth". This view should also meet with ecumenical agreement. Küng regards it as possible that it will prevail in the Catholic Church. In that case the present crisis of authority would not have been in vain. In place of the present juridical doctrinal primacy Küng suggests a "primacy of service" as a programme for the Church. "Carrying it into effect requires patience, and fearless and continuous effort. That in one form or another it will be carried into effect it is impossible to doubt. The only question is whether it will not once again be too late and thus involve excessive losses."

Is Küng "still Catholic"? Perhaps it would be better not to raise this question at all. But it has been raised more or less openly from the Catholic side and should therefore be considered from the Protestant side too. This much is certain, that even twenty years ago this question would have been answered with an unequivocal no. If anyone had disputed the 1870 dogma of infallibility so uncompromisingly, he would have been anathematized. But throughout the hundred years since 1870 covert opposition to this dogma has certainly not been lacking. It was assumed to be without practical effect: the Pope would in future take good care not to speak *ex cathedra*. Pius XII refuted that by his proclamation of the dogma of the Assumption in 1950. But subtle methods of theological interpretation were applied in the attempt to derive a tolerable sense from this definition, and in the process its actual content was often turned very nearly into the exact opposite.

It is to Küng's honour that he has declined to use methods of this kind. Even against Rahner he has to bring the charge of a speculative interpretation of dogma that goes beyond what can be demonstrated by the biblical and historical evidence. It is this evidence that in Küng's view should be decisive, and according to him adequate proof cannot be furnished on these grounds. In this he is in complete agreement with Protestant criticism. Nevertheless the bishops have not decided on a clear condemnation of Küng. Are the guiding principles they lay down addressed perhaps to Rome rather than to Küng? In any case the opening up of the Church brought about by John XXIII has not been without its influence on them.

The reproach often used to be made to Protestants taking part in talks held under the auspices of the Una Sancta movement: "One doesn't know what it is that is really 'Protestant' – your confessional formulations or your modern theology." To a considerable extent the practical policy of Evangelical Church leadership was a *felix inconsequentia*, a happy lack of logic. Officially one clung to the old doctrinal formulations, while modern theologians were left to go their own way in their divergences from these credal statements. In my view this compromise was, despite its confusion, the right one for the situation. It looks as if something similar is now happening in contemporary Catholicism. Evidently there can today no longer be an unequivocal answer to the question "What is Catholic?" Is this a misfortune or an advance that can still appeal to a centuries-long tradition that since the Counter-Reformation has been the victim of growing constriction? Küng's aim is to serve such a Catholicism of the future that will also bring suppressed truth once more into play.

The decisive question, therefore, in the case of Küng should not be: "Is Küng still Catholic?" It should rather be: "Will Catholicism succeed in struggling out of the constriction caused by a juridical understanding of doctrinal authority to reach genuine catholicity?"

HANS KÜNG
A Short Balance-Sheet on the Infallibility Debate[3]

As the author of the book *Infallible? An Enquiry*, I have always freely admitted that I am not infallible. It surprises me that I have not been found guilty of more errors than confusing three ecumenical patriarchs in different centuries in such a complex book, in which I had to define my attitude with regard to so many questions at the same time. May I recall the motto of St Augustine which prefaced the book: "Let me ask of my reader . . wherever he recognizes me to be in error, there to call me back."

I. THE BACKGROUND TO THE BOOK

My "enquiry" into infallibility gave rise to the greatest debate among Catholic theologians that has taken place since Vatican II. The debate has extended far beyond the frontiers of theology and a balance-sheet is urgently required. The many criticisms of my book merit a detailed reply and this will be published this year, together with contributions by fifteen other theologians, a full documentation containing the correspondence with the Congregation of Faith and a bibliography. In this book will be found full arguments and evidence for what is dealt with so briefly here – what has emerged from the debate on infallibility so deliberately unleashed after twelve years of preparation.

Ever since this preparation began with the publication of the German original of my book *Justification* (*Rechtfertigung*) in 1957, I have again and again asked the question implicit in the very historicity of all dogmas, that is, their possible fallibility. I asked it very clearly in my *Structures of the Church* (1965), but it was ignored. It is precisely because of this long period of preparation that I chose to write my "enquiry" in a different style. The more gentle notes of my previous works had not aroused those in responsible positions in the Church, so I had to sound the alarm and they woke up suddenly and complained loudly. What did they complain about? The failure of leadership in the Church since Vatican II? The old and new forms of Roman imperialism? The enormous loss of credibility in the Church? The tens of thousands of priests who have given up their ministry because of the law of celibacy and the established structure of the Church or the crisis among the younger generation that has reached catastrophic proportions? The great suffering caused by wrong decisions concerning mixed marriages, the regulation of births, the appointment of bishops, celibacy and many other matters, in which the ordinary people have no say at all?

No, their complaints have been about the outspoken language of my book. There are cases, and this is one of them, where it is expedient to engage in polemics. The replies to my fair polemics have been polemical enough in themselves and I do not accept that serious polemics are necessarily unscientific. In other words, it is desirable to engage in polemics where it is expedient to do so.

In 1970, after the publication of my *The Theologian and the Church* in 1965, *Truthfulness* in 1968 and *The Church* in 1969, I came back to the old question and concluded that the time had come (1) to strip the Church's teaching office of the mythology and the false ideology that surrounded it and to free the Church from the dishonesty and the pretensions that have for so long characterized Vatican theology and administration; (2) to draw certain conclusions from the initiatives of Vatican II, at which no infallible definitions were made and a positive proclamation of Christian teaching was preferred to the traditional dogmatism of the Roman Church; (3) to make a loyal protest against the doctrinaire leadership in the post-conciliar Church, which has, in many ways – the regulation of births, mixed marriage, celibacy, the election of bishops, the Dutch Church, and so on – resulted in human suffering; (4) to work for a solution to the four-hundred-and-fifty-year-old problem of reunion between the churches in the West; (5) to consider once again the historical aspect of truth in the Church and to try once again to

further Catholic renewal and to facilitate a breakthrough of
the structure of the Church which is in so many ways contradictory to the Christian message.

II. RESULTS

1. My Catholicity can only be called into question if no distinction is made between authentic Catholicity in time and
space as defined in *The Church* and the Roman Catholicism
of the Church especially since the eleventh century. The
juridicalism, imperialism, triumphalism and absolutism of
this Roman system was sharply criticized during Vatican II
and bishops, theologians and lay people have continued to
criticize these characteristics of the Church ever since the
Council as the main reason for the schism with the Eastern
churches and the Protestant Reformation in the West.

2. My "enquiry" has been fully justified because no one
has yet been able to raise any really convincing objections
to my interpretation of the painful "infallibility" texts of
Vatican I and II. The equally painful question about the
"infallibility" of the teaching represented by *Humanae
vitae* – which only formed an opening to the book and was
not central to my argument – proved to be a very suitable
catalyst and was, significantly enough, supported even by
"Roman" theologians when they found themselves unable
to say anything constructive about the infallibility of the
"ordinary" teaching office of the world episcopate.

3. The Catholic basis common to all participants in the
debate is apparent from the fundamental agreement between
myself and even my sharpest opponents. This is clear in
three important ways.

(a) It was universally admitted with unexpected frankness
that the Church's teaching office could be fallible and had in
fact often erred.

(b) Even conservative theologians often regard the concept of infallibility as susceptible to misunderstanding and
even as largely unintelligible today. If the infallibility of the
Pope had not already been defined, it would hardly be possible to define it now, as the social and historical conditions
for such a definition would be lacking. The exaggerations

37

and abuses of this dogma which have occurred in the hundred years since its definition and which, in my view, have their basis in the definition itself, are, of course, a frequent cause of complaint.

(c) Again, even conservative theologians regard the Church's remaining in the truth as more important than the infallibility of certain definitions. Therefore, since any errors on the part of the Church's teaching office cannot, at least in general, be disputed, at least fundamental and general consent is given to my positive argument, namely that the Church is maintained, despite all errors, in the truth of the Gospel.

4. Are there perhaps pronouncements, definitions, dogmas or propositions which are not only true (this is not disputed), but also infallibly true, since certain office-bearers are unable, because of the special help they receive from the Holy Spirit, to err in a given situation? It was precisely to this that the question mark in the title of my book *Infallible?* pointed. Yet there is general agreement that, in the whole of the debate so far, including the special seminar on infallibility held at Tübingen and attended by members of different schools at the university, not one theologian has been able to produce any proof of the possibility that the Holy Spirit guarantees the infallibility of certain pronouncements. Even the Congregation of Faith has not answered this question, which I have asked again and again in the correspondence.

5. Several other questions require further discussion (and this will in fact be found in the book to be published this year).

(a) What is the situation with regard to the dialectic of truth and error?

(b) How does a proposition that, according to its verbal formulation, that is in the abstract, can be true and false, become a true proposition in a given situation, that is, in the concrete?

(c) How can a proposition persist in history?

(d) How can a proposition about faith be both conditioned by its situation and at the same time binding?

6. Since the appearance of my book, my position has been

unexpectedly confirmed from the Catholic side.

(a) The authentic but fallible authority of Peter and the question of Petrine succession has been further developed in recent exegetical investigations. However important Peter may have been to the Church in the post-apostolic period as a symbolic figure, there is little support in the New Testament for his infallibility – both positive and negative characteristics are to be found in all the biblical evidence. This applies *a fortiori* to any question of infallibility in the case of the Bishop of Rome. What is more, the canonists of the Middle Ages never used, as evidence for papal infallibility, Luke 22:32, which contains a promise to Peter not of inerrancy, but that he would preserve his faith to the end. The medieval canonists did not, moreover, apply this promise to the Bishop of Rome, but to the whole Church.

(b) At the same time, recent studies in the development of dogma have also shown that, according to Athanasius and the early tradition of the Church, the authority of ecumenical councils is not based simply on their "ecumenical" character or on their definition of infallibly true propositions with the help of the Holy Spirit. On the contrary, their authority is derived from the witness they bear to Scripture and to the apostolic faith. In other words, they are authoritative in so far as they authentically and credibly proclaim the Gospel.

(c) Finally – and this has been perhaps the most surprising fact to emerge during the debate – recent historical research has revealed that the doctrine of papal infallibility did not develop slowly, but that it was quite a sudden creation at the end of the thirteenth century by Peter Olivi, a Franciscan theologian who was accused of heresy. It was not the classical medieval theologians and canonists or even the theologians of the Counter-Reformation who were ultimately responsible for the 1970 definition of infallibility, but rather the secular political and rationalist thinkers of the Counter-Reformation, de Lamennais and above all de Maistre. The medieval canonists – ecclesiology was at that time within their province – taught not that the faith of the Church was preserved by an infallible head, but that, however much the head of the Church might err from the truth, God would preserve the whole Church from error. This, of course, is completely in line with what I said in my book.

The result of these recent exegetical, dogmatic and historical studies is simply that my whole argument is even more in accordance with the great Catholic tradition than I originally believed.

III. THE POSSIBLE CONSENSUS OF THE FUTURE

In the light of the debate that has so far taken place on the subject of infallibility, it would seem that it should be possible to reach a further consensus of opinion. In other words, an even more positive definition of how the Church can remain in the truth even without any infallible pronouncements is now a distinct possibility. This idea is more fully developed in the book about the debate that is to appear this year, but, in the meantime, a few brief notes will be of interest.

The indefectibility of the Church as the whole community of believers is in itself a truth of faith. This statement can be justified not merely by referring to a few classical texts, but by appealing to the whole Christian message, which finds faith as God's word addressed to man and which founds a community of believers. The Church is maintained in the truth wherever Jesus himself remains the truth for the individual or for a community and wherever man follows in his footsteps. This remaining in the truth is more a matter of orthopraxis than of orthodoxy. It is more a matter of individuals and of individual communities than of institutions. Truth is, after all, life lived in the fullness of the good news brought in Jesus Christ. This remaining in the truth is revealed – whenever it is not visible, as it often is not, in the hierarchy or in the teaching of the established Church – in the lived faith of the ordinary people, both inside the Church and outside it. The offices of the Church do not constitute truth in the Church. They have to serve truth in the Church and people in the Church.

The result of this is that the Church continues to live even in the case of serious error in faith or morals and that the

Church must learn again and again how to live with errors. Errors are serious, but they do not threaten the life of the Church. The Church's criterion for truth in the Church is the Christian message as found in the New Testament and ultimately in Jesus Christ himself. This Christian message can be interpreted critically within the Christian community and the tradition of the Church. The Christian does not, in other words, ultimately believe in dogmas, statements or propositions, nor does he believe even in the Bible or in the Church. He believes in God himself and in Jesus Christ in whom God is revealed. His faith is certainly to some extent dependent on statements or propositions whenever he has to confess it, but it cannot be cancelled out by false statements or propositions.

In this way, the proclamation of the Christian message – both from day to day through the ordinary teaching office and in the extraordinary form of the teaching office – can be maintained in spite of individual errors, and bishops and the Pope as well as councils can "function" and carry out their task even if they cannot define infallibly in cases of doubt who is right. The conflicts that are always likely to occur in the Church can also be more easily endured in this way.

A fallible teaching office must be accepted as providing an opportunity for the Church of the future to deal more easily with its errors. It may also be possible for a fallible Church to recover its earlier freedom and thus for the truth of the Gospel to be heard again more freely and despite all errors. Again, it may mean that, since sin can also be a *felix culpa*, error may similarly be a *felix error*. The truth of the Gospel will, after all, perhaps be more powerfully experienced through the Church's errors. Possibly too, the history of the Church will come to be viewed much more realistically and the Church's remaining in the truth will be seen in a much more convincing light.

A consensus of opinion of the kind that I have outlined so briefly here would also have to be an ecumenical consensus, implying possible faith on the part of other Christians in the indefectibility of the Church. This would remove the most serious obstacle to Christian unity. Even more important, however, is that it would make the Christian message much more credible to men living in the modern world. This is ultimately the only worthwhile reason for the continued practice of theology today.

One final comment in conclusion – the heated discussion that has been taking place has shown clearly that a question of the complexity of "infallibility" cannot be settled by a unilateral decision on the part of the Church's teaching office. It is ultimately no more and no less than a question of truth. I can always be convinced by reasons, but we have to wait for these.

Notes
1. John L. McKenzie, S.J., born 1910, one of America's leading biblical scholars, was professor of Biblical History, Loyola University, Chicago, 1960–5, professor of Theology, Notre Dame, 1966–70, and professor of Theology, DePaul University, Chicago, since 1970.
Taken from *National Catholic Reporter*, 26 March 1971, and used by kind permission of the Editor.
2. Walther von Löwenich, born 1903, is professor emeritus of Church History at Erlangen.
Taken from *Christ und Welt*, 5 March 1971.
3. First published in *Concilium*, Vol. 3, No. 9, March 1973, pp. 226–30, this translation by David Smith is used by kind permission of the Editor.

VI: The Christological Question

THE INCARNATION: An Introduction to Hegel's
Theological Thought as Prolegomena to a Future
Christology (1970). (Published only in German.)

WALTER KERN
A Theological View of Hegel[1]

The interest in Hegel's philosophy, that to some extent has
been growing more intense in all quarters, has since the early
1960s addressed itself to a considerable degree to the hitherto
neglected philosophy of religion of the man whose work
crowned the movement of German idealism (and who is
labelled the philosopher of the Prussian state). The two
hundredth anniversary of the Swabian philosopher's birth
brought an immediate boom in literature on the subject.
Hans Küng's 704-page work is flanked by three other imposing volumes.[i] We shall concentrate on Küng's book –
not because of its compass, nor because it comes from a committed Catholic theologian who is known to be much occupied in other fields, but simply because of its quality, because
of the wealth of stimulating suggestions it outlines for our
understanding of the Christian faith. In all these respects the
only comparison can be with the work of Franz Anton
Staudenmaier, professor of Dogmatic Theology at Freiburg-
im-Breisgau, which appeared as long ago as 1844.[ii] At that
time, a few years after Hegel's death, when the influence of

(i) M. Theunissen, *Hegels Lehre vom absoluten Geist als theologisch-
politischer Traktat* (Berlin 1970); A. Léonard, *La foi chez Hegel* (Paris
1970); D. E. Christensen (ed.), *Hegel and the Philosophy of Religion*
(The Hague 1970). The following year there appeared: P. Cornehl, *Die
Zukunft der Versöhnung, Eschatologie und Emanzipation in der Auf-
klärung, bei Hegel und in der Hegelschen Schule* (Göttingen 1971) and
F. Wagner, *Der Gedanke der Persönlichkeit Gottes bei Fichte und Hegel*
(Gütersloh 1971).
(ii) *Darstellung und Kritik des Hegelschen Systems aus dem Standpunkte
der christlichen Philosophie.* On the new edition of this work that appeared in 1966 see *Stimmen der Zeit*, 183 (1969), pp. 354 f.

the old Hegelian school was at its peak, though already beginning to abate, it had above all to be a matter of drawing lines and fixing boundaries on a basis of defensive criticism that did not in any way correspond to Hegel's status as a thinker. But was it necessary for more than a century to elapse before the attempt was undertaken on a large scale in the Catholic world to make positive use for theological endeavour of this philosopher's dialectical findings and systematic outlook? In order to do this an essential preparatory process was to master the material contained in the emergence and systematic arrangement of Hegelian thinking. This difficult task has been accomplished by Küng, not without effort. Indeed, it is probably only because his preliminary studies go back to his student days and were followed by a wide acquaintance with the growing literature on the subject, that the success of this undertaking was possible. It should be an exemplary case of an established professor of Catholic[iii] theology occupying himself in this kind of intensive way with the thought of a modern philosopher whom the bulk of his academic colleagues have hardly caught sight of in the distance.

Hegel's theological and more precisely his Christological thought, to which Küng's aim is to provide an introduction, turns out to be the history of his entire development. Küng devotes a hundred and fifty pages just to the young, presystematic Hegel, whom many outlines of his philosophy wrongly pass over or dispose of too briefly. This provides the most dramatic chapters in Hegel's life as in Küng's book. "The young Hegel did not think much of Jesus Christ" (p. 41): this was as a pupil at the *Gymnasium* at Stuttgart and even later when he was a fairly indolent student of theology at Tübingen. In the flat wake of Enlightenment

(iii) Among a larger selection of Protestant theologians W. Pannenberg particularly deserves mention. The two books listed at the end of note (i) above are both dissertations by pupils of his, as is the book published in 1966 by T. Koch, *Differenz und Versöhnung. Eine Interpretation der Theologie G. W. F. Hegels nach seiner "Wissenschaft der Logik"*. Rumour has it that Pannenberg himself is engaged on a major work of his own about Hegel.

religion, the only thing to make noticeable waves was enthusiasm for the French Revolution; and like his fellow-
students Hölderlin and Schelling, Hegel was constantly fascinated by the ideals of Greece. Christ was placed on about
the same level as Socrates (Kierkegaard would establish the
decisive difference); popular religion must be based on
reason. But the young Hegel was not uncritical with regard
to the Enlightenment too. And above all he could not escape
from this Jesus. Was he simply a great man who set an
example, *the* teacher of virtue, the personification of Kant's
moral rationalism? Jesus's proclamation of the message of
goodwill towards men and surrender to God had as early as
primitive Christianity become rigid in the form of an authoritarian violation of conscience, of priestly domination, of
ascesis turned into a matter of torment, etc. It was here that
there arose the problem of "positivity", of what is positively
given in religion and life generally, a problem so important
for Hegel's development as a thinker. Christianity was criticized by the young Hegel in a way that formed an unmis-
takable prelude to Feuerbach's and Marx's critique of religion: the treasures that had been squandered on heaven
were to be claimed once again for the earth . . . "The consequence for Hegel of this unprecedentedly strong criticism of
historical Christianity was clear: no mere change of attitude,
but the rejection of the orthodox theological system as of
the political feudal system, the disentangling and separation
of state and Church, the religious as well as the political
renewal of a moral society" (p. 122). In Küng's view the
widespread theological ambiguities of that age explain a great
deal: an unsubtle doctrine of original sin, the Protestant
assertion of the total corruption of human nature by sin and
the corresponding pessimism about salvation. But the decisive question is directed at Hegel's own nationalistic misunderstanding of what Christian faith means (pp. 97ff).

A certain change took place with Hegel's move from
Berne to Frankfurt in 1796. "A movement away from the
deism of the Enlightenment towards a pantheistic outlook
was characteristic of the age" (p. 135). Spinoza's ideas had a
new effect when placed within the context of Goethe's view

of the world. A major piece of evidence is Hegel's poem "Eleusis". Man's separation from God was overcome by man's rational, not mystical (p. 139), participation in the life of the absolute. The distant and alien God of Israel upset man even in his self-alienation. Abraham was the archetype of being torn apart in this way (Kierkegaard, once again, as elsewhere). Hegel's intention was to criticize Kant's isolated subject. It meant the re-Judaization of Christianity. But in God's son Jesus as seen afresh in the Johannine writings man's life is reconciled in love for the heavenly father. The unity of the divine and the human nature in Jesus became the basic pattern of the "kingdom of God". Profound analysis of the unity and totality of what is alive and of love between human beings also led to a re-evaluation of what had come into being and is present as a datum: "There was now an attack on the rejection by the Enlightenment (and Kant) of any form of positivity, a rejection that . . . rested on a completely abstract, allegedly familiar and universally valid human nature in the face of which everything positive must appear to be going against or beyond nature, against or beyond reason. There was now an acceptance of the affirmation of a positivity included in the structure of all religion and all spiritual and intellectual life" (p. 124). The historicity of human nature and thus of the religion of mankind was perceived and recognized. Above all by the end of his time at Frankfurt Hegel had already gone a considerable way with the dialectic of love, something which, with a change of philosophical structure, as the dialectic of discerning reason, would determine his later system.

"In keeping with the New Testament?" is Küng's laconic question at the conclusion of the story of Hegel's younger days. Did Hegel develop a doctrine of reconciliation that was in keeping with the times and at the same time genuinely Christian? Essential elements of classical Christology were included by him: sin as not merely a moral and juridical fact but as a fatal event, "and in keeping with this reconciliation as a living event brought about by God in the spirit, in which man united with God simply appears as the ideal of mankind" (p. 172); "over against all external piety imposed by law an infectious new freedom and subjectivity" (p. 171). But should biblical faith and the love of the New Testament be understood simply as a recognition of the spirit by the spirit, as a feeling of harmony and of being at one, as being in God and being reunited with the totality of life . . .? Above all, can "Jesus in God" simply be turned into a "Godhead in the world, in nature and in man" everywhere and at all times? To sum up: "Pantheism in the sense of 'everything being God' was something Hegel in his time at Frankfurt definitely did not want to recognize. But pantheism in the sense of a living 'being in God' on the part of man and the world, in the sense of a differentiated unity of life, love and the all-embracing spirit, was something he could well have affirmed" (p. 170).

Here of course we cannot discuss in similar detail the Hegel of the years at Jena, of *The Phenomenology of Mind*, of his fully worked out system and of the later Berlin lectures on world history, on art and particularly on the philosophy of religion; all this is dealt with by the subsequent chapters of Küng's work. All we can do here is to throw a few side-lights on this. From 1800 onward Hegel, now thirty years old, seemed to have left the theological ground floor for a philosophical and metaphysical upper storey that was quite different and could only be reached with difficulty by ordinary people, having as close neighbours Schelling and Fichte, who sanctioned the consistent and logical development of his spiritual monism (cf. p. 193). But that already means that a profound continuity underlay all the changes that were ventured on. It shines through in the concluding sentences of *Faith and Knowledge* of 1802, a passage much quoted by the "God is dead" theology of today (or yesterday?) and one that is widely misinterpreted: Good Friday, now a matter of speculation, becomes the colossal image of what happens in the re-emergence afresh of reconciled unity from the unending pain of dissociation and disunity. (On Hegel's clarification of contemporary atheism cf. Küng's chapter on "The death of God", pp. 207–22.) In 1806 Hegel called "the immanent dialectic of the absolute God's curriculum vitae"; God's incarnation, his becoming man, is the presupposition for the spirit becoming the universal world-reality (cf. pp. 230ff). As far as the *Phenomenology* of 1807 is concerned, religion, which reaches its perfection in Christianity, is the recapitulation of the path of consciousness through the world towards its freely and consciously becoming spirit. The view of this work is that in the Christian religion the incarnation became directly real from having before Christ been a mere myth: the divine essence now has "essentially and directly the form of self-awareness". One cannot simply impute to these formulations "the accepted Christian meanings" (p. 263): what they are concerned with above all is the universal fate of the spirit. The divine substance divested itself to enter into the self-awareness of a single individual human being (Jesus of Nazareth), who in turn (in his death) divested himself to enter into the universality of human spiritual reality (equivalent to the Christian community): thus arose the "true reunion" of God and mankind.

Here we stand at the "birth of the spirit becoming self-awareness". Hegel understood the incarnation from the point of view of the development of the spirit: "Christ cancelled and at the same time preserved [*aufgehoben*] in knowledge" (pp. 277–302). The *Science of Logic*, dating from the Nuremberg years 1812 to 1816, is, as one can put it following Hegel, "the representation of God as he is in his eternal essence before the creation of nature and of an infinite spirit". The subject of this logic is the divine logos, which is not a Platonically static element but a dynamic and indeed dialectical one. God before the world must be God in the world and through the world. This development is pursued by the philosophy of nature and of the spirit to be found in the *Encyclopaedia* (1817, third edition 1830): from the realm of pure logical thought the idea divests itself to enter material nature and in the emergence of human self-awareness reaches the consummation of its realization on the individual plane and on the vast stage of human cultural development in law and the state and in world history. The effect of the idea in history is as "the cunning of reason" that turns the history of the world into the world's court of

justice – into the "glorification of God". Hegel's onto-
theology is a single comprehensive theodicy as historiodicy,
in other words the speculative justification of history (p.
467). What is sketched out in brief in the *Encyclopaedia* is
developed on a broad scale by the lectures on the philosophy
of religion[iv] (but as a teacher at the Nuremberg *Gymnasium*
he had already been talking the same language as the professor at Berlin university: pp. 309ff). The idea's process of
becoming has a trinitarian structure: it leads from the realm
of the father through the realm of the son to the realm of the
spirit; and for the sake of most people's powers of com-
prehension this dialectical process is interpreted by means
of religious concepts of the creation of the world, the incarnation in Jesus Christ, his death, the imparting of the
spirit that this made possible, and the universal spiritual
community, the Church, that was founded in this way.

Hegel as a systematic thinker is also met with critical
questions from Küng. Does not a religion of revelation –
along with the history of the world (pp. 398ff, 469, 473ff) –
become constrained by the demands of a system? Is not
Christ "confined in the necessity of a system of knowledge"
(p. 354)? And is not the decisive historical dimension of the
future omitted along with all eschatological expectation (pp.
489–95)? Probing theologically beyond favourable and
adverse critical judgements Küng also sees in the system,
which in its nature is alien to theological thought (pp. 347ff),
a justified protest against an arbitrary God.

Let us now turn to the positive indications that Küng
finds in Hegel. Küng sees the point where Hegelian philosophy and Christian theology come closest together in the
problems they tackle in a point on which criticism is apt to
concentrate: in Hegel's identifying dialectic of God and
man. For Greek metaphysics, which had a strong influence
on Christian theology, too strong an influence despite efforts

(iv) These later lectures attempt to think along lines closer to Christian
belief. Küng mentions some of the points Hegel clarified (p. 468). But
it still remains true that these do not add up to an orthodox dogmatic
theology.

at correction, God is incapable of change, immeasurably distant from and beyond the world, incapable of suffering, eternally blessed in himself. How can this concept of God be combined with the God who became man in Jesus Christ (the title of Küng's book can be literally translated as "God's becoming man") and who died on the cross? The heretical Christological models simply push the difficulty to one side: either the divine unity in Christ is made predominant (Monophysitism), but then the word did not truly become flesh; or the duality is overemphasized for the sake of the genuine humanity (Nestorianism), but then it is no longer the word itself that became flesh.

The orthodox Christology of Chalcedon, which does not duck the difficulty, must be the subject of further thought with regard to "the historicity of God" (pp. 522–62 and the excursus on the history of dogma, pp. 611–70). The Christian God is not a colourless absolute that lives separated from everything: he is the living God who settles contradictions "by bringing them into the world and reconciles them in unity by enduring their suffering", who "in this renunciation to enter into creation, a process which reaches its manifest culmination in the incarnation and the death on the cross, makes plain his deepest and most inward nature" (p. 526). But how, asks Küng, can we talk of God suffering? "God must not suffer. And yet he does so in his son. This is God's mystery from God's free grace . . ." (p. 540). God suffers in his son, not through any need to be supplemented, but out of the fullness of love, in freedom. And what can be said about God's capability or incapability of change? Certainly, God has no need of any process of realization, of becoming himself, of the development of the world. But this is not the whole final truth that has been given to us. For the word did become flesh. God himself became man in Jesus Christ. He who is in himself unchangeable changed himself and appeared as the other of himself.

All this, however – and this is the decisive distinguishing mark of what is Christian – was done by his free grace. "It is precisely because God is not only any reality whatsoever but the purest reality, not only any activity whatsoever but

actus purissimus, that he can identify himself with suffering
and dying under Pontius Pilate" (p. 546). "In its glorious
freedom God's unalterable, transcendent essence includes
the 'possibility' of becoming: 'possibility' not in the sense
of unrealized potentiality but in the sense of superabundant
power, of omnipotence" (p. 552). Hence there can be no
ontological proof of this "becoming" of God, no transition
from essence to activity that can be deduced philosophically
and constructed dialectically. No speculative necessity for
God's suffering and becoming exists. "The difference between
finite and infinite spirit, between God and man, which Hegel
certainly took note of but tried to transcend in the absolute
knowledge of the absolute spirit," remains and is indeed
heightened by Christian theology to become the "contradiction of God's grace and friendship and man's guilt and
sin" (p. 553). Hence finally the God who in his "fundamental historicity and power over history" makes the world
and its history possible at all is not simply "the God who
appears in and is visible through" the world and world
history in general, "who would here be capable of being
unambiguously perceived and understood and of being the
subject of speculative knowledge" (p. 559). God has indeed
involved himself in this obscure history, but not in such a
way that would allow one to argue its obscurity away, nor
as if God willed it and was obliged to will it thanks to the
laws of dialectical contradiction, as if he ratified and sanctioned it.

   We have had to pass over in silence the splendid things
Küng has to say about the inner dialectic of God's qualities
(pp. 543–9).[v] We have also had to pass over in silence

(v) Quoting Luther's phrase *absconditas Dei sub contrario* he describes
it as "God's hiddenness made manifest": "In the cross the resurrection
is hidden and at the same time revealed to the believer. Closed up in
the flesh God discloses his spiritual nature, his immeasurability in
limitedness, his eternity in being subject to time, his omnipresence in
being confined to one place, his unchangeability in growth, his infinity
in deficiency, his omniscience in silence" – "and the height of the para-
dox is that the supreme good 'has become a curse' (Gal. 3:13), the
holiest 'made to be sin' (2 Cor. 5:21)" (pp. 544–5).

what he says, supplementing his remarks about the historicity of God, about the historicity of Jesus in the context of biblical criticism since D. F. Strauss.

Notes
1. Walter Kern, S.J., born 1922, is professor of Fundamental Theology and Philosophy at Innsbruck and enjoys an international reputation for his work on Hegel.
Taken from *Stimmen der Zeit* 189 (1972), pp. 125–33 (with the omission of the discussion of the other works mentioned in note 1), and used by kind permission of the Editor.

VII: The Essence of Christianity

ON BEING A CHRISTIAN (1974)

JOSÉ GOMEZ CAFFARENA
A Summa for People of Today[1]

At 49, Hans Küng can look back on a dozen books of high theological value, some of which are of considerable length. This is already a record. Even more important, however, is the fact that in his books and in his work, both for the periodical *Concilium* and at the Institute for Ecumenical Studies of the University of Tübingen – an institute which he founded and directs, he has managed more than any other contemporary theologian to plumb the human depths of those problems with which Christianity today is faced.

He has done this clearly and bravely, combining scientific seriousness with intellectual honesty. Possibly he was helped in this – apart from his personal gifts – by the "ecumenical", by which I mean universal or at least pan-European nature of his life history. It is almost as if this was destined to combine Germanic and Latin values. Hans Küng is Swiss and for eighteen years has been teaching at German-speaking universities; but before that he studied for seven years in Rome and for two in Paris, as well as spending varying periods in Amsterdam, Berlin, Madrid and London.

Four qualities come to my mind when trying to express his theological personality:

Ecumenical: This time in the sense of the movement to restore unity to Christianity. His thesis on "Justification according to Karl Barth" was, as Barth himself recognized in the foreword which he wrote for it, a decisive step towards the breaking down of secular prejudices which divided Protestant and Catholic theology.

Prophetic: Küng, who is familiar with and uses the results of scientific exegesis and the history of the Church and its dogmas, is not a man to put science before everything. On the contrary, he understands the need to harness science to the service of the spiritual, and without confusing his own work as a theologian with prophecy he has put it to serve prophecy.

Modern: Culturally Küng is a man of our century, with all that that means. If we read chronologically through his work we find ourselves brought face to face in a manner ever more stimulating with the questions which occupy the mind of an educated man today, a man of a scientific and technological age imbued with the spirit of history and with a Promethean humanism. His study of Hegel was vital for this understanding and there is little doubt that this, too, was the source of his most polemical book *Infallible?*.

Radical: In the specific, etymological sense of *getting to the root*. And therefore also in the sense of speaking clearly and without compromise which has made him well known as a polemicist. But it is important to emphasize that the second form of Küng's radicalism derives from the first. And it is perhaps in his latest book *On being a Christian* more than in any other that Küng has embarked upon the glorious adventure of getting to the root of things.

I will now try to convey something of my own impressions as a reader of the book and in doing so will be forced to omit much of the praise and admiration that is his due – for the scope of his learning, sound judgement on difficult questions of exegesis, his capacity for synthesis, for his grasp of his subject. I should like to deal with more basic matters.

Certain of Küng's German critics would be ready to withdraw many of their objections were he to hold up his book less as a *Summa theologica* – or compendium of considerations of faith – pure and simple and look upon it more as a "Summa for pagans".

It seems to me that there is a grain of truth here but that it could be better expressed. Küng has not written a "Summa for ecclesiastics", which is what all the academic Summas have been to date, but rather a *Summa for the men of today*. There is a pagan lurking inside each one of us, perhaps always on the point of conversion but never fully converted, and we all need theology as a help in our conversion, particularly in our complex and sophisticated civilization today. Even those of us who are ecclesiastics are less concerned with theology as ecclesiastics than vitally as men.

Should theology not become the reflection of the faith of every responsible, educated believer: a reflection extending to the root of his being as a man where – naturally – he is pagan?

I believe that this is so and that consequently theology today should be ready to accept considerable pruning and, especially, to change its point of view – should be less "immanent in its own system" and have more *fundamental theology* which will always renew the path of the man of faith. Küng's latest book seems to me to contain, if not all the theology possible, at least a summary of what is most important, and to be a definite step towards this new way of looking at things.

THE RETURN TO THE CHRIST OF HISTORY

Many of the objections which have been levelled at Küng's book by his colleagues from their German chairs of theology and in a book criticizing *On being a Christian* refer to his method. They would like to trace the faults they find in the book – most of which are omissions – to the critical attitude which Küng adopted towards the Church's magisterium in his book on infallibility. Obviously, Küng is a single consistent being and his works must necessarily be linked one with another. However, he himself wished in his new book to put before us the more positive aspect of his thought – well aware of the fact that in doing so he was bringing forward what might well have been a work of many more years. It would be unjust to the author not to read the book *in and for itself*.

Whatever the case, Küng shows himself to be an innovator in what concerns method. How can I express it? I consider that there are three principles which must combine in any theological reflection. The first is a return to the origins of Christianity, the second an acceptance of the tradition of the Church and its doctrinal pronouncements, and the third an awareness of the signs of the time and of the practice of the Faith as it is today. I doubt whether in theory any modern theologian would argue against the importance of any of those principles. But there is room for varying emphasis and this is the source of three different types of theology, the first of which might be described as more historical, the second more traditionally orthodox and the third more charismatic.

In the case of Hans Küng's theology the main emphasis is on the origins of Christianity, the second on the reality lived by the believers today and only the third on doctrinal tradition. The choice is understandable and reasonable and one which I consider Küng manages to keep within its due limits.

It might, perhaps, be worthwhile considering how this emphasis influences Küng in his actual choice of subject. Somewhat less than a third of the book is taken up with setting it in the context of present-day problems. Thus there are 120 pages of introduction on the questions which a Christian asks himself today and 90 concluding pages offering the mainly practical reply which derives from the book as a whole. A good third, some 290 pages, follows on from the initial statement of problems and is a rich and variegated presentation, written with learning and affection, of the "Jesus of history". That leaves something less than a third for the rest – which includes the Resurrection, the Christ of Faith, the Trinity and the Church, the subjects which in classical academic theology would claim the lion's share. The inversion of methodology here is obvious.

JESUS CONVERTS US TO CHRIST . . .

In the eyes of some of Küng's critics, the defect of this inversion presumably lies in the fact that behind this return to the Jesus of history is hidden the granting of a privilege to the learned historian who is the one who knows by what methods it may be achieved. Thus when it comes to determining the guide for Christians he in some way replaces the Church's magisterium. And is not historical science nowadays only too conscious of its limits? Is it not very obvious that learned men have differing opinions and attitudes? And above all, is this not something far above the normal believer?

I consider these difficulties to be real but consider, too, that they are difficulties for all of us and inevitable in a religion of a given, and now remote, historical origin. To abandon the return to the origins of Christianity as too difficult would seem to me to be simple suicide. To submit it to a principle of traditional authority is merely to beg the question. The way to overcome them is rather by efforts such as that of Küng: to gather patiently the harvest, now fairly ripe, of historical criticism and present it to the believer who already today but even more so in the future will not be an uneducated spirit unable to grasp what is offered to him in this effort at synthesis.

Because this is not a case of a learned man assuming the role of the Church's magisterium in order to dictate an image and a doctrine. It is an attempt to introduce a critical way of reading the documents relating to Jesus in the confidence that Jesus – the historical Jesus – will make himself accessible in his essential features, which is what is important, to those who read the documents. In my opinion, any denial of this by a theologian would indicate a dangerous enclosure in a ghetto. To be a Christian in its intellectual dimension would mean to consider the teachings of a magisterium whose history is complex and problematical but above all whose legitimacy it is logical to question. And this brings us to Jesus as the only possible source – a question which is a very real one to the man of today.

The pagan we recognize as being within each one of us and whom we cannot honestly silence will not be converted to faith in Christ by the magisterium of the Church. If the historical Jesus himself does not convert us, no one nowadays will make us believe in the Christ of Faith. And this, it seems to me, is the logical expression of the core of Küng's thinking: Jesus brings us to Christ and from this comes Jesus Christ.

... WITH THE VITAL COLLABORATION OF
THE FIRST ECCLESIAL COMMUNITY

Here we have a point closely linked with what we have just been saying but which is quite specific and the key to any understanding of Christianity. The first community is the Church and thus belongs to the tradition which mediates between Jesus and the Christian of today. However, it is not just any link in this tradition but belongs to the origins of Christianity as much as to Jesus himself. The faith of the first Christians who experienced the first Easter and believed the man who had been crucified to be alive is a fundamental, and what we might call a "constituent" part of Christian faith. If I said that Jesus converts us to Christ, I must add that this is brought about with the vital collaboration of the first ecclesial community.

Küng has touched accurately upon a number of points concerning the first community – one of the most important of these being the whole question of the "appearances" of the Risen Christ, the memory of which is linked to the Paschal faith, as also that of the meaning of the Christian writings which constitute the origin of the tradition of Jesus and, especially, the question of the personality of Saint Paul. I wonder, in fact, whether this might not be the source of some of the criticisms already referred to and, more specifically, whether it would not have been advisable and more in line with Küng's theology to deal more in depth with the history of the development of the Faith during the first two generations of Christianity (possibly extending this to the whole period covering what is known as the "Canon" of the New Testament) and thus to all that which makes for a qualitative difference in the Early Church and gives its faith a certain constitutive character in relation to later faith.

Obviously I am not suggesting that we should think of it as a quasi-magic golden period in which alone was given the "revelation" in the sense of a deposit of truth of which the later Church was merely the custodian. I regard this idea as outdated. Nonetheless I believe there to be something essential in the faith of the first generations of Christians which it is important to explain critically. Without it – and Küng is in agreement on this point – we cannot take the step from Jesus to Jesus Christ in a critical, responsible manner.

One question which it is the fashion of a certain type of exegesis to discuss (and I think of Brandon as the most typical representative) might well be illuminated by this study. This is a question which now occupies many of those among us who today tackle the subject of the origin of Christianity from a Marxist standpoint, namely that of whether Christianity did not undergo an essential change of direction with the fall of Jerusalem in the year AD 70 from a more historically revolutionary messianism to an ideologically conservative spiritualist and universalist gnosis. I feel it would have been worthwhile establishing more firmly the coherent character of the development of early Christianity.

FATHER, SON, HOLY SPIRIT:
THE ACTION OF GOD IN THE WORLD
This brings me to the last of the points I feel it necessary to make in a discussion of *On being a Christian*, namely that of the reinterpretation of the basic Christian dogmas which Hans Küng undertakes in his book. Here we see an example of everything that has already been said about his originality of method. And this no doubt will be the part of the book which readers less familiar with Küng's work will find different – some a source of scandal and others a means of regaining for Christianity the credibility which it had lost for them in its more familiar versions.

"Jesus is the Son of God made man, one person in two natures". "God is one in essence and three in persons, Father, Son and Holy Spirit". Do these formulas not summarize the very essence of Christian faith?

In one sense they do. But on the other hand it is impossible to hide the fact that we are not concerned with a routine repetition of formulae but of their affirmation within the context of a responsible, critical faith; otherwise they will only scandalize and offend men of today in a sense very different from the "Scandal of the Cross" which Paul already saw Christianity would become to ordinary men. Today the scandal comes from the fact that the formulas which were so highly valued are liable not to be understood or to be understood in a manner which sounds absurd without it being clear that this was the sense that it was intended they should have when they were coined. But perhaps the most serious aspect of this new "scandal" is the fact that they are accidental to Christianity in its original form. Neither Jesus of Nazareth in his words and deeds, nor the faith in the Risen Christ in its first expressions consisted of these formulas which were only the result of problems and concepts from the Hellenistic world after stormy controversies in the fourth and fifth centuries.

Küng's fundamental option is clear and it is widely shared today. It is a matter of giving preference to the first formulas and, with them, to a Christology "from below" and to a Trinity "more economical than essential" (in which the terms Father, Son and Holy Spirit refer primarily to the action of God in the world). Those Catholics most liable to be scandalized by what Hans Küng has to say in this connection would probably be equally scandalized by reading a lot of other serious books of theology today. Hans Küng, it is true, does go a bit further than some other writers, but he does so, to my mind, without breaking the obligatory link with tradition and, specifically, with the Councils quoted.

Küng expresses his thought largely in terms which on the one hand are easily understood in our language and on the other hand express undeniably an absolutely unique relationship of Jesus to God. The omission in this context of certain formulas or the lesser insistence on others do not imply a denial of what they were intended to state. This is not a ᵴe of a convenient playing down of Christian truth nor of a concealed denial of the dogmas concerning Christ and the Trinity. It is a case simply of a *selective interpretation sufficiently faithful to tradition* made on the basis of a primacy of method given by the author to the original kerygma and to the present practice of the faith. In my reading, therefore, Küng says "yes" to Nicaea and Chalcedon, but it is a conditional "yes" given from the original kerygma: the absolute yes of his faith to the primary truths.

To be able to justify this reading as against the opposite, which would be "Küng rejects Nicaea and Chalcedon to return simply to the original kerygma" one must add another, viz.: the prevalent functionalism – by which I mean the fact that the divine sonship of Jesus is expressed particularly in his acting as God's "deputy" and that the application to God of the symbols "Father, Son, Spirit" should be understood "for us and from us" does not deny an essential context, a kind of *fundamentum in re* (without which they would also have no functional truth). I see Küng not as denying this ontological context; he merely considers it excessively ingenuous of human reason to wish to develop it in categories belonging to our conceptual thought, thereby producing a sort of "higher mathematics of God", the worst effect of which would be to dissipate the one starting point we had for everything, which is the human reality of the Man Jesus of Nazareth.

HEINZ ZAHRNT
Mutual Recognition[2]

I can now give an answer to the question that is often asked: where can one find out about Christianity, about Christian belief and Christian behaviour, from a source that respects both the facts and the nature of the world we live in? The answer is to read Küng. And it is an answer that can be given not just to Catholics but to Protestants too, not just to Christians but to non-Christians and atheists as well. What this adds up to is that Küng's latest book, *On Being A Christian*, is a genuinely ecumenical work. And this is true in five different respects.

First, Küng's book is ecumenical because it is based on the Bible. At its centre stands the "programme" of Jesus Christ, which Küng outlines in such a way that it describes Jesus's character and message, his proclamation and his conduct, his life, suffering, death and new life. In this Küng naturally includes the findings of historically based biblical criticism, so that in reading it one completely forgets that it is a Catholic author one is dealing with. Here there is further proof that the effects of biblical criticism, for all the attempts to belittle it, have been positive rather than negative: it was indeed biblical criticism that established the first theological bridge between the two Churches. In view of this fact one can only ask its opponents in both confessions: "Why are ye fearful, O ye of little faith?" and at the same time console them with the discovery that there is no truth that is not from God and that where truth is to be found it has been ordained by God.

Secondly, Küng's book is ecumenical because its conspectus covers the entire inhabited world. In the first part – entitled "The Horizon" – Küng comes to grips with the different varieties of modern humanism as well as with the major religions of the world other than Christianity, and this debate is carried through the whole of the rest of the book. In this he is following an important principle for any and every ecumenical dialogue: Rome and Geneva can only talk to each other in such a way that in doing so they are mindful of the fate of Nineveh, in other words that the outside world is drawn into the dialogue between them. In this way Küng is addressing his contemporaries in this book. True, he does so without displaying a frantic eagerness for conversion at all costs. But he is still making a case for conversion, since the ultimate aim of his reflections and argumentation, of his discoveries and explanations, is to convince the reader too of what he the author is himself so deeply convinced of.

Thirdly, Küng's book is ecumenical because it incites the separate confessional Churches to growing integration as Churches on the basis of the programme of Christ that is common to them. As far as Küng is concerned the decisive distinctions between the Churches today are to be found no longer in the various individual traditional differences of doctrine but in the different traditional basic attitudes. But in fact it is overcoming these that can in certain circumstances be the more difficult task. Hence Küng's aim is not to make short work of demolishing them. Rather he would prefer to dismantle their various forms of onesidedness and in this way to overcome their mutual exclusiveness, so that in the future "Protestant Catholicity" and "Catholic Protestantism" could exist not just side by side but intermingled with each other.

For this kind of integration Küng puts forward a series of practical suggestions: the reform and mutual recognition of ministries, joint services of the Word, open communion and also to an increasing extent joint celebrations of the Eucharist, shared church buildings and full co-operation in carrying out the Church's ministry of service towards society at large, increasing integration of theological faculties and of religious education, and finally the drawing up of detailed plans for union by Church leaders at the national and international level. But to prevent Protestants agreeing too easily to this kind of integration I should go out of my way to add that Küng would like to maintain the papacy (the "Petrine ministry", as he calls it) in his Church and this not just as a primacy of honour but as a ministerial and pastoral primacy.

Fourthly, Küng's book is ecumenical because it draws the world's other major religions into the dialogue between the Christian Churches. Gone is the age of *extra ecclesiam nulla salus*, the claim that outside the Christian Church there is no salvation; gone too is the method of one-sided monologue impelling its listeners towards conversion because it sees all other religions as simply the constructions of men. While Küng abandons all arrogant claims to exclusivity on the part of Christianity, not least because of the impact of the failure of the Christian missions in Asia, his aim is not simply to level out the differences that exist between the various religions. Nor is he at all interested in an "anonymous Christianity", nor in a syncretistic religion of unity. He holds firmly to the uniqueness of Christianity while seeing in the other religions partners of equal rank in the common search for the divine truth. To the extent that in this way Küng expands the dialogue of the Churches among themselves into a dialogue between the Churches and the other religions of the world, he instigates a genuinely ecumenical theology in the broadest sense of the word.

Fifthly, Küng's book is ecumenical because it seeks to overcome the polarization that threatens Christendom today. There is a dispute between those who concentrate above all on man's relationship to God and hence are one-sidedly concerned about the conversion of the individual and those who are only interested in the relations between human beings and hence are one-sidedly concerned to press for a change of present conditions. In this dispute Küng occupies a position of mediation and reconciliation. He does so with reference to the "programme" of Jesus Christ. Jesus advocated God's cause; but God's cause was man's cause: God became man not so that man might become God but so that man might at last be able to be really and truly man. Thus, because they believe in God's friendship towards man, Christians are radical humanists.

There is no need for any special prophetic gifts to predict that Hans Küng has written the most important theological book to appear this Autumn – for both Catholics and Protestants. To make this prediction all that is needed is a sound theological judgement. It is a book that shows once again that today the decisive lines of theological division do not correspond with the boundaries between the individual Churches but instead run right through the middle of the Churches themselves.

Notes

1. José Gomez Caffarena, S.J. born 1925, is director of the *Fe y Secularidad* institute in Madrid.
The article was first published in *El Ciervo* 25 (1977), pp. 40f, and is used by kind permission of the Editor.
2. Heinz Zahrnt, born 1915, theologian, lives in Hamburg, and is a former president of the German Evangelical *Kirchentag* and editor of the *Deutsches Allgemeines Sonntagsblatt*. Taken from *Deutsches Allgemeines Sonntagsblatt*, 13 October 1974, and used by kind permission of the Editor.

C. An Interview with Hans Küng

An Interview with Hans Küng

by HERMANN HÄRING and KARL-JOSEF KUSCHEL

Once at a meeting of the executive committee of the international theological journal Concilium, *among colleagues from a wide variety of different countries, you asked yourself the question: "How have I changed?" – as a theologian, of course. If you look back today, Professor Küng, have you changed and how have you changed?*

I can't answer this in a single sentence, but, if I may give some kind of general answer, I have continually been changing and hope to go on doing so in the future. If I look back over thirty years of theology, then there haven't really been any very abrupt conversions. I don't like tacking from side to side to keep up with the prevailing trend. I'd sooner follow something like a definite line. Of course I have always tried to be completely open to new questions that were being raised and to new methods and insights. I am possessed by a boundless intellectual curiosity that can never be satiated.

But surely certain definite stages can be distinguished?

Yes, certain definite stages can be distinguished, but it is something I would really prefer not to do because such stages of one's development can't be summed up in a few key words. But I can simply go through the various places where I've been since leaving home. To start with there was the *Gymnasium* [grammar school] in Lucerne. For me, a young Catholic brought up in the traditional Catholic way and moulded by the Catholic youth movement, this meant becoming open, in the best liberal spirit, to what was modern, particularly in literature and art and contemporary intellectual life in general. It meant coming into contact in the same class with Catholics, Protestants and Jews. It also meant coeducation, with boys and girls together in the same school. Then I was changed by my seven years in Rome from 1948 to 1955, by the intensive contact all day and every day with the Roman Catholic system in both theology and discipline as well as in the Church at large. You must not forget that it was a system that at that time still stood in all its impressive, unbroken strength and determination. Then at the same time during my final years in Rome there was the intensive study of Protestant theology in the form of Barth's *Church Dogmatics*. I was also changed, though perhaps to a lesser extent, by Paris and by studying at the Sorbonne and the Institut Catholique. After the strict Roman training Paris was for me a period of new freedom and it also meant coming into contact with the then French avant-garde *nouvelle théologie*. At the same time I was able to go abroad for extended visits to Spain, England and Holland and to develop and deepen the knowledge of people of other languages and nations that I had begun to acquire when still at the *Gymnasium*. It was also during this phase of my life that I came into close personal contact with Karl Barth. Then back to Lucerne. Between 1957 and 1959 there were eighteen months of being very involved in pastoral work, which showed me most of the problems of pastoral work today and also provided me with a test of how applicable and feasible a particular theology was. The single year as a research assistant at Münster that followed this was in fact the first time, although it was rather late in my career, that I came into contact with the German university with all its problems. Finally, I have also been changed by Tübingen from 1960 on. There has been the intensive business of coming to grips with the historical and critical method, first of all in exegesis and then with all its consequences in systematic theology too. Then at the same time there has been the enormous upheaval in the history of the Church in connection with Vatican II and its effects in the period after the Council.

18

Naturally all you have been able to do in this is to sketch the broad outlines of your development. So we trust you will not mind if we question you in somewhat greater detail about the individual stages of your career. Let us start with Rome. Presumably with the relatively liberal education you had been receiving you went there with a certain spirit of opposition?

Not at all. I went to Rome completely voluntarily and in full knowledge of what lay in store for me there: an education in the strict Tridentine spirit that would last a total of seven years, during which I would be able to visit my home only once, possibly twice at the most. However astonishing it may seem to you today, what I wanted was precisely this contrast to the worldliness and freedom I had been enjoying up till then. Above all I wanted a thorough scholarly training, something which seemed to be guaranteed by the Gregorian with six semesters of philosophy and eight of theology. I wanted the strict internal and external discipline of the German College, which like the Gregorian was run by the Jesuits. I wanted something that would in every way be a thorough intellectual and spiritual training. Of course with all due diffidence we regarded ourselves as an élite and were in fact trained as such. But that was what was fascinating and challenging about it all. And all this was something I saw not as preparation for academic work at a university but as preparation for the active pastoral work that I hoped to undertake, if possible in one of the bigger cities, first as a curate and eventually, I hoped, as a parish priest. They were great years in Rome, that period from 1948 to 1955, years when streams of Catholic pilgrims never stopped coming in their millions to the Holy City. I had the opportunity of joining in everything on my very doorstep: the holy year pilgrimages of 1950, the display of papal pomp and ceremony, the Roman curia. Pius XII was then at the pinnacle of his power and reputation, and that did not fail to leave its mark on us students. The publication of the encyclical *Humani generis* directed against theological deviations was something that I experienced as it were on the spot. It had been drawn up in essentials by my own professors at the

Gregorian. Then in the same year, 1950, there was the triumphalist definition of the Assumption. And so on.

Did you accept all this then without any reservations at all?

Yes, I did to start with. The definition of the Assumption for example struck me as a suitable expression of the Catholic understanding of the faith on the basis of the organic theory of the development of dogma being served up to us at that time. And in talking to students from German universities I used to criticize the "arrogance" and the "mania for criticism" shown by the German professors of theology who had their doubts on this question and who were described as rationalistic. For the rest I used to be pretty slavish in keeping to the uncommonly strict rules of the German College, rules that in some respects weren't even sensible, and I didn't understand at all the freer attitude of my older fellow-students who had come into the German College straight off the Italian campaign and just could not come to terms with this Tridentine regulation of their entire life.

You say you began by identifying yourself with the system without any reservations. When did the breach come?

It wasn't really a breach. There wasn't any single dramatic event, any sudden conversion. It was a matter of slowly becoming aware of certain definite problems, a process that really crystallized out in certain issues and indeed conflicts some time after my first five years in Rome.

What kind of issues and conflicts were involved?

One was the crisis of Church leadership. Pius XII's final years were marked by an ever-increasing ossification on the part of the Roman curia and an ever-increasing isolation of the Pope himself. Then, after the suppression of modern theology in France, there was the suppression of the French worker priests, something that shocked me because of the

very abrupt way it was done. There was a continuous in-
flation of statements by the Church's teaching authority in
the form of addresses and encyclicals by a Pope who had
learned it all by heart and who ended up by merely reading
what had been written by others who I happened to know
only too well. So, if you like, being able every day to look
behind the scenes of this pontificate brought about a de-
mythologization of this Pope whom formerly we had all
idealized. A second was the development of theology.
Despite good professors at the Gregorian, the neoscholastic
system of theology didn't deliver what it promised. Its thesis
form covered the problems up more than it solved them. And
a problem that was particularly debated among a small
circle of students I belonged to that met to discuss theological topics was the problem of the supernatural and what
can best be described as the neoscholastic two-tier way of
looking at these questions. Problems that neoscholastic
theology was incapable of solving like nature and grace,
reason and faith, the natural and the supernatural, could not
in our view be divided up in theory and practice in the way
that this happened in the neoscholastic system and in the
ecclesiastical system that corresponded to it. A third was
that in this context college discipline seemed more and more
problematical to me. Something that may well seem today
of no significance at all but that was anything but, given the
completely rigoristic way we had been trained, was that the
obligation to have to attend lectures when one could have
read their contents up much more quickly in text-books was
for me the first test case of ecclesiastical obedience. The
question was whether I should follow the system or my own
personal convictions. A fourth and final issue arose from
my work as chaplain to the Italian employees of the college,
a post I had applied for (and also prepared for) on my own
initiative. I saw it as part of my job to intervene on their
behalf to get an improvement in their conditions with regard
to accommodation, pay, and the possibility of getting
married. Just like the problems over college discipline and
over theology this brought me into very serious conflict with
the college authorities. However, I wasn't sent down.

In all this process of your finding Roman theology and discipline more and more questionable, were there people whom you could look to for guidance?

Well, we weren't isolated. Practically every week at the Germanicum we had visitors from all over the world – bishops, professors, politicians, even artists. Usually they gave lectures or took part in discussions in which they talked about the problems they were facing. We were always in touch with what was going on in the Church and the world in general. Then there were a number of professors at the university who helped me through the crisis in theology both by means of their lectures and, most importantly, by means of personal conversations and who showed understanding for a student who had noticed a little of the crisis that was going on. I am thinking particularly of my professor for the history of philosophy, Alois Naber, under whom I did my dissertation on Jean-Paul Sartre's atheistic humanism for my licentiate in philosophy, as well as my professor for dogmatics, Maurizio Flick, who accepted the idea of my doing my licentiate in theology on Karl Barth's doctrine of justification. I didn't have the slightest difficulty with either of them; on the contrary both showed me a great deal of understanding. Then in the field of philosophy there was the Frenchman René Arnou, with whom one could have a very good discussion on contemporary problems, or in theology the young Spanish dogmatic theologian Juan Alfaro who had a good knowledge of German theology and was also interested in coming to grips with recent problems. Finally, I must not forget Gustav A. Wetter, then rector of the Russicum, for whom I ran a study circle on dialectical materialism, nor must I forget the social scientist and papal adviser Gustav Gundlach, whose sociological study circle I was keenly involved in and indeed chaired for one year. From all these men I didn't just learn a great deal with regard to their particular fields of study, but also they were very often able to act as models and examples of how to behave and be involved in a system under the most difficult circumstances. Nevertheless I probably would not have been able to survive these seven years without the help of my spiritual director at the Germanicum, Fr Wilhelm Klein, who brought to his job a remarkably wide outlook that was the fruit of varied activity as a professor of philosophy, as provincial of the North German province of the Jesuits, and as the Society's visitor from Scandinavia to Japan, and who put me on the path of making personal decisions of conscience in fundamental questions of ecclesiastical obedience. He was also someone who was the first to make me aware of many urgent philosophical and theological problems. I discussed Hegel and later Karl Barth with him. And he was the one to whom I first showed my own first efforts at theological work, writings that for the most part he was merciless in pulling to pieces so as to force me into a genuinely dialectical way of thinking that always included the antithesis too in the final synthesis.

Looking back now on your whole period in Rome, what apart from your studies really made a lasting impression on you?

Without a doubt my seven years in Rome had a lasting effect on my basic attitudes. The fundamental decisions, too, did not, as is often believed, take place in Paris or in Germany but in Rome. Perhaps the biggest effect on my fundamental spirituality was brought about by something that may surprise you – Ignatius of Loyola's *Spiritual Exercises*, which I followed in Rome in the widest possible variety of forms and under a wide variety of spiritual directors. Despite all the reservations one might have about Ignatius's rules for thinking with the Church a triple criterion has become decisive for me. First, the supreme norm for my attitude and behaviour should not be some earthly, worldly or ecclesiastical authority or discipline but, if you will allow me the grandiloquent but very precise expression, only the will of God – in other words what in a particular situation I recognize as God's will for me. Second, a Christocentric approach, in other words a growing process of aligning myself with reference to the person of Jesus Christ, in which I recognize the will of God in concrete form: this is a process that has been strengthened by Barthian theology and by increased preoccupation with the New Testament. Finally, as far as living in the world and society of today is concerned, active indifference with regard to all earthly things, which may be important but are not ultimately decisive: they can and should be made use of inasmuch as they help towards the goal one has set before one, but in certain circumstances they must also be renounced if they become an impediment, an obstacle.

What do you mean in practice by active indifference? Where does it operate?

Its effects are or should be pretty well universal. It means an ultimate inward distancing from, an ultimate but thoroughly positive indifference towards, all the things of the world, towards everything, if you like, that is not God. Thus this means money, possessions and prestige to begin with and goes on to embrace human relationships. But I must emphasize the adjective. It is active indifference. This does not mean holding everything at arm's length and practising a cold-blooded inaccessibility or even using people simply as a means to higher religious ends and ideals – something that can be a real danger with this kind of spirituality. Complete and profound human involvement and commitment are comprised in the idea and they only run up against a definite limit in certain circumstances when the fulfilment of the task one has undertaken would be impeded.

Has this had its effects on your conflict with the ecclesiastical authorities?

A certain ultimate imperturbability in all the tough fights there have been no doubt has its roots in this fundamental attitude and not just in a certain temperament or even in a Swiss appreciation of freedom and independence. With regard to the Church and its representatives it operates in a

critical loyalty which is continually striving afresh for unity
with the community of the Church and its authorities and
for the unity of this community, despite all the disappoint-
ments. It also operates in a spirit of loyal criticism – and
this is only the other side of the coin – which does not let its
voice be silenced but, in season or out of season, tries to
speak the truth in truthfulness and also to write it down.
This is really what has always carried me through the disputes with Rome and the bishops that have lasted for nearly
twenty years: this, and truly not the accusation that is always
brought against me, a desire to parade my own person,
taking myself too seriously, a lack of humility, an unwilling-
ness to listen to reason, thoroughgoing obstinacy, etc. On
the basis of this fundamental attitude I have never sought
publicity, but also I have never shunned it if it served the
cause I had to champion. I have criticized the Church not
because I have distanced myself from it but because I am
involved in it and committed to it. The Church is and remains tremendously important for me, but it has never been
the ultimate absolute for me and will not be so in the future.
"Church" only makes sense in the service of men and women
and ultimately of God himself. And the Christian Church
only makes sense if it is guided not by the laws and dogmas
it has created for itself but by the norm of the Gospel of
Jesus Christ himself.

*Karl Barth's name has already cropped up more than once.
It's rather surprising that someone like yourself, trained in
Roman theology in the days of Pius XII, should become involved with* the *Protestant theologian. How did this come
about?*

What attracted me to him was his very Protestantism. In
him I saw the strictest possible development of the Protestant
thing and at the same time a striving after a Catholic breadth.
And to begin with doubtless no small part was played by the
fact that he was a fellow-countryman of mine and that his
name had been known to me since my schooldays. Wilhelm
Klein played a decisive role in encouraging me to choose

Barth's theology as a subject for my dissertation, and it was Barth's great partner in dialogue on the Catholic side, Hans Urs von Balthasar, who in Basle proposed three subjects from among which the topic of justification suggested itself as the subject for my doctoral thesis in talking it over with my teachers in Paris in 1953.

Wait a moment: how did you run into Hans Urs von Balthasar?

I had known of him for a long time as another fellow-countryman of mine. When I had finished my three years of philosophy and started to occupy myself more seriously with theology I read several of his books, particularly the one on Bernanos and St Teresa of Lisieux and finally the one on Karl Barth. The style of dialogue that he used with Karl Barth struck me as the model of what was needed for ecumenical discussion. Even today Balthasar is a theologian of a mental and spiritual breadth of outlook without equal, and that not just in the Catholic world. I still remember my first visit to his home in Basle when I was twenty-five. I was fascinated by his library, which seemed to cover not just the whole field of theology but the whole of the world's literature in all its different languages. It was Balthasar, too, who encouraged and supported me in my work on Barth, corrected me when I went wrong, and finally published the work from his Johannes-Verlag with a personal letter of introduction from Karl Barth himself. He too – and this is something I shall never forget despite the extraordinary fuss he has been making about *On Being A Christian* – came all the way to Paris when I had to defend my thesis at the Institut Catholique.

Can we stay for a moment with your work on justification? Could you sketch out briefly what the problems were for you at that time?

What I was concerned about first of all was quite simply Protestant theology and in particular that of Karl Barth, which I wanted to get to know as thoroughly as possible. At the same time it was of course well known to me that according to the general view all the differences between Catholic and Protestant theology and between the Catholic and Protestant Churches were based on their different understanding of justification. But for the general run of Catholic theology and preaching justification still played a relatively insignificant role that didn't really affect or concern people at all. Despite all its intensive efforts the Council of Trent ultimately failed to understand Luther on this point, not to mention the theology of the Counter-Reformation or neo-scholasticism. And as far as I was concerned it was only while I was working on this subject that the significance of our understanding of justification first dawned on me. It is only with time that the extent has become clear to me to which the whole existence of the Christian depends in a much more profound way than I had hitherto accepted on faith, a faith that has confidence in what it believes in, and not on his or her own efforts.

Where do we find the significance for the history of theology that many of the reviewers of this book were pretty well unanimous in ascribing to it?

What was completely surprising was the fundamental agreement that this book established between the Barthian doctrine of justification and the Catholic one when the latter was correctly understood. This was something nobody had thought possible, and without exaggeration it meant something like an ecumenical sensation, especially after Barth had explicitly confirmed his agreement in his accompanying introductory letter. And in fact this agreement had a long-lasting pioneering effect and was confirmed not only by various other books and articles but finally also by official documents, particularly the Malta Report drawn up by an official commission of the Lutheran World Federation and the Unity Secretariat in Rome. In addition there was another point that affected internal Catholic difficulties. It was the first time that the two-tier theory with nature providing the foundations and the supernatural the super-structure had been overcome, inasmuch as even the level of creation was seen entirely in the light of Jesus Christ. As a result, from start to finish the "natural/supernatural" ter-minology was avoided, even though it had dominated dis-cussion particularly since de Lubac's work *Surnaturel* of 1946, and more down-to-earth language was used to replace it. So one was no longer talking about human nature but about human beings, about people, no longer about the various graces as accidents but about the effectively gracious God. The person who then agreed most clearly with me on this point of neoscholastic terminology having got bogged down was Professor Josef Ratzinger, who is roughly the same age as me and who meanwhile, as is well known, has gone his own way.

What you are saying is that the problem of justification can no longer be described in physiological and ontological but only in personal categories. Does this doctrine still really have significance for you today or is it just a subject of theological controversy that is now left behind?

Not at all. Its significance and importance cannot be valued too highly, especially in the Catholic world. As you know, I was particularly pleased that I succeeded in making the entire book *On Being A Christian* culminate in a con-temporary interpretation of what justification is all about in the two sections "What is not ultimately important" and "What is ultimately important". It is precisely in our con-temporary society that is based on the idea of achievement, that is characterized by the pressure on people to achieve and to be successful, in this society in which it is only through his or her achievements that a person means some-thing, has his or her place in society and is respected – it is precisely in this kind of society that it is of enormous com-fort to know that through all his or her achievements, through all that he or she does man or woman does not in any way gain being, identity, freedom, personhood, does not in any way attain to the confirmation of his or her ego and the sense and meaning of his or her existence. Not that we should renounce achievements and as a matter of course treat them as something diabolical. But contemporary men and women can and should know that the person is more than his or her role, that achievements are indeed important but they are not decisive, and this applies both to those that are good and those that are bad. Briefly, before God it is ultimately not a matter of achievements but of something else: that in good as in evil, man in every case places his unconditional trust in God and maintains it. That protects him or her from false pride over his or her achievements as well as from despair over his or her failures.

But aren't you in fact a prize example yourself of someone whose whole being is geared to success and achievement? You've got nearly twenty books to your credit, you've been on a lecture tour round the world more than once, you're internationally famous as a prominent theologian, you've got a whole host of academic honours. And there's all the effort that you demand of yourself (and of us) every day and that of course lies behind all your achievements. Don't you in fact depend on your successes? Don't you in fact need all this to confirm your identity?

It's not exactly easy to answer a difficult personal question like this. Of course success isn't something I'm indifferent to: that's something I have in common with many people. And I also want to see the things I'm concerned about succeed. I think I can say without being conceited that I can rejoice with an easy conscience at my own successes but also at those of others. But you would be completely misunderstanding me if you thought I based my own personal existence on my achievements and successes. I know the other side of this only too well: the perpetual risk of failure, the insecurity and the all too frequent disappointment. And I think I can say honestly that on the basis of my understanding of the message of justification I do not pride myself on my achievements, since I know I have not been able to give anything that I have not first received. And so my whole activity has not primarily been directed towards success. If it had there is much I would have had to leave undone. And there has been much I have had to get involved in where success just didn't come into the picture at all. If one had had an ecclesiastical career in mind one could certainly have done things differently. If you want to become a cardinal today in Germany you need to start practising early. But to a greater extent than may appear from outside the most important things in my life are not things I have seized hold of on my own initiative but things that as it were I have let happen to me. Thus a university career wasn't something I was pushing myself into: instead I was asked to take it up by others. I never thought of going to the Second Vatican Council: instead I was invited to do so, against all expectation, by the then Bishop of Rottenburg. Most of my books weren't planned long in advance nor did they arise from a mania for boosting my ego, but they were shown to be necessary by the development of the life of the Church. Often I would have been happy for someone else to have taken the job over for me. I'm not at all the person hooked on success and achievement that I may seem to the outside world. The fact that I have been able to write books like *The Church* or *On Being A Christian* is for me anything but a matter of course. If it doesn't seem too pompous, it is something I am aware of as a definite grace for which I can only be thankful.

If it isn't success that provides the basis for your life, what does?

I can only hope that what is able to support me in success and failure is this unconditional trust in God that is what Christian faith is all about. There is something that made a very deep impression on me that I mentioned in the speech I gave at the memorial service for Karl Barth in Basle cathedral. Right at the end of his life, when he was facing death, Barth did not want to appear before God with all his works piled up in a basket ("That would make all the angels laugh," he said). But nor did he wish to appear just with good faith, as if he had always had the right intentions. At that moment, he told me – and this for me sums up this unconditional trust – there was only one thing he could say: "God have mercy on a poor sinner like me."

Before we return to Barth, can we ask how it came about that on the one hand in 1957, the year your book on justification was published, a Küng dossier was begun in the Holy Office in Rome with the later well-known file number 399/57i while on the other hand Rome did not open any proceedings against a book which in the days of Pius XII was claiming to be able to establish a consensus between Protestants and Catholics with regard to such fundamental axioms of the Reformation as sola gratia (*by grace alone*), *sola fide* (*by faith alone*), *simul iustus et peccator* (*justified and a sinner at one and the same time*), *etc.?*

In fact people from the Holy Office told me at the time that numerous denunciations had come in to Rome with regard to this book. But it was in part external circumstances that protected my book from a condemnation. My former teachers at the Gregorian, and particularly Fr Sebastian Tromp, who together with Fr Franz Hürth played a decisive role in the Holy Office, took me under their wing. Fr Tromp used to tell anyone who would listen that what my book was concerned with was a possible interpretation of the Tridentine decree on justification, even if one didn't therefore have to agree with everything in it. My professors at Paris, too, especially Louis Bouyer, my supervisor for my doctorate, and Guy de Broglie, who taught half the year in Rome and the other half in Paris and was held in high regard in Rome, shielded me from the cruder attacks through their public statements in the book's favour that were printed on the cover. I think the decisive thing was that I myself knew and had mastered the official Roman doctrine and had gone to endless trouble to adduce, as Barth said, a cloud of witnesses from the Catholic tradition to support my view. As a result even traditional-minded Catholic theologians could not deny that what was involved was a view that could not *a priori* be dismissed as un-Catholic. For myself I regarded the situation as serious, as was confirmed by the opening of the dossier on me, the existence of which I only learned about later. I thought the chances of this book ending up on the Index were about fifty-fifty. If it had done so, my life would have taken a completely different course. It was only after the book had been well received that I decided to enter the field of academic theology. Otherwise I would perhaps be a parish priest in some Swiss town or village today – something that no doubt would make many people in Rome and elsewhere sleep more peacefully.

To revert to Karl Barth himself, what has he meant for you both as a theologian and as a man?

As I've already said, Barth opened up the way into Protestant theology for me. Beyond that Barth aroused my enthusiasm for theology as such. Before, theology was for me an essential and obligatory exercise and a preparatory phase for the pastoral work that was to come later. To begin with it had comparatively little fascination for me, certainly less than philosophy, art, music, psychology . . . It was only now, brought up against Barth's theological system, which is enormously spacious and at the same time organized down to the smallest detail, that I could see clearly what theology as a field of study was capable of. Barth's critical and constructive grappling with the entire Christian tradition of the past two thousand years and thus with the Catholic tradition too, his grappling with the great thinkers of the past and with the spirit of the age, his involvement in practical questions not only in connection with the Church's resistance to Hitler and the Nazis but also in other Church disputes, all this established for me lasting standards of theological thought and activity. And in this you mustn't forget that for seven years it was only in Latin that I had been listening to lectures, only in Latin that I had been doing examinations, and hence it was Latin books in particular that I had been studying. It was Barth who reintroduced me to decent German in theology with his powerful theological language that may indeed often be a bit long-winded but is nevertheless honed down to a fine polish.

When did you get to know him personally?

Comparatively late. It was only in 1955, when I had just left Rome and had sent him in Basle the dissertation I had done for my licentiate in theology on his doctrine of justification. He was filled with amazement on reading it. The first question he put to me the first time I got in touch with him – by telephone – was: "Are you in fact an old man or a young man?" I was twenty-seven at the time. Right from my first visit I was able to establish a rapport with him at the human level to a greater extent than with most of the other people I have met in my life. I regarded him as friend and father-figure, while his concern the whole time was that I should go on putting everything to rights in theology and that I should continue to tread surefootedly the dangerous path within Catholic theology. Thus he read the manuscript of my book on the Council and reform (1960) and after a few days' consideration it was he himself who suggested the title: "The Council and Reunion: Renewal as a Summons to Unity". He wanted the word "reform" avoided in the title, because otherwise I could all too easily be written off as a crypto-Protestant. Barth at that time read everything I wrote with much approval, although as early as *Structures of the Church* (1962) I had to apply myself more to the historical difficulties in order to come to grips with the problems of Church reform and in particular the questions of the ministry and the papacy. His first serious criticism was aroused by a section I included on the historical Jesus in my book *The Church* (1967) – a work that struck him as "profoundly Protestant" – before going on to develop the ecclesiological aspects of the work. Barth regarded this as unnecessary. But as far as I was concerned the necessity of a section of this kind became clear to me when I saw everything else that had to be said about the Church otherwise hanging in the air. It struck me as impossible to talk about the historical foundation of the Church without talking in detail about the Jesus of history. With regard to *Truthfulness* (1968) his view was that in Catholic theology too one should now talk not so much of truthfulness as above all of the truth, of which indeed there was of course enough talk everywhere in Catholic theology even if not always on the right lines. Truthfulness, however, had not up till then been discussed by anyone in connection with Catholic theology and the Catholic Church (already at that time the question of infallibility was clearly indicated). With Karl Barth it became evident, as it did to me in connection with other great teachers of theology, that I wanted to learn as much as possible from all of them and never be lacking in gratitude. But ultimately I had all the same to go my own way.

Are you affected by the reproach of the Catholic historian of dogma Fr Grillmeier, who said Karl Barth would have given your book On being a Christian *a decisive "No"?*

This kind of reproach makes little impression on me if it comes from Catholic theologians who are merely making use of Barth as a convenient apologetic shield for their traditionalistic theology and who otherwise never in any way face up to the challenge of Barthian theology. Karl Barth often said to me: "I'd like to be as young as you again, then I'd be manning the barricades once more." And I have no doubt that if Barth were my age once again and were manning the barricades once more, then he would do things differently and unexpectedly – to the disapproval of his teachers and older colleagues – as he did in 1919 with his commentary on Romans.

There is however a real problem lurking behind this reproach. Where is the difference to be found between your theological approach and Barth's?

I must begin by stressing that in my view I have adhered to the fundamental intentions of Barth's approach up to and including my latest book, *Does God Exist?*, despite all the changes which indeed Barth himself carried through to a considerable degree, as with the shift from the divinity of God to the humanity of God. Both now and then what strikes me as fundamental for a serious theology is immense respect and reverence before God himself, what is meant by Barth's saying about the infinite difference between God and man: an attitude that abhors all frivolous and superficial theological talking about God. It is the *Deus semper maior*, the God who is always greater, as according to the New Testament witness he revealed himself decisively in Jesus Christ: an event that cannot simply be explained on the basis of history, of the history of ideas, or of psychology but that is to be understood as an event of revelation that man can only adequately respond to in faith. God's divinity, rightly understood, Christocentricity, the fundamental significance of the attitude of faith – these and very much else in line with Barth's thinking are things people will be able to find even in my latest books.

Where then do the differences lie?

What is involved is above all a difference in our theological starting points and in theological method. Barth in his day, in an attack for which there is virtually no parallel, stormed and overran the positions of that liberal theology that had to far too great an extent reduced the event of revelation to history, psychology and human subjectivity. He rightly made the radical change of beginning from above and made the starting point of his theology God and his free sovereign activity in Christ. But one must nevertheless agree with Rudolf Bultmann without thereby surrendering Barth's intentions that in doing so Barth had overrun rather than assimilated the important results of liberal theology. It seemed to me important above all for pastoral reasons, which can however easily be given a theological underpinning, to try to begin from below and once again to make a fresh start from human experience and history. Thus with regard to Christology it would be a question not so much of starting from Jesus Christ as the son of God, as of trying to place oneself in the situation of Jesus's disciples who had to ask themselves who this man was. This perspective of slowly fumbling one's way towards the person of Jesus Christ and thus towards God himself too ought also to be better adapted to contemporary men and women. What the Christian message has to say to us is not thereby reduced to the level of the history of religion in general but is however seen within the context of the history of religion. Right from the start this was a major point of difference between me and Barth, who indeed rejected any true knowledge of God that was not based on Christian revelation. My view on the other hand – and here I find myself in the great Catholic tradition and indeed that of the Reformation – is that even according to the Old and New Testaments, whose statements in this context Barth did violence to, it is necessary in fact to accept a knowledge of the one true God even among non-Christians, among "the heathen". Of course, along with Barth I am convinced that it is only with the Christian message that God is made manifest to me in his complete unambiguity with all the consequences that flow from this. But this must not be understood in an exclusive sense. There is a way – and it is one I have followed particularly in my last two books – between dialectical theology in Karl Barth's sense and natural theology in the neoscholastic sense. The possibility of non-Christians being able to know God must be accepted in the sense of Vatican I as against dialectical theology. But as against natural theology it must, in the sense of what Barth is driving at, be made clear that even a non-Christian's knowledge of God is not simply a natural or purely rational knowledge. A matter of trust, of confidence, is fundamentally involved in all knowledge of God. The knowledge of God oversteps in every case the boundaries of our experience, and God can only be affirmed and accepted if man deals with him on the basis of a trust that can exist before reason comes into play and if man thus comes to depend on him.

The next important stage in your career was Paris: the Sorbonne, the Institut Catholique. What did this period in Paris mean to you?

First of all Paris meant an immense liberation after all the business of being isolated and segregated in a Roman college, after all the compulsion and regulation of a life regimented from morning till night. At last one was free to plan one's life oneself again. It may sound rather odd even for seminarists today, but once again, as earlier during my days at the *Gymnasium*, I could freely go to the theatre, to the cinema, to talks and lectures, when I had the time to do so. This contact with French cultural life and above all with the French university, with the Sorbonne and of course particularly with the Institut Catholique and with French theology, meant an undreamed-of enrichment for me.

Were there teachers here who had a particular influence on you and subjects that were to crop up in your lectures and work later?

Yes, I recall the Protestant New Testament scholar and author of the well-known book on Peter, Oscar Cullmann, under whose guidance at the Sorbonne, at the *École des Hautes Études*, I took part for the first time in a serious seminar on exegesis, on this occasion on confessions of faith in the New Testament. His were practically the only Protestant lectures I went to, and I have several times in Basle visited this man who has done so much for ecumenism, the last time while I was a visiting professor at the Protestant faculty of theology there. Then I had the luck to be able to go to lectures by experts on the philosophy of Descartes and on the French seventeenth century like Henri Gouhier – something that stood me in extraordinarily good stead when I came to give my first lecture at Tübingen in 1960. Like my book *Does God Exist?* this began with the antithesis between Descartes' *Cogito, ergo sum* and Pascal's *Credo, ergo sum*.

French theology at that time meant above all nouvelle théologie, *the new direction in theology banned by Pius XII. And one of your examiners for your thesis at the Institut, Henri Bouillard, was an exponent of this direction who had himself at one time been dismissed. What was your attitude to this theology?*

Someone coming straight from Rome was greeted with a little suspicion by that side. But this evaporated with time. At all events I was glad to be able to discuss with living people – the Jesuit Henri Bouillard with regard to Barthian theology, but also the Oratorian Louis Bouyer – what I had previously only known from books. Of course it wasn't possible for me to fit myself into and see myself as a member of a theological faction. This was not only because I had friends on both sides but also and above all because the kind of questions that were being asked struck me as being out of date. As I have already indicated, I did not see any solution possible within the framework of natural and supernatural. And in fact when Fr de Lubac was at last under John XXIII freed from the ban on writing on this subject and published his defence of his position practically no one was interested in this any longer. And the tragic thing, to which this contributed in no small way, is that Fr Henri de Lubac, for whom I had the highest respect, lapsed into a state of resigned bitterness with regard to the way the Church and theology developed after the Council.

What were the positive things you drew from your time in Paris?

There is a great deal that ought to be mentioned but which I cannot go into now, such as the efforts which at that time were completely new towards creating living worship, or the chants of the French Jesuit Fr Gélineau, who followed a course with me at the Institut Catholique. From the theological point of view there were two things of especial importance for me. The first was the significance for the renewal of theology of the Latin and particularly the Greek fathers of the Church. This patristic-based theology was something I was in complete agreement with, just as in later life I would gladly apply myself to the fathers once again. At all events, even at that time an examination of the view of the Greek and Latin fathers in the light of the New Testament and thus of a historical and critical exegesis struck me as unavoidable. This very point had been neglected in the *nouvelle théologie*, and this in turn was connected with the suppression of the French school of exegesis in connection with the struggle against modernism. The idea was that in place of a rigorous exegesis on historical and critical principles one could solve the problems with a spiritual, "pneumatic" exegesis somewhat along the lines of the fourfold meaning of scripture proposed by Fr de Lubac.

And the second thing?

Ecclesiology, and here the first figure to be mentioned must be that great French theologian Yves Congar. I had already got to know him when I was a member of a small group as a student in Rome, when in the aftermath of the worker-priests' affair he had been dismissed and banished from France and thus spent some time in Rome as well as elsewhere. It was only relatively late that I read his major work *Vraie et fausse réforme dans l'Église*, which at the time was promptly suppressed by Rome. Then I discovered that in this book Congar had thought through from the theological, historical and systematic point of view and had brought together in a large-scale synthesis a number of fundamental insights with regard to the reform of the Church that had dawned on me at the practical level in Rome when in contact with the Roman system and Roman theology. Congar's book was extraordinarily important for my work *The Council and Reunion*. Even at that time, however, I was not attracted by his distinction between true reform, understood as reform of the Church's life and regarded as Catholic, and false reform, understood as reform of the Church's doctrine and seen as Protestant. It struck me even then as important that we should set about a reform of doctrine. But what remains significant for me personally up to the present is that, in contrast to many others of his generation in France and elsewhere, Congar has not given up and simply decided to reject the efforts of his younger colleagues in theology, as to some extent Karl Rahner tends to do. Instead he has always backed and shared in them and has also maintained his friendship with me.

In this context the way in which conflicts within the Church used to be settled has a paradigmatic significance for today: the condemnations, dismissals, accusations of heresy and modernism. In your work today do you see a link with those who were then proscribed? Do you advocate the concerns of the modernists of the past? In a word, are you what you are often accused of being, a neomodernist?

You will be surprised to learn that I can hardly answer this question for you. The reason is that I don't know what a modernist really is, just as most of those who talk about modernists haven't read them. The term modernism was coined by the opponents of the theologians of that time advocating renewal and reform, particularly in France and Germany. The encyclical directed against the modernists, as even traditional theologians admit today, was cobbled together from all the available views possible so as to construct something that in this coherent form had never existed at all: in other words, modernism. In this field there is still some research to be done. One of my students, an Italian Franciscan, Bernardino Greco, has already done some work on Ernesto Buonaiuti, who is the best known of the Italian modernists and who was a friend of Angelo Roncalli, later John XXIII. This shows me two things. First, many questions that were dealt with by the progressive theologians of that time are still questions for us today, and in fact not just for me. I am decidedly in favour of justice at last being done to all those who were then labelled heretics. Here there is a great deal to be done which should not be done uncritically. The reason is – and this is the second point – that the solutions found then were very inadequate, which is not to be wondered at. To too great an extent – and this applies to Buonaiuti just as much as to the Frenchman Loisy – people followed the liberal German theology of the turn of the century and thus shared its weaknesses and strengths. A eturn to the original gospel, which is what Buonaiuti and others were striving after, is without a doubt more than ever necessary today. But the original gospel must not be seen imply in the light of Adolf von Harnack's theology.

To raise a completely different and additional subject: as ou know, we have often been amused by the title of one of he earliest articles you published. Right at the start of his areer Küng wrote about "Our girls in Paris" – but presumably this doesn't mean what one might think.

I'm afraid I have to disappoint you on this one. Just as in Rome I took on the pastoral care of the Italian employees t the college as an extra job, so in Paris I undertook, on ehalf of the Swiss bishops, the pastoral care of the numerous Swiss au pair girls who were living with families in Paris n order to improve their French. This additional pastoral work was something I very much enjoyed doing.

Then what at that time was a sideline became your chief ccupation in Lucerne from 1957 to 1959, didn't it?

It was a short but a very pleasant time, those eighteen months as assistant priest at the Hofkirche in Lucerne. They were sufficient to enable me to have a clear picture throughout my entire life of the practical problems, anxieties and needs of the pastoral clergy. I saw how important a good theological preparation is for pastoral work in practice, for proclaiming the word, for preaching, for giving instruction. also saw – and this, you will recall, was before the Council – ow relatively easy it is to carry out reforms in worship, in he structure of the parish, in religious instruction, and in the fe of parish organizations, provided one at the same time ffers positive solutions alongside all the negative criticism hat may be necessary, and provided one does not go over he heads of the people involved but draws them into cooperating in the project. I have warm memories of working ith my then parish priest and the other members of the parish team.

Your academic career began in 1959 with your post as assistant for dogmatic theology in Münster and then only a year later your succeeding Heinrich Fries in the chair of fundamental theology at Tübingen.

Yes, being summoned to Tübingen was a little startling. I was only thirty-two, and while in Münster I had not yet found time to hand in the thesis I had completed for my *Habilitation* [the examination which establishes a candidate's fitness to hold a professorship at a German university]. Meanwhile *The Council and Reunion* had appeared, a book I had completed while research assistant in Münster to Professor Hermann Volk, now Bishop of Mainz and a cardinal. But my work on Hegel's Christology, which had originally been intended for a doctorate in philosophy at the Sorbonne and then as a thesis for the theological *Habilitation* in Münster, stayed tucked away in a drawer and was only published ten years later after it had undergone a third and a fourth revision.

This book Menschwerdung Gottes *is perhaps the most difficult that you have written and hence probably the least read. Could you describe briefly what you were concerned about in it?*

A body of work as difficult and comprehensive as that of Barth or of Hegel is something that if possible one should study when one is young when to some extent one still has time, if you will allow me this pedagogical comment. There were several things I was concerned about in *Menschwerdung Gottes*. Hegel – whom I tried to present as simply as possible – attracted me from the years when I was studying philosophy. In my book I presented his biography and the development of his thought from the theological writings of his youth through his major published works to the lectures that he himself did not publish on world history, the philosophy of art, the philosophy of religion, and the history of philosophy. But everything was focused on his understanding of God and his understanding of Christology as God becoming man, something I followed through all its phases from his early years in Stuttgart and Tübingen to his final years in Berlin. Each chapter works its way through five interwoven layers, for the most part curving inwards in a spiral, so as to attain to a wide-ranging and penetrating initiation into and discussion with Hegel that is equally significant for theologians and for philosophers. At the same time I tried to provide an introduction to the world of German idealism that is so important for the contemporary discussion both of Marx and of Kierkegaard, for both Catholic and Protestant theology. The motive that lay behind what was in fact a difficult and extensive investigation was on the one hand to attain, with the aid of Hegelian dialectical thought, a more dynamic understanding of God, and on the other a more profoundly based Christology that as far as possible avoided the weaknesses of the static, classical Christology as it has been handed down to us from the time of the great Christological councils of the first millennium.

This book Menschwerdung Gottes *certainly has a strange history behind it and takes a completely surprising course that very few Catholic theologians have taken note of up till now. To put it in the right perspective, did you begin to develop an interest in Hegel because you wanted to provide a philosophical support for the "high" Christology which in your book on justification you continually presuppose and indeed develop further in an excursus? Then when later in Tübingen you began work once more on the draft of your book on Hegel did you not have to make a change of course that is made clearly explicit in the last section of the final chapter of the book – a change from a Christology from above on Hegel's lines to a Christology from below? If this is right, what occasioned this change?*

In fact in my first years it was exclusively a Christology from above that I advocated. My view then was that it was precisely with Hegel's help that this Christology from above, as it had been elaborated once more in Karl Barth's magnificent synthesis in several volumes, but also as it had been hinted at by Karl Rahner in a handful of articles – that this Christology could be renewed for the present day with the aid of Hegelian speculation. How this had to happen is expressed in the book, especially with relation to a possible becoming on the part of God and the dialectic that is thereby posited within God himself, as it is actualized in a dialectical conception of the divine attributes. But you are right: the more in Tübingen I occupied myself intensively (and this was the first time I had done so despite numerous lectures on exegesis at the Pontifical Biblical Institute and also in Paris) with exegesis on historical and critical principles, as exemplified in a very lively fashion for me by my colleague in the Protestant faculty of theology, Ernst Käsemann, who was a pupil of Bultmann's, the more difficult it became for me to maintain this speculation in connection with the understanding of God and with Christology. This doesn't mean at all that I had abandoned the positive intentions of a Christology from above. But what increasingly became my goal – and I remember a long conversation with my then colleague at Tübingen Professor Ratzinger, who endorsed me in this – was that it was from below that people of today could more convincingly strive to attain and could reach the statements of a "high" Christology. Thus I then devoted myself with growing intensity to research into the historical Jesus and dealt with the Jesus of history in my private study as well as continually in my seminars and lectures. What exercised no little influence on me in this was that when I was celebrating Mass every day at the local hospital at home in Switzerland I had preached my way through the entire gospel according to Mark with the help in particular of the commentary that had just appeared by Eduard Schweizer, as I did later on with the Sermon on the Mount and other passages from the New Testament. In this I was able to discover how Jesus himself is again experienced in a much fresher way that is closer to the original if one does not simply as a matter of course proclaim him as the son of God come down from heaven but rather as the man Jesus of Nazareth whom his disciples learned to recognize in faith as the son of God.

We shall come back to Christology again later. Ernst Käsemann became particularly important for you with regard to a future ecclesiology. Illustrative of this is perhaps your evaluation of Acts for the question of the ministry. In The Council and Reunion *you are still saying that Acts shows in prototype the unchangeable Petrine and apostolic constitution of the Catholic Church. In* The Living Church, *however, you say that Catholic ecclesiology has overvalued the pastoral epistles and Acts as against a charismatically structured Church order as is to be found in the major Pauline epistles. Is Ernst Käsemann responsible for this re-evaluation of yours?*

That's right. If in this case we disregard Heinrich Schlier, who was Käsemann's fellow-student at Bonn and Marburg and who later was converted to the Catholic Church on the basis of a different evaluation of early Catholicism, then Käsemann was the only pupil of Bultmann's who grappled intensively with the problem of the Church in the New Testament and in the present, doing so particularly on the basis of his personal experiences as a minister during the Third Reich. And for me as a young professor who on the basis of his own studies in Rome, Paris, and even in Münster understood little of what was involved in a radical critical exegesis, Käsemann in Tübingen, a generation older than myself, meant a major challenge which I realized I had to accept, not only in this regard but also with respect to the hermeneutical questions tied up with it of the New Testament canon. I buried myself in the relevant literature and also discussed the question intensively with my Catholic colleague for New Testament studies, Karl Hermann Schelkle. As a result I was able to venture to conduct a three-cornered discussion both with Bultmann's pupil Käsemann and with Barth's pupil Hermann Diem – with in the background the traditional ecclesiology which in actual fact needed fundamental revision.

Was this how in 1962 you came to write your article on

"Early Catholicism in the New Testament as a Problem in Controversial Theology"?

Yes, the first result was this article on early Catholicism in the New Testament. Thanks to Käsemann I had become aware of the decisive charismatic dimension of the Church, particularly in the Pauline epistles, with all the consequences this has for the Church's ministry in the present. At the same time it was right from the start more than Käsemann that persuaded me to take seriously the "early Catholic" Church order of Acts and the pastoral epistles that are fundamental for the traditional Catholic and Orthodox understanding of the Church. It was not a question of becoming a Protestant but of a synthesis in the broader Catholic sense of that word. On the one hand this meant taking the charismatic dimension in the Church seriously along with a new freedom, and particularly also the possibility of a free charismatic vocation to the ministry of the Church even outside the traditional apostolic succession in office (which is important for a recognition of the validity of Protestant ministries and of the Protestant eucharist). On the other hand this meant the defence of the relative justification of apostolic succession when that is correctly understood and of the threefold ministry of bishops, presbyters and deacons. In other words, there was no need for a revolutionary upheaval of the Catholic Church order, merely for it to be filled with a new evangelical spirit and evangelical freedom and thus renewed.

Käsemann was apparently so much in agreement with your position on the ministry, especially in the form in which your synthesis of it was presented in your book The Church, *that he stated publicly in a lecture that the schism between him and you was ended: a truly unusual step for so combative a Protestant. But this gave Rome cause enough to open doctrinal proceedings against your book* Structures of the Church, *something that at the time was relatively little known.*

That book contains a vast amount of historical research. It arose from my inaugural lecture at Tübingen in 1960 on the theology of the Council. Various questions were involved here that caused grave offence in Rome. For the first time I had become involved in coming to grips with Luther's and Calvin's understanding of the Church and of councils, even if in no way uncritically, and at the same time in coming to grips with our own great conciliar tradition in a self-critical spirit. Even before coming to Tübingen I had recognized more or less instinctively that the ecumenical Council of Constance – which a hundred years before the Reformation defined the supremacy of the council over the Pope and compelled three Popes to resign – provided the opposite pole in the history of the Church to the First Vatican Council which, as is well known, established as doctrines of the Church in 1870 the supremacy of the Pope over the council and the Pope's infallibility in matters of faith and morals. My Catholic colleague specializing in Church history, Karl August Fink, encouraged me to see not just the Council of Constance but the entire conciliar tradition in a historically clearer light. The doctrinal conclusions I had of course to draw for myself. And naturally they were not inoffensive. Much that traditional dogmatic theology and traditional canon law declared to belong to the papacy by divine right and thus to be unalterable now appeared as an at least problematical historical development – if not indeed as a false development when seen from the point of view of the original Christian message. Traditional dogmatic theology and canon law saw the summoning, leadership and confirmation of an ecumenical council and thus its ecumenicity as a right of the Pope granted by God, whereas historical research showed that the most varied possibilities had existed with regard to the summoning, leadership and confirmation of an ecumenical council and thus continued to exist now. As so often, people in Rome recognized the neuralgic points with a surer awareness than in the German faculties of theology, where people are happy to play down such awkward questions, and they were afraid that the established Roman system would be threatened.

How did these Roman proceedings turn out?

Well, it was the period of the Council, and so I was for-given a certain amount. At all events a solemn session took place in Rome with Cardinal Bea in the chair and with the Bishops of Basle and Rottenburg in attendance along with professors from the Gregorian. I had to answer various questions that had been drawn up in the Holy Office. Later I had to repeat my answers in writing and in Latin. Without a doubt it was thanks to Cardinal Bea. whom I had got to know during my first years in Rome when he was visitor of the German College, in the days when he was still a simple Jesuit priest and Pius XII's confessor. that the proceedings came to a happy conclusion and in fact were discontinued without any obligation of any kind being laid upon me.

Isn't there a danger lurking in becoming involved with the exegesis of scripture along historical and critical lines – that of the individual interpreting it subjectively for himself or herself? In the discussion that followed your book On Being A Christian *your Tübingen colleague Walter Kasper charged you with letting the precedence of scripture over tradition, something completely in line with Vatican II, increasingly turn into a precedence of scripture over the Church. You did not bear in mind that while the Church might stand under the word of God at the same time it stood above the individual's sub-jective interpretation of scripture. Kasper can indeed appeal to you yourself, since in your book on justification you had raised the objection against Karl Barth that it was always the isolated individual that passed judgement on the tradition of the Church and indeed on holy scripture. In that context you were even talking of covert arbitrariness. Are you not now doing basically the same as you were then accusing Barth of doing?*

I'm always a little amused when someone tries to play the younger Küng off against the older Küng. In twenty years one ought to have learned something, and I don't think Walter Kasper would dispute that. And, while I wouldn't want to stop anybody taking their stand on my doctoral thesis, I have no wish to remain stuck at that point of my development. In fact it is precisely on this issue that the continuity between that period and today is completely visible. I have been and am against a subjectivist interpretation of scripture and I have always stood out against this danger of Protestant exegesis and systematic theology. For this reason I have continually been concerned to grapple with the official documents of the Church's teaching and have thus investigated councils that other theologians know only by hearsay. At the same time in my own interpretation both of councils and of scripture I am concerned not to put forward some personal view of my own but to work out the consensus of scholarly opinion. Competent critics have always recognized this with regard to my book *The Church* as well as with regard to the historical Jesus in my book *On Being A Christian*. What I am always concerned with – and in this way I regard myself as a Catholic theologian – is that the link with my fathers in the faith is the tradition of the Church. But, so as not to give a one-sided picture, the other side of it is that over the past twenty years I have learned to see a lot more clearly how subjectivism finds expression in the theology of the schools and even in the doctrinal statements of bishops and councils. One can just presuppose as taken for granted that every council is *a priori* in agreement with the Christian witness or in real terms with Jesus Christ himself. It is in fact he who now is the immovable norm as far as I am concerned. Jesus Christ himself as he is testified to in the original evidence of the New Testament is the *norma normans*, the absolute standard, which applies not just to individual theologians but also to the community of the Church and its representatives and councils. Everything else can also provide a norm or standard and is one to varying degrees – but always only as a standard controlled by this Jesus Christ. In brief, the primary norm is Jesus Christ, and the Church with its authorities and documents is only a secondary norm.

The same hermeneutical question about the problem of the interpretation of scripture also comes up in connection with the picture you present of Jesus of Nazareth in On Being A

Christian. You maintain that you have worked out a reliable picture of the Jesus of history. Is this in fact still possible after the continual warnings of theologians that all that is reflected in certain pictures of Jesus is the lord of one's own mind? Thus your American colleague Avery Dulles is of the view that your Jesus looks very like an anti-establishment Jesus who was just as much harried by the scribes and pharisees of his time as progressive theologians are today by the Church's teaching office. Is your Jesus then a Jesus as Küng would like him to be, a useful weapon in the fight against the Church establishment?

It is remarkable the way in which Catholic theologians who fundamentally approve of research along historical and critical lines always proclaim their reservations about it and point to what they term its limits whenever the results of this kind of research are inconvenient to them. Apparently they are too little aware that in them too a certain attitude of mind is speaking (possibly even the official attitude of mind, which is in no way superior) that would like to enlist the Jesus of history on behalf of the predominant ecclesiastical system. If the parallels, as Dulles sees them, should turn out to be only partially right, it would be urgently necessary to break off the self-satisfied style of Catholic apologetics and to press for the change that would be needed in the Church system. The fact that Jesus was not in fact on the side of the hierarchy but was instead liquidated by them in collaboration with the political powers-that-be may not suit the hierarchs and theologians of today but is in fact, as practically no one disputes, the historical truth from which the actual practical consequences ought to be drawn. The fact that in certain cases one has Jesus on one's side doesn't excuse or justify one but rather obliges one. Meanwhile even the more cautious Catholic exegetes have recognized that I have throughout been concerned not to sketch a Jesus *à la* Küng but, as has hitherto happened hardly anywhere else in systematic theology, have taken exegetical research into Jesus and worked it up, and that for this reason the Jesus of history portrayed in *On Being A Christian* has in its decisive traits the consensus of New Testament exegetes behind it.

With your reliance on the Jesus of history as the criterion of Christian faith and life are you not, from the point of view of the history of theology, retreating to a position that has long since been surpassed. the position that predominated in the liberal Protestantism of the turn of the century and that had its chief advocate in Adolf von Harnack? Isn't one of your Tübingen colleagues right when he said of your book On Being A Christian *that it indulged in Harnacking?*

If one of my Tübingen colleagues said that, then he can hardly have read the book thoroughly or at least he can't have understood it – though of course this is something that can happen even in Tübingen. In this book what is quite obvious to anyone who knows the subject is the extent to which, as I have already indicated, I have been influenced by the school of Karl Barth and thus of dialectical theology, so that it would be completely impossible for me to see Jesus as he was seen by this kind of liberalism as simply a teacher of virtue and morals for a better bourgeois life. The cross and the resurrection stand at the centre of this book to such an extent that in no way is it possible to see in it anything like a "liberal" account of Jesus. But it was precisely in concentrating in this way on the cross and resurrection that it struck me as necessary – and this was what Ernst Käsemann was appealing to at the start of the 1950s – to go back once again to the pre-Easter Jesus, to the Jesus of history, and to bring him before the eyes of contemporary men and women as a living person, as far as this is possible, in his historical setting and in his relevance for the course of human history.

Would you say that the choice between a Christology from above and a Christology from below offers a real alternative or only an illusory one?

The task of every true Christology is to combine in thought both the "above", that is that which comes from God, and the "below", that which comes from man. It is this that I have tried to do in section C of *On Being A Christian*. And on this question I am not prepared to come down on either side: in Jesus Christ both God and man are involved, both God and man belong together. What is different is the way this combination, this balancing of both aspects, is reached. One cannot simply as it were climb the mountain from the foot, from among men, and at the same time be landed by a helicopter on the summit so as to descend the mountain starting from a full knowledge of the divine aspect. I have no fundamental objection to the method of starting "from above" and have myself made a thorough trial of it, as has been noted in the case of *Menschwerdung Gottes*, and have re-examined it yet again in connection with its most impressive representatives in theology and philosophy, Hegel and Barth. But despite everything, the method of starting from below strikes me as the most suitable. Jesus's disciples, after all, didn't have the chance of seeing him from the viewpoint of heaven and couldn't make the knowledge that he was the son of God their starting point. For Jesus himself, according to what is probably the general view of leading exegetes, did not use the title "son of God": it was ascribed to him only after his resurrection by the first community to form round him. When he was alive, as the gospels continually make apparent, the disciples had to ask themselves who this man was. And my view is that this is precisely how the problem presents itself to men and women today. No longer can they rely as in the Middle Ages on taking for granted the fact that he is the son of God. Instead they begin by asking, as in the gospels, "Who is this man?" My task as a theologian, and it is not an easy one, is to guide my contemporaries, who are often so sceptical and yet at the same time open-minded, carefully and cautiously towards the real mystery of the person of Jesus that for the disciples only became evident after his resurrection to eternal life.

If on the one hand you say that God and man belong together in Jesus Christ but on the other that Jesus seems most probably never to have himself used the title "son of God", what does it mean to say Jesus is God's son? Can you still adhere to this?

I have in fact done so in *On Being A Christian*, even if I have often used other terms, such as God's advocate, representative, plenipotentiary, Messiah, Christ. And in *Does God Exist?* I have once again given a positive and comprehensive interpretation of this faith in Jesus as the son of God. The decisive point at issue seems to me to be whether the fact that Jesus is the son of God, which is the common Christian conviction, must necessarily and solely be explained with the help of the categories and concepts of the Hellenistic age, as was done not of course in the original community but to begin with in the early Hellenistic Christian communities and above all in the first general councils. Or is this not necessarily so? To put it more clearly, can the fact that Jesus is the son of God only be explained by the doctrine of the two natures, which means that Jesus is not a human person but a divine person with two natures, one divine and one human? I notice that, to mention only some of the best-known names, other dogmatic theologians like Rahner, and the Dutchmen Schoonenberg and Schillebeeckx, have their difficulties in this field, as now also do the New Testament scholars. For example, my Tübingen colleague Walter Kasper affirms in his book *Jesus the Christ* as against this traditional doctrine that Jesus was also a human person, which in fact brings him into conflict with the dogma – not that that strikes me as cause for anxiety. But at least I openly acknowledge the difficulties. In this way, and this applies both to other theologians and to the bishops, I feel people should finally put a stop to acting as if I were the only person to have difficulties in this field or as if I had invented the difficulties for myself. What may perhaps distinguish me from others is simply that I am looking for a clear, honest and consistent solution. In doing so all I am doing is fundamentally to bring together and summarize what many exegetes are saying and what many dogmatic theologians, even Catholic ones, are thinking when I explain Jesus's being the son of God along such lines as these: that according to the New Testament the man Jesus of Nazareth is in his whole person the genuine revelation of the one God and Father and is thus rightly called God's true word and God's real son. Who sees Jesus sees the Father, says the gospel according to John. In Jesus, therefore, God himself is present to me, God is at work, God speaks, God acts, and this in a unique and definitive (eschatological) way. All this appeals to my faith and can in no case be affirmed of the founder of a religion like Mohammed or an important saint like Francis of Assisi. Jesus and only Jesus is for me the son of God.

If in this way you are able to fit such central doctrinal statements as Jesus being the son of God and God's revelation in Christ into your system, how do you explain the criticism that is made against you in a statement by the bishops that as far as you are concerned Jesus was "only an exemplary human being" who had a particular relationship with God?

The charge I must bring against the bishops and many theologians in return – and this is something I have been able to see confirmed in personal discussions – is that many of them have clearly only dipped into the book and have not understood it as a whole. I have several times publicly protested against the imputation in the bishops' statement to the press on *On Being A Christian* of 3 March 1977 that as far as I am concerned Jesus Christ is "only an exemplary human being and only God's spokesman and advocate". These protests of mine have for the most part not been published by the Church press. A falsification of my ideas that I find incomprehensible is also involved in the imputation that I have denied the Christological statements contained in the Nicene creed. Why cannot it be admitted that I have gone to the greatest possible trouble to make them understandable to people of today? The question naturally often comes up of what the point is of being ready to enter into discussion, of talking to and corresponding with bishops in the hope of clarifying things, in the face of a teaching authority that just doesn't want to know. The charge is often raised of misleading and confusing the reader, but in this situation it is completely open to question whom this charge is directed against. One thing that fits into this picture, along with a number of flanking measures, is the volume of essays that was launched against *On Being A Christian* in 1975 by selected theologians with the knowledge and approval of the German bishops' doctrinal commission under the innocuous-sounding title "Discussion of Hans Küng's *On Being A Christian*". Yet in the various contributions it is less a matter of discussion than of misunderstanding, misinterpretation, disparagement and insinuation. The most striking thing about it was that all these theologians hardly had any better alternative proposals to offer and that once again, as had happened with the volume of essays directed against *Infallible?*, I was refused the opportunity of answering my critics in a contribution to the same volume. Clearly people are afraid of the truth.

In fact while we have been talking a new episcopal statement on On Being A Christian *has come out together with accompanying documentation. Isn't this completely extraordinary?*

It is, I think, almost unparalleled in the recent history of theology. I cannot in fact understand why the German bishops' conference has now issued its third statement against a book that, according to the witness of countless men and women, both clergy and laity, has done so much to help them with regard to their faith and life as Christians. When I was informed of this by telephone the day before it was made public, I protested as strongly as possible against the publication without my permission of personal letters to the successive presidents of the German bishops' conference, Cardinal Döpfner and Cardinal Höffner. This was, unfortunately, in vain – not that I had any reason to be afraid of their publication. But this is something I see as being clearly a breach of confidence. Beyond this I regard it as intolerable that the German bishops' conference could not wait until the actual theological questions in dispute were tackled once

more in my book *Does God Exist? An Answer to the question
of God in our time* which was already in the press – and not
just tackled but deepened and, I hope, clarified. This was
something I had held out the prospect of in several letters
to the German bishops' conference, as people can see for
themselves by reading the one-sided selection of documentation produced by the bishops. Because this collection of
documentation not only represented a biased selection but
was also provided with tendentious comments I see myself
forced for my part to agree to the publication of a more
comprehensive and objective collection of documentation
that would be intended to bring the complete truth to light.
This is something I regret, because throughout I wished to
maintain good relations with the bishops. But it is something
the bishops have provoked by publishing their selection of
documents, and the publishing house of Piper asked me at
once for permission to publish this documentation supplemented by important additional documents, because these
were in fact documents of contemporary historical interest
that were involved and because there were quite a lot of
people who would like to know what the position really
was with regard to the truth. Because this, ultimately, is
what it is all about, and that is why the book of documentation bears the title "Nothing but the Truth: the German
Bishops' Conference versus Hans Küng". The fact that
Walter Jens, my colleague at Tübingen and president of
German PEN, edited the volume and wrote the introduction
shows that the importance of these questions extends far
beyond the confines of the Church.

*Now, you have yourself taken part in an ecumenical
council . . .*

 . . . Yes – and unfortunately did not discover as much in
the way of the immediate activity of the Holy Spirit as people
have often thought they have been able to do in retrospect
with regard to the early councils.

On several occasions in your writings you have expressed a conflicting evaluation of this council: progress, but not going far enough, hope for renewal that has often been disappointed. What were the reasons for this?

To answer this I would need to tell you a long story, but that is the last thing you want from me. To begin with I went to Rome in a very sceptical mood. But then, against all expectation, the first session turned into a genuine break-through – above all because the curia overreached itself in trying to influence the choice of members of the council commissions. And it was very pleasant then to help the new pastoral and ecumenical awareness (for which essentially we were indebted to John XXIII) to come to life by talking to various bishops' conferences from all over the world – though not the German – in as wide a range of languages as possible. The reform of the liturgy, the introduction of the vernacular, the new attitude towards the other Churches both in theology and in practice, the new relationship to the Jews and to the other major religions of the world, and in this context too, in diametrical opposition to previous papal doctrinal statements, an approval and acceptance of freedom of religion and of conscience, and connected with all this a new attitude on the part of the Church towards the world's needs and hopes up to and including atheism, as well as numerous internal Church reforms: all this was what made Vatican II an epoch-making turning-point in the history of the Church which can no longer be annulled. I continue to regard all these positive results as being so important that the question that is often put whether Vatican II was worth while has never seemed to me to be a genuine question.

You personally experienced more and more disappointment the longer the council continued. During the second session you refused to join the extremely important doctrinal commission because this continued to be chaired by Cardinal Alfredo Ottaviani, head of the Holy Office, and thus remained under the control of the Curia.

Unfortunately John XXIII died after the first session of

the council, and the longer his successor Paul VI reigned the less did he fulfil the hopes that the council's progressive majority had placed in him. He banned discussion of birth control and celibacy, made several authoritarian interventions and had conciliar documents drawn up by the council fathers amended "by higher authority" to fit in with what he wanted. He proclaimed Mary as the mother of the Church without consulting the council and established a synod of bishops which was anything but an organ of collegial co-decision but increasingly showed itself in the period following the council to be a farce, a collegial figleaf, a talking shop that produced no serious results. And so on ... During the second session I drafted an assessment that was concerned particularly with the election of a fresh doctrinal commission and the replacement of Cardinal Ottaviani by a president to be elected by the council. This assessment was handed over to Paul VI personally by the Melkite Patriarch Maximos IV Saigh. The result of this and many similar initiatives was merely that a few more members were elected on to the commissions, a second secretary was appointed, and other steps were taken along these lines. For the rest, however, everything stayed as it was. This made it clear that there could be no thought of recasting the fundamental conciliar constitution on the Church to place it on a more solid biblical basis. In particular no decisive change would be possible in what is now the third chapter on the Church's hierarchical structure which confirmed Vatican I with its problematical definitions of the papal primacy and infallibility without introducing any differentiation and even partly extended this to the episcopate. This was the reason why I was not ready to take part in the work of this commission, whose first secretary, incidentally, was my old teacher Sebastian Tromp. Another demand to remain unmet was one I expressed on several occasions to the effect that a number of competent and critical exegetes should be added to this commission. The German critical school of exegesis was in fact not represented at the council.

But did you not all the same lose the opportunity of exer-

*cising influence on the theological shape of the council docu-
ments by refusing to join the commission?*

Of course there was much I would have been able to attain
inside the theological commission, and I was always of the
opinion that other people, including many of my friends,
ought to belong to this commission. But in this situation I
would not have been able to make any decisive changes. And
for this reason other things struck me as more important.
All the same I still had opportunities of introducing important amendments into the constitution on the Church,
whether directly or indirectly, inasmuch as I drafted various
important council speeches for various bishops: on the
charismatic dimension of the Church, on the significance of
the local Church, on the sinful Church and the necessity of
continual reform, on the threefold ministry, and on similar
questions. And it was also possible to exert influence by
making public statements in the international press. Indeed,
tipping off the major newspapers in time about curial efforts
to scrap the declaration on the Jews, as well as that on
religious freedom, put a stop to these tricks. To sum up: I
was present at the council even if not a member of the
theological commission. The decisive thing was indeed something different. At the start of the second session, after a
careful study of the revised schema on the Church, I decided
after considering the matter for several days to start work
on my book *The Church*. I had indeed set myself the goal for
the future to write something like a *Spirit of Catholicism* on
the lines of the model established by my great predecessor in
the chair of dogmatic theology at Tübingen, Karl Adam. But
now the time seemed to have come to write a book about the
nature and essence of the Church in what is indeed a very
different fashion. And I started a private contest with the
council's theological commission to have my book ready at
roughly the same time. A year after the council ended the
manuscript was finally completed, after endless trouble, and
it was published in 1967. It was not surprising to receive an
order from Cardinal Ottaviani – and this bang in the middle
of the Christmas holidays – to stop the distribution of the book

and also to call a halt to its translation into other languages pending my taking part in a "colloquium" in Rome. My reaction was to ask the work of translation to be speeded up. And then a few months later in the middle of the semester the order came from Rome at the weekend for me to turn up at the Holy Office in the middle of the next week. I replied by telegram: "Sorry, can't make it; letter follows." And then the virtually endless negotiations began to ensure fair conditions for a colloquium of this kind, negotiations that you can read about in the book edited by H. Häring and J. Nolte, *Diskussion um Hans Küng "Die Kirche"*. Then with the appearance of *Infallible? An Enquiry* these negotiations entered a new and tenser phase.

Was it because of the personal experience you had had of the Pope's continual authoritarian interventions on many very important issues, interventions that could be the result of his ultimately infallible teaching authority, that later in 1970 you raised at a fundamental level the question of papal infallibility?

No, as you know the question had already come up as far as I was concerned in connection with the work on *Structures of the Church*, which was published in 1962, and thus when John XXIII was still Pope. It was then that I had the first heated discussion of this and other dogmatic questions with Karl Rahner, admittedly between just the two of us: the occasion for this was whether Rahner would recommend the book for an official imprimatur and for inclusion in the series *Quaestiones disputatae*. This conflict only came out into the open in 1970 when Rahner said he saw a fatal threat to "Catholic faith" posed by my book *Infallible? An Enquiry*. But the only threat I could see was to Karl Rahner's theological method, which did not seriously go back to the Bible but made dogmas the starting point for ingenious theological speculations. There is no doubt that these were a real help during the transitional phase when neoscholasticism started to decay. But seen as a whole the longer this method persisted the more it was shown to be an ultimately ineffective continuation of neoscholasticism by other means. Of course in the time of John XXIII I would not have written the book in its present strongly worded form: that would not have been necessary. But in the period after the council, when already during the council itself Paul VI's customary authoritarian interventions had been piling up – to see what I mean you need only read the foreword to *Infallible?* – things were different. In addition, the frequent warnings I had given on this point were at first not generally heeded by my fellow Catholic theologians, as is usual with awkward questions. The relevant section on infallibility in *The Church*, published in 1967, essentially offers the same solution as *Infallible?* – a solution that Vatican I, which just did not take any notice of the theology of the Reformers, was simply not aware of as a possibility. Even the sections in *Truthfulness*, published in 1968, that dealt with the manipulation of doctrine, the presupposition for that unhappy encyclical *Humanae vitae* on birth control, were passed over in silence in the reviews by my professional colleagues. There is too much at risk if you go into these questions honestly, as is indeed shown by the consequences that followed. And thus, as I pointed out when drawing up a balance-sheet of the debate in *Fehlbar? Eine Bilanz*, published in 1973, the alarm had to sound in order to wake the sleeping theologians from their admittedly not that gentle slumbers. Any further information about the history that led up to *Infallible?* you can find in this later volume, which also includes a whole series of extremely constructive contributions by Catholic theologians to the question of infallibility. Catholic theology in fact remains divided in its views on this issue.

Did the alarm really have to sound? Were there not more genuinely important issues in theology in 1970 than this typically Catholic question about papal infallibility?

It depends on the angle from which you are looking at it. If you are concerned merely with the objective significance of the questions at issue, then obviously the question of God, like the question of Christ, or indeed the question of the justification of the sinner, is infinitely more important than the question about infallibility, of which Karl Rahner indeed once acknowledged that Jesus himself would not have understood anything. But with regard to infallibility what is involved is a formal question that precisely as such has a decisive influence upon theological method and that in practice affects all the Catholic Church's doctrinal statements on matters of faith and morals. There is indeed an immense difference between the possibility of probing and testing the truth of each and every doctrinal statement and being obliged to accept it as true on *a priori* grounds, because it is guaranteed by the alleged special assistance of the Holy Spirit. I would not have been able to write *On Being A Christian* and *Does God Exist?* at all if this question, which had long been waiting in the wings, had not previously been faced up to at a fundamental level. In this connection I would like to stress that I have put forward a positive and constructive solution that tries to do justice both to the biblical promises and to the actual errors in the history of the Church, of dogma and of theology, and a solution too that meets with ecumenical agreement. I do not in fact deny each and every form of infallibility or, what strikes me as a better term, indefectibility, the Church's indestructibility in the truth. All I am denying is that indefectibility of the Church in the truth is tied to definite propositions or cases. The positive meaning of this – and the New Testament and the early Catholic tradition say no more than this – is that the Church will be maintained in the truth of the Gospel on the basis of the promise given to it by Christ, not because its leaders or teachers make no mistakes, but despite all the errors of professors of theology, bishops, and possibly even Popes.

A final question about ecclesiology: is there not a clearly detectable tendency at work with you always to play down the significance of the Church in favour of Christianity in general? In The Church *a chapter on the reign of God precedes the detailed ecclesiological discussion, in* On Being A Christian *the Church appears as it were as merely an annex to the weighty chapter on the earthly Jesus. Is this not too great an accommodation to Protestantism?*

One doesn't need in every book to repeat everything one had written before. If I have written a book of some six hundred pages like *The Church*, then, when I am dealing with the question of being a Christian and not just the Church, I do not have to repeat everything. In *On Being A Christian* I have made it clear that everything that I said in *The Church* is presupposed and only a brief summary of this is offered. And in this connection I came out in *On Being A Christian* more strongly than others have done in favour of staying and remaining active in the Church. All these years it has been painful to have to watch the way in which many friends of mine from earlier days from among the theologians of Europe and other continents have in the meantime given up their teaching posts and one or two of them have even left the Church, to a considerable extent because of this tiresome question of celibacy, while other colleagues have thought they need to conform in all possible things to the present conservative trend.

A remarkable coalition of interests is to be observed in your case. From both left and right equally the demand is made for you to leave the Church as a consequence of your critical attitude towards it: the right, because they want to rescue the Church from Küng, the left, because even with Küng the Church is no longer capable of being rescued.

This merely shows that despite all the official caricatures I am a man of the centre – if you like, of the left of centre, in other words with the stress on reform. Hence on the one hand I find myself in virtually unavoidable conflict with the German episcopate, which seen as a whole today forms the right wing of the ecclesiastical spectrum, in contrast to other episcopates. And on the other hand, I am involved in conflict with a number of theologians, especially those with views to the political left, who identify the Christian message with a socialist party programme and who thus strike me as involuntarily sacrificing elements that are decisive for the Church and Christianity. What matters for me I have already indicated, and there isn't any contradiction involved in it:

critical loyalty towards this Church and at the same time loyal criticism of this Church. If people ask questions about the consistency of this attitude, I offer the same reason for both aspects of it. I remain a loyal member of this Church because it is ultimately in the community of this Church that the gospel of Jesus Christ can continue to live and prevail, at least at the grass-roots. But at the same time I criticize this Church because, and this is especially so at its hierarchical summit surrounded by all its court theologians, it does not seem to me sufficiently to correspond to this same gospel of Jesus Christ – despite the good will of all concerned, which is something I do not dispute.

You are well known as a convinced ecumenist. You call for an ecumenical style of Christian living. But are not Catholics right to be afraid that over the past fifteen years you have had to conform ever more rigorously to Protestant positions without the Protestants on their part being compelled to make equivalent concessions? Is not your demand for Christian unity therefore basically a demand that Catholics must turn Protestant?

Even from Protestants one can in practice hear that on the Protestant side there is often much less ecumenical enthusiasm and much less ecumenical involvement visible than among Catholics. This shows the weakness of the Protestant Churches, which, in view of the often frightening extent to which their loss of membership has dropped, are plagued by fear that they could possibly be taken over by the Catholics. But here, too, fear is a bad adviser. Beyond this, however, there is a lack of Protestant theologians who provide a hearing for the concerns of Catholics with the same decisiveness in the Protestant world as I have done in the Catholic world for the concerns of Protestants. There are hardly any books by Protestant theologians that provide a similar evaluation and recognition of Catholic concerns. But having admitted t..is much there is this to be said clearly on the other side: that is that quite clearly the Catholic Church and Catholic theology have a certain need to catch up, because with regard to liturgical reform as with regard to theology, and finally Church discipline too, it has to some extent waited for four hundred years before eventually carrying out certain reforms. I myself have always drawn attention to the fact that all these demands on the Catholic Church and theology have their reverse side. Thus for example it is right to demand of the Catholic Church greater attention to scripture in worship and in theology, but on the other side the neglect of the sacraments, and especially the eucharist, in the Protestant Churches represents a genuine ecumenical scandal. Similar points could be made about taking the Church's two thousand years of tradition into account and about the problem of what is termed natural theology and much else, where on the Protestant side people often take the rather superior line that all this has already been taken into account and that one is a stage beyond all that. Today it can be established that in pretty well all fields Catholics and Protestants have drawn closer together and that even Catholic and Protestant theologians have done so. And in the future it will not be a matter of Catholics turning Protestant or Protestants turning Catholic but rather of each taking the other's justified concerns into account and putting them into practice and thus of both sides becoming more Christian.

Do you therefore fail to discern any longer any decisive theological reasons that would justify a schism today? Why does the actual unity of the Churches then not come about? Where is the blockage?

I would not say that we have already solved all the controversial issues of the past. There still remains much work to be done on the doctrine of the sacraments, and I myself started work quite a time ago on a book on the sacraments that aimed at working out the same kind of ecumenical consensus on the sacraments as on the Church. But even here unity would be possible from the theological point of view, as has been shown by the debates on the most difficult point, that of the papacy as the chief obstacle to ecumenical

union. Proposals I have put forward in various publications
have found their way meanwhile into the agreed statement
of the joint Anglican-Roman Catholic International Commission and deal with such difficult questions as primacy
and infallibility. Similar things could be said of other ecumenical documents in Europe, North America and to some
extent also in other continents. The decisive opposition –
indeed, one must often talk of blockage and even of ob-
struction – comes from the ecclesiastical apparatus and particularly from the Catholic ecclesiastical apparatus. Under
the influence of Rome – something that can hardly be dis-
cerned in public but that is extremely effective behind the
scenes – the bishops, even in Germany constantly refuse to
sanction the joint building of new churches and the shared
use of existing ones, to press on with ecumenical religious
instruction, to purge the treatment of mixed marriages of its
final insulting elements, and to bring about the recognition
of the ministries of other Christians. Whenever proposals
are put forward they are either not taken note of or, in
certain circumstances when there is fear of what their effect
might be if made public, quite brutally suppressed. Such
was the fate of the memorandum on the reform and mutual
recognition of ministries drawn up by the Association of
Ecumenical Institutes of German Universities. Instead of
the bishops' conference being constructively concerned
about reaching a practical solution, it had a statement issued
by its doctrinal commission that was irresponsible and in-
excusable both from the point of view of theology and from
that of Church politics. Similar measures are used to frus-
trate any change of position over birth control as well as any
lifting of the obligation of celibacy in favour of voluntary
celibacy on the part of the Church's ministers, even when it
is becoming clearer every day that our communities are
continually being deprived of their priests and that in just
a few years the situation will become catastrophic in countless Catholic communities all over the world. Everywhere
people will not acknowledge what is true; one often thinks
back to the Pope and bishops of the Reformation period.
Those who do not create the problems but merely bring

them out into the open are then accused of disturbing the peace. With regard to the question of celibacy I cannot help wondering how long people can go on fighting against a reform the whole aim of which is merely to help the freedom to emerge that Jesus Christ himself gave us, the freedom of choosing celibacy or marriage according to one's personal vocation.

As far as the Church is concerned you are regarded as being on the radical outside left, but in secular politics and in university life you count rather as a conservative. How do you explain this contradiction? Why are you not more deeply involved in secular politics?

I am neither a radical outside-left in the Church nor politically conservative. This is something that depends on the point of view from which you are making the judgement. I have already made it clear that I can with reason place myself with regard to the actual spectrum of opinion within the Church as belonging to the *centro-sinistra*, as being centre-left, between the conservatives on the right and the revolutionaries on the left. And to the extent that anyone is interested I would see my own personal political position in a similar light: centre-left, between restoration and revolution, with the stress on reform both in the state and in the university and society generally. But in this I seek to avoid becoming over-involved and over-committed. I've got nothing against theologians, and indeed some of my colleagues in the faculty here, becoming involved in party politics, whether of the right or of the left, especially since the German bishops' conference somewhat one-sidedly favours a conservative political line and must be regarded as somewhere to the right of the CDU – compare its statement on the abortion question. For my part I refrain from all party political statements, however keenly I may follow political developments in Germany and in my own country, Switzerland, and in the world in general, and however many conversations I may have had with politicians everywhere. In this it is not merely a question of becoming over-involved, of the fact that I have to make public statements on more than enough topics with regard to my own subject. There is also the fact that I think I have to avoid any connection that would make me appear the man of only one particular political party, and this precisely because of my position as a theologian who is involved in and committed to the life of the Church and its pastoral work. The concerns that it is my job to champion from the point of view of the Gospel of Jesus Christ affect all political parties and groupings, and it is these that I would like to stand up for. In this one's own job can only be helped by seeing one's own limits. This does not of course exclude my having taken up a very decided position on political questions that demand a response from the point of view of the Gospel such as the questions of liberation theology in South America or the question of violence and terror. This can above all be seen by reading *On Being A Christian*. But I don't think much of expressing one's solidarity simply by appending one's signature to a petition or document or letter and nothing more. If I knew that it was precisely my signature that was needed and that it would have some effect, then I would be ready to join in campaigns of this kind.

In your address at the celebrations to mark the five hundredth anniversary of Tübingen university you directed the request to science and scholarship to include the religious and ethical dimension in their reflection to a stronger extent. Indeed, you spoke of breaking a final taboo, that of bringing God into science. Are you not here appearing in the role of one crying in the wilderness? Hasn't the bus gone long ago, so that it would be illusory to think science today could still be interested in God?

Many scientists and scholars begin by appearing as voices crying in the wilderness when the demands they are making are new, and there is a whole series of demands that today are recognized, although they were originally heard and understood by only a few, such as those concerning the protection of the environment, a more careful use of raw materials, or reconciliation between states. But the response to this address of mine from among my colleagues in the natural sciences and among public opinion at large shows me that people are aware not just of the long neglected social and political dimension in the various fields of study but also of the ethical and religious dimension. What is concerned is not the influence of theology but rather the immense relevance and explosive power of the question of God, which no serious person and above all no serious scholar or scientist can deny even if he or she should give it a negative answer. In this of course everything depends on the way in which this question is presented, and it is the task of theology and subsequently also of the Church's proclamation of the Gospel, to bring contemporary men and women, and scientists and scholars, into contact with God in such a way that this is not at the expense of people, or of their rationality or freedom or humanity. Here, as I showed in my address, there have been countless sins committed by the Church and by theology. But we should let the past be past and apply ourselves jointly to the future that lies before us.

How would you see the task of a theology of the future?
What direction will you be taking in theology?

For my part I would really sooner let things come to me and not play at providence. But the general line has indeed already to some extent become visible. I have increasingly turned from internal Church problems to devote myself to the problems of contemporary men and women, of contemporary science and scholarship, and of contemporary society. This does not mean that I subsequently find what I have done earlier not to be important or that I do not go on doing it. I have already said that I would like to write a book on the sacraments and probably also a short one about grace that would clear up the classic controversies between Catholic and Protestant theology. But in *On Being A Christian* and *Does God Exist?* I have in a new fashion become involved in the questions of my contemporaries, including those outside Church institutions, and as far as internal theological matters are concerned have tried to promote not only a unity of exegesis, the history of dogma and dogmatic theology, but also a unity between dogmatics and ethics as well as practical theology. But, if I may say so openly, I have honestly had enough of continually defending myself against bishops and their tame theologians, and my very modest hope is that I will finally be allowed to go on working in peace. Questions of ecclesiastical and theological politics dominate only the periphery of my theological consciousness. What honestly fascinates me is everything that is of significance for us theologians today in astrophysics, in atomic theory, in microbiology, in psychoanalysis, in philosophy and scientific theory – but also in literature, art, and music. These are all things that pose countless questions to us theologians, but they are questions that only few devote themselves to, even though for the people of today they are infinitely more important than the theological topics disputed within the Church at the moment.

And how do you see the Catholic Church developing in the future?

This development is not something to be predicted in advance. To no small extent it depends on the successor of Paul VI. What strikes me as most important is finally to provide a solution to the problems that under Paul VI have been neglected and in part suppressed and that have been waiting so long to be dealt with. In a comparatively short time we could be in a situation that is no longer characterized by defeatism and despair but once again by hope and initiative, a situation in which rapid progress would be thinkable in the ecumenical field too. When this time will come, nobody knows. But we should get ourselves ready for it. This is the background to the initiative we took when the executive committee of the international theological periodical *Concilium* combined with the Catholic Theological Society of America to hold a conference at Notre Dame University in Indiana on the theme: "Vatican III: The Work That Needs to be Done". There contemporary problems were discussed with a view to a third Vatican council. Not as if I took the view that this council will be summoned tomorrow or the day after. But, following the example of our predecessors in theology and its practical applications under Pius XII, we should prepare ourselves both theologically and as a Church for a time that will come sooner or later – whether we ourselves live to experience it or not.

D. Complete Bibliography of Hans Küng's Published Works 1955-1978

My thanks are due to Ruth Sigrist for her invaluable help with the laborious task of sorting and co-ordinating all the material for this section.

Margret Gentner

Complete bibliography of Hans Küng's published works, 1955–1978

compiled by MARGRET GENTNER

I: Books

1: RECHTFERTIGUNG. DIE LEHRE KARL BARTHS UND EINE KATHOLISCHE BESINNUNG. Johannes-Verlag, Einsiedeln, 1957; fourth enlarged edition 1964.

American edition: *Justification: The Doctrine of Karl Barth and a Catholic Reflection*, Thomas Nelson and Sons, New York, 1964.
English edition: *Justification: The Doctrine of Karl Barth and a Catholic Reflection*, Burns and Oates, London, 1965.
French edition: *Justification: La doctrine de Karl Barth – réflexion catholique*, Desclée De Brouwer, Paris, 1965.
Spanish edition: *La justificación: Doctrina de Karl Barth y una interpretación católica*, Estela, Barcelona, 1967.
Italian edition: *La Giustificazione*, Queriniana, Brescia, 1969.

2: KONZIL UND WIEDERVEREINIGUNG. ERNEUERUNG ALS RUF IN DIE EINHEIT. Herder, Freiburg-Basle-Vienna, 1960, seventh edition 1964.

French edition: *Concile et retour à l'Unité*, Editions du Cerf, Paris, 1961 (no. 39 in the series *Unam Sanctam*).
English edition: *The Council and Reunion*, Sheed and Ward, London, 1961.
American edition: *The Council, Reform and Reunion*, Sheed and Ward, New York, 1961; paperback edition with new introduction, Image Books, Doubleday, New York, 1965.
Dutch edition: *Concilie en hereniging*, Paul Brand, Hilversum, 1962.
Spanish edition: *El concilio y la unión de los cristianos,*

Herder, Santiago de Chile, 1962.
Polish edition: *Sobór i Zjednoczenie*, Znak, Cracow, 1964.
Japanese edition: Herder-Enderle, Tokyo, 1964.
Italian edition: *Riforma della chiesa e unità dei cristiani*, Borla, Turin, 1965.
Malayalam edition: *Pazhya Sabhayum*, Prakasam Publications, Alleppey, 1967.

3: DAMIT DIE WELT GLAUBE. BRIEFE AN JUNGE MENSCHEN. J. Pfeiffer, Munich, 1962, fifth edition 1968.

English edition: *That the World May Believe: Letters to Young People*, Sheed and Ward, London, 1963.
American edition: *That the World May Believe*, Sheed and Ward, New York, 1963.
French edition: *Pour que le monde croie: Lettres à un jeune homme*, Editions du Cerf, Paris, 1963.
Dutch edition: *Opdat de wereld gelove: Brieven aan jonge mensen*, Paul Brand, Hilversum-Antwerp, 1964.
Italian edition: *Perché il mondo creda: Lettere a un giovane*, Borla, Turin, 1964.
Spanish edition: *Para que el mundo crea: Cartas a un joven*, Herder, Barcelona, 1965.
Japanese edition: Herder-Enderle, Tokyo, 1965.
Danish edition: *For at verden måtro*, Pauluskredsens, Copenhagen, 1966.
Portuguese edition: *Para que o mundo creia*, Agir, Rio de Janeiro, 1966.
Czech edition: *Aby svět uvěřil: Dopisy mladým lidem*, Krestanská Akademie, Rome, 1968.

4: STRUKTUREN DER KIRCHE. Herder, Freiburg-Basle-Vienna, 1962 (*Quaestiones disputatae* no. 17), second edition 1963.

Dutch edition: *Strukturen van de Kerk*, Paul Brand, Hilversum-Antwerp, 1962.
French edition: *Structures de l'Église*, Desclée De Brouwer, Paris, 1963.

American edition: *Structures of the Chruch*, Thomas Nelson and Sons, New York-Edinburgh-Toronto, 1964.
Spanish edition: *Estructuras de la Iglesia*, Estela, Barcelona, 1965.
English edition: *Structures of the Church*, Burns and Oates, London, 1965.
Italian edition: *Strutture della Chiesa*, Borla, Turin, 1965.

5: KIRCHE IM KONZIL. Herder, Freiburg-Basle-Vienna, 1963 (Herder-Bücherei no. 140), second enlarged edition 1964.

Dutch edition: *Kerk in Concilie: Tussentijdse balans*, Paul Brand, Hilversum-Antwerp, 1963; *Kerk in Concilie 2: Resultaten van de tweede zitting*, Paul Brand, Hilversum-Antwerp, 1964.
English edition: *The Living Church*, Sheed and Ward, London, 1963; *The Changing Church*, Sheed and Ward, London, 1965.
French edition: *Le Concile, épreuve de l'Église*, Editions du Seuil, Paris, 1963, second enlarged edition 1964.
American edition: *The Council in Action*, Sheed and Ward, New York, 1963.
Italian edition: *La Chiesa al Concilio*, Borla, Turin, 1964.
Spanish edition: *Iglesia en Concilio*, Sigueme, Salamanca, 1965.
Japanese edition: Herder-Enderle, Tokyo, 1966.

6: FREIHEIT IN DER WELT. SIR THOMAS MORE. (Theologische Meditationen 1.) Benziger, Einsiedeln, 1964.

Dutch edition: *Vrijheid in de wereld: Sir Thomas More*, Paul Brand, Hilversum-Antwerp, 1963.
English edition: *Freedom in the World: Sir Thomas More* (Theological Meditations 3), Sheed and Ward, London-Melbourne-New York, 1965.
American edition: see no.17.
Italian edition: *Libertà nel Mondo: Sir Thomas More* (Meditazioni teologiche 1), Queriniana, Brescia, 1966.

French edition: see no. 17.
Korean edition: Taegu, 1971.

7: THEOLOGE UND KIRCHE. (Theologische Meditationen 3.) Benziger, Einsiedeln, 1964.

Dutch edition: *Theoloog en Kerk*, Paul Brand, Hilversum-Antwerp, 1964.
English edition: *The Theologian and the Church* (Theological Meditations 1), Sheed and Ward, London-Melbourne-New York, 1965.
American edition: see no. 17.
French edition: see no. 17.
Italian edition: *Teologo e Chiesa* (Meditazioni teologiche 3), Queriniana, Brescia, 1966.

8: KIRCHE IN FREIHEIT. (Theologische Meditationen 6.) Benziger, Einsiedeln, 1964.

Dutch edition: *Kerk in Vrijheid*, Paul Brand, Hilversum-Antwerp 1965.
English edition: *The Church and Freedom* (Theological Meditations 6), Sheed and Ward, London-Melbourne, 1965.
American edition: see no. 17.
French edition: see no. 17.
Italian edition: *Libertà nella Chiesa* (Meditazioni teologiche 6), Queriniana, Brescia, 1967.

9: CHRISTENHEIT ALS MINDERHEIT. DIE KIRCHE UNTER DEN WELTRELIGIONEN. (Theologische Meditationen 12.) Benziger, Einsiedeln, 1965.

Dutch edition: *De christenheid als minderheid*, Paul Brand, Hilversum-Antwerp, 1966.
Flemish edition: *De christenheid als minderheid*, Davidsfonds, Louvain, 1967.
English edition: in J. Neuner (ed.), *Christian Revelation and World Religions*, Burns and Oates, London, 1967.
American edition: see no. 17.

French edition: see no. 17.
Italian edition: *Cristianità in minoranza* (Meditazioni teologiche 11), Queriniana, Brescia, 1967.

10: GOTT UND DAS LEID. (Theologische Meditationen 18.) Benziger, Einsiedeln-Zürich-Cologne, 1967.

French edition: *L'homme, la souffrance et Dieu* (Méditations théologiques 5), Desclée De Brouwer, Paris, 1969.
Italian edition: *Dio e il dolore* (Meditazioni teologiche 13), Queriniana, Brescia, 1969.
Dutch edition: *God en het lijden*, Desclée De Brouwer, Bruges-Utrecht, 1971.
Polish edition: *Bóg a cierpienie*, Pax, Warsaw, 1973, second edition 1976.

11: DIE KIRCHE. (Ökumenische Forschungen I, 1.) Herder, Freiburg-Basle-Vienna, 1967, fourth edition 1973; paperback edition, Piper, Munich, 1977.

Dutch edition: *De Kerk*, Paul Brand, Hilversum-Antwerp, 1967.
English edition: *The Church*, Burns and Oates, London, 1967; paperback edition, Search Press, London, 1971.
American edition: *The Church*, Sheed and Ward, New York, 1967; paperback edition, Image Books, Doubleday, New York, 1976.
French edition: *L'Église* (two volumes), Desclée De Brouwer, Paris, 1968; fourth edition in one volume, 1970.
Spanish edition: *La Iglesia*, Herder, Barcelona, 1968.
Italian edition: *La Chiesa*, Queriniana, Brescia, 1969.
Portuguese edition: *A Igreja* (two volumes), Moraes, Lisbon, 1969–70.
Japanese edition: in preparation.

12: WAHRHAFTIGKEIT. ZUR ZUKUNFT DER KIRCHE. (Kleine ökumenische Schriften 1.) Herder, Freiburg-Basle-Vienna, 1968, eighth edition 1970; paperback edition, Herderbücherei 390, 1971.

Dutch edition: *Waarachtigheid: over de toekomst van de Kerk*, P. Brand/J. J. Romen en Zonen, Roermond, 1968.

English edition: *Truthfulness: The Future of the Church*, Sheed and Ward, London-Sydney, 1968.

American edition: *Truthfulness: The Future of the Church*, Sheed and Ward, New York, 1968.

French edition: *Être vrai: l'avenir de l'Église*, Desclée De Brouwer, Paris, 1968.

Italian edition: *Veracità: per il futuro della Chiesa*, Queriniana, Brescia, 1968.

Spanish edition: *Sinceridad y veracidad: en torno al futuro de la Iglesia*, Herder, Barcelona, 1969.

Portuguese edition: *Veracidade: o futuro da Igreja*, Herder, São Paulo, 1969.

13: MENSCHWERDUNG GOTTES. EINE EINFÜHRUNG IN HEGELS THEOLOGISCHES DENKEN ALS PROLEGOMENA ZU EINER KÜNFTIGEN CHRISTOLOGIE. (Ökumenische Forschungen II, 1.) Herder, Freiburg-Basle-Vienna, 1970.

Italian edition: *Incarnazione di Dio: Introduzione al pensiero teologico di Hegel, prolegomeni ad una futura cristologia*, Queriniana, Brescia, 1972.

French edition: *Incarnation de Dieu: Introduction à la pensée théologique de Hegel comme prolégomènes à une christologie future*, Desclée De Brouwer, Paris, 1973.

Spanish edition: *La Encarnación de Dios: Introducción al pensamiento teológico de Hegel como prolegómenos para una cristologia futura*, Herder, Barcelona, 1974.

English and American editions: in preparation.

14: UNFEHLBAR? EINE ANFRAGE. Benziger, Zürich-Einsiedeln-Cologne, 1970.

Dutch edition: *Onfeilbaar?*, P. Brand/J. J. Romen en Zonen, Roermond, 1970.

Italian edition: *Infallibile? Una domanda*, Queriniana, Brescia, 1970; second edition, Anteo, Bologna, 1970; revised edition with summing up from *Fehlbar?* (no. 19), Monda-

dori, Milan, 1977.
French edition: *Infaillible? Une interpellation*, Desclée De Brouwer, Paris, 1971.
English edition: *Infallible? An Enquiry*, Collins, London, 1971; paperback edition, Fontana, London, 1972.
American edition: *Infallible? An Inquiry*, Doubleday, New York, 1971; paperback edition, Image Books, New York, 1972.
Spanish edition: *Infalible? Una pregunta*, Herder, Buenos Aires, 1971.
Japanese edition: Shinkyo Suppansha, Tokyo, 1973.

15: WAS IST KIRCHE? Herderbücherei (376), Freiburg-Basle-Vienna, 1970; Siebenstern-Taschenbuch (153), Munich-Hamburg, 1970; second edition, Gütersloher Taschenbuch (181), Gütersloh, 1977.

Dutch edition: *Wat is Kerk?*, P. Brand/J. J. Romen en Zonen, Roermond, 1970.
French edition: *Qu'est-ce que l'Église?*, Desclée De Brouwer, Paris, 1972.
Italian edition: *Chiesa*, Queriniana, Brescia, 1972.
Finnish edition: *Mikä on kirkko?*, Kirjapaja, Helsinki, 1975.

16: WOZU PRIESTER? EINE HILFE. Benziger, Zürich-Einsiedeln-Cologne, 1971.

French edition: *Prêtre pour quoi faire?*, Editions du Cerf, Paris, 1971.
Italian edition: *Preti perchè? Un aiuto*, Anteo, Bologna, 1971.
Dutch edition: *Waarom Priester? Een Handreiking*, Romen, Roermond, 1972.
English edition: *Why Priests?*, Collins, London, 1972.
American edition: *Why Priests? A proposal for a new Church ministry*, Doubleday, New York, 1972.
Spanish edition: *Sacerdotes, para que?*, Herder, Barcelona, 1972.

Portuguese edition: *Padres, para quê?*, Moraes, Lisbon, 1973.

17: FREIHEIT DES CHRISTEN. Buchclub Ex libris, Zürich, 1971; Siebenstern-Taschenbuch (167), Hamburg, 1972; second edition, Gütersloher Taschenbuch (167), Gütersloh 1976.

American edition: *Freedom Today* (Theological Meditations 1), Sheed and Ward, New York, 1966.
French edition: *Liberté du chrétien* (Méditations théologiques 1), Desclée De Brouwer, Paris, 1967.
Spanish edition: *Libertad del Cristiano*, Herder, Barcelona, 1975.
Other editions: see nos. 6, 7, 8, and 9.

18: WAS IN DER KIRCHE BLEIBEN MUSS. (Theologische Meditationen 30.) Benziger, Zürich-Einsiedeln-Cologne, 1973.

Dutch edition: *Wat blijven moet in de Kerk* (together with the summing up from *Fehlbar?* [no. 19]), Gooi en Sticht, Hilversum, 1974.
Italian edition: *Che cosa deve rimanere nella Chiesa*, Queriniana, Brescia, 1974.
Spanish edition: *Lo que debe permanecer en la Iglesia*, Herder, Barcelona, 1975.
Portuguese edition: *O que deve permanecer na Igreja*, Vozes, Petrópolis, 1976.
English edition: *What Must Remain in the Church*, Collins, Fount Paperbacks, London, 1977.

19: FEHLBAR? EINE BILANZ. (With contributions by 16 other scholars.) Benziger, Zürich-Einsiedeln-Cologne, 1973.

Italian edition: see no. 14.
Dutch edition: see no. 18.
Other editions in preparation.
Earlier partial editions (containing Hans Küng's reply to

Löhrer, Lehmann and Rahner):
Italian: *Risposte: sulla discussione per 'Infallibile?'*, Anteo, Bologna, 1971.
Spanish: *Respuestas a propósito del debato sobre 'Infalible? Una pregunta'*, Ediciones Paulinas, Zalla (Spain), 1971.

20: CHRIST SEIN. Piper, Munich, 1974; paperback edition, DTV-Taschenbuch (1220), Munich, 1976.

American edition: *On Being A Christian*, Doubleday, New York, 1976.
Dutch edition: *Christen zijn*, Gooi en Sticht, Hilversum, 1976.
Italian edition: *Essere cristiani*, Mondadori, Milan, 1976.
Portuguese edition: *Ser cristão*, Imago, Rio de Janeiro, 1976.
Spanish edition: *Ser cristiano*, Ediciones Cristiandad, Madrid, 1977.
English edition: *On Being A Christian*, Collins, London, 1977, Fount Paperbacks, London, 1978.
French edition: *Être chrétien*, Editions du Seuil, Paris, 1978.
Japanese edition: in preparation.

21: 20 THESEN ZUM CHRISTSEIN. Piper, Munich, 1975.

Dutch edition: *Profiel van een christen: Twintig stellingen*, Gooi en Sticht, Hilversum, 1977.
Danish edition: *20 teser om det 'at være kristen'*, Niels Steensen, Copenhagen, 1977.
American edition: see no. 27.
Other editions in preparation.

22: WAS IST FIRMUNG ? (Theologische Meditationen 40.) Benziger, Zürich-Einsiedeln-Cologne, 1976.

Italian edition: *Che cosa è la confermazione?*, Queriniana, Brescia, 1976.
Dutch edition: see no. 27.
American edition: see no. 27.
Other editions in preparation.

H.K.   G

23: JESUS IM WIDERSTREIT. EIN JÜDISCH-CHRIST-LICHER DIALOG. (With Pinchas Lapide.) Calwer-Kösel, Stuttgart-Munich, 1976.

English edition: *Brother or Lord? A Jew and a Christian talk together about Jesus*, Collins, Fount Paperbacks, London, 1977.
Dutch edition: see no. 27.
American edition: see no. 27.
Other editions in preparation.

24: GOTTESDIENST – WARUM? (Theologische Meditationen 43.) Benziger, Zürich-Einsiedeln-Cologne, 1976.

Dutch edition: see no. 27.
American edition: see no. 27.
Other editions in preparation.

25: HEUTE NOCH AN GOTT GLAUBEN? ZWEI REDEN (together with *Mut zu kritischer Sympathie* by Walter Scheel). Piper, Munich, 1977.

26: EXISTIERT GOTT? ANTWORT AUF DIE GOTTES-FRAGE DER NEUZEIT. Piper, Munich, 1978.

Translations in preparation.

27: WEGZEICHEN IN DIE ZUKUNFT (in preparation).

Dutch edition: *Wegwijzers naar de toekomst*, Gooi en Sticht, Hilversum, 1977.
American edition: *Signposts for the Future*, Doubleday, New York, 1978.
Other editions in preparation.

II: Series, symposia and journals edited by Hans Küng

1: THEOLOGISCHE MEDITATIONEN (Theological Meditations).

German: Benziger, Einsiedeln, 1964 onwards.
Dutch: Paul Brand, Hilversum-Antwerp, 1964 onwards.
English: Sheed and Ward, London, 1965 onwards.
American: Sheed and Ward, New York, 1966 onwards.
French: Desclée De Brouwer, Paris, 1965 onwards.
Italian: Queriniana, Brescia, 1966 onwards.

2: SYMPOSIA, ETC.
(a) *Konzilsreden*, edited by Y. Congar, H. Küng and D. O'Hanlon, Benziger, Einsiedeln, 1964.

American edition: *Council Speeches of Vatican II*, Paulist Press, Glen Rock, N.J., 1964.
English edition: *Council Speeches of Vatican II*, Sheed and Ward, London, 1964.
Dutch edition: *Concilie-Toespraken*, Paul Brand, Hilversum-Antwerp, 1964.
French edition: *Discours au Concile Vatican II*, Editions du Cerf, Paris, 1964.
Spanish edition: *Discursos conciliares*, Guadarrama, Madrid, 1964.
(b) *Towards Vatican III: The Work That Needs To Be Done*, edited by D. Tracy with H. Küng and J. B. Metz, Seabury Press, New York, 1978.

3: ÖKUMENISCHE FORSCHUNGEN (Ecumenical Studies). Founded by H. Küng and J. Ratzinger, edited by H. Küng and J. Moltmann with the co-operation of E. Jüngel and W. Kasper: Herder, Freiburg-Basle-Vienna, 1967 onwards.

I: Ecclesiological section.
II: Soteriological section.

III: Sacramentological section.
Supplementary section: Minor ecumenical writings.

4: JOURNALS AND PERIODICALS.

(a) Associate editor of the *Tübinger Theologische Quartal-schrift* from 1960 onwards; editor from 1972 to 1974; introductions (together with J. Neumann) from vol. 152 (1972) no. 3 to vol. 154 (1974) no. 4.

(b) Member of the executive editorial committee of the international theological periodical *Concilium* and editor (together with W. Kasper from 1965 to 1976 and J. Moltmann from 1977 onwards) of the section on ecumenism from 1965 onwards, consisting of the following numbers (vol. 4 1965 to 1972, vol. 10 1973 onwards):

1 (1965) (various subjects).
2 (1966): *Other Christian Churches – Do We Know Them?*
3 (1967): *The Debate on the Sacraments.*
4 (1968): *Apostolic by Succession?*
5 (1969): *Courage Needed: Ecumenism at Present and in the Future.*
6 (1970): *Post-ecumenical Christianity.*
7 (1971): *A Papal Primacy?*
8 (1972): *Mutual Recognition of Ministries?*
9 (1973): *A Risk of Factions in the Church?*
10 (1974): *Christians and Jews.*
11 (1975): *Church Renewal and the Petrine Ministry at the End of the Twentieth Century* (special number edited by G. Alberigo and W. Kasper).
12 (1976): *Luther Then and Now.*
13 (1977): *What Are We On Earth For?*
14 (1978): *An Ecumenical Creed.*
(c) Associate editor of the *Journal of Ecumenical Studies* (Philadelphia) from 1964 onwards.

III: Contributions to encyclopaedias

1: *"Christozentrik"* in *Lexikon für Theologie und Kirche*, Freiburg-im-Breisgau 1958, vol. II cols 1169–74.

2: *"Kirche: IV, Reform"* in *Handbuch theologischer Grundbegriffe*, Munich 1962, vol. I, pp. 822–7.

3: "Freedom, intellectual" in *New Catholic Encyclopedia*, New York and London 1967, vol. VI pp. 100–2.

4: "Justification" in *Encyclopedia Britannica* (14th edition), Chicago and London 1967, vol. 13 pp. 162–3.

5: *"Konzil"* in *Sacramentum Mundi*, Freiburg-im-Breisgau, Basle and Vienna 1969, vol. III pp. 47–51, and in *Herders Theologisches Taschenlexikon*, Freiburg-im-Breisgau, Basle and Vienna 1972, vol. 4 pp. 248–51.

English translation: "Council: I, Theology" in Karl Rahner et al. (edd.), *Sacramentum Mundi*, London 1968, vol. 2 pp. 8–9, and in Karl Rahner (ed.), *Encyclopaedia of Theology: A Concise Sacramentum Mundi*, London 1975, pp. 296–7.

6: *"Katholisch – evangelisch: eine ökumenische Bestandesaufnahme"* in *Meyers Enzyklopädisches Lexikon*, Mannheim 1976, vol. 17 pp. 609–12.

IV: Contributions to symposia, etc.

1: *"Ihr seid eine königliche Priesterschaft, ein heiliges Volk"* in *Arbeitsmappe für die Frauen- und Mütterseelsorge*, Faszikel 2, Lucerne 1958–9, pp. 2–31.

2: *"Rechtfertigung und Heiligung nach dem Neuen Testament"* in M. Roesle and O. Cullmann (edd.), *Begegnung der Christen: Festschrift O. Karrer*, Stuttgart and Frankfurt-am-Main 1959, pp. 249–70.

English translation: "Justification and Sanctification according to the New Testament" in D. J. Callahan and others (edd.), *Christianity Divided: Protestant and Roman Catholic Theological Issues*, New York 1961, paperback edition

London and New York 1962, pp. 309–35.
French translation: *"Justification et sanctification d'après le Nouveau Testament"* in D. J. Callahan and others (edd.), *Catholiques et Protestants*, Paris 1963, pp. 290–314.

3: *"Konzil und Ökumene"* in A. Dänhardt (ed.), *Theologisches Jahrbuch*, Leipzig 1961, pp. 393–416.

4: *"Karl Barths Lehre vom Wort Gottes als Frage an die katholische Theologie"* in J. Ratzinger and H. Fries (edd.), *Einsicht und Glaube: Festschrift G. Söhngen*, Freiburg, Basle and Vienna 1962, pp. 75–97.

5: *"Das theologische Verständnis des ökumenischen Konzils"* in A. Dänhardt (ed.), *Theologisches Jahrbuch*, Leipzig 1963, pp. 23–40.

6: "Reunion and Doctrine on Justification" in *The Church: Readings in Theology*, New York 1963, pp. 101–11.

7: *"Die Liturgiereform des Konzils und die Wiedervereinigung"* in W. Kampe (ed.), *Das Konzil im Spiegel der Presse*, Würzburg 1963, pp. 280–7.

8: "Theological Currents in Europe Today" in R. Graubard (ed.), *A New Europe?*, Boston 1964, pp. 560–80.

9: *"Der Frühkatholizismus im Neuen Testament als kontroverstheologisches Problem"* in A. Dänhardt (ed.), *Theologisches Jahrbuch*, Leipzig 1965, pp. 150–77; also (with a postscript) in E. Käsemann (ed.), *Das Neue Testament als Kanon*, Göttingen 1970, pp. 175–204.

10: "God's Free Spirit in the Church" in J. C. Murray (ed.), *Freedom and Man*, New York 1965, pp. 17–30.

11: *"Anmerkungen zum Axiom 'Extra Ecclesiam nulla salus'"* in R. Schippers and others (edd.), *Ex auditu verbi: Festschrift G. C. Berkouwer*, Kampen 1965, pp. 80–8.

12: *"Karl Barths Lehre vom Wort Gottes als Frage an die katholische Theologie"* in A. Dänhardt (ed.), *Theologisches Jahrbuch*, Leipzig 1967, pp. 66–86.

13: *"Katholische Besinnung auf Luthers Rechtfertigungslehre heute"* in *Theologie im Wandel: Festschrift zum 150-jährigen Bestehen der Katholischtheologischen Fakultät an der Universität Tübingen 1817–1967*, edited by the Catholic faculty of theology at Tübingen university, Munich and Freiburg-im-Breisgau 1967, pp. 449–68.

14: *"Deus o que é?"* in *Deus o que é?*, Lisbon 1968, pp. 118–22.

15: *"Das Petrusamt in Kirche und Konzil"* in G. Otto (ed.), *Glauben heute*, Hamburg 1968, vol. 2 pp. 115–23.

16: "Comment" (on § 25 of Vatican II's constitution on the Church) in *Church: Vatican II's Dogmatic Constitution on the Church*, New York 1969, p. 55.

17: *"Ansprache"* in *Karl Barth 1886–1968: Gedenkfeier im Basler Münster*, Zürich 1969, pp. 43–6.

18: "The Freedom of Religions" in M. E. Marty (ed.), *Attitudes Towards Other Religions: Some Christian Interpretations*, New York and London 1969, pp. 191–217.

19: *"Zur Zukunft der Kirche"* in G. Otto (ed.), *Sachkunde Religion*, Hamburg and Düsseldorf 1969, pp. 215–21.

20: *"La participation des laics aux décisions dans l'Église: Une lacune dans le Décret sur l'apostolat des laics"* in Y. Congar (ed.), *L'Apostolat des laics* (commentary on the decree *Apostolicam actuositatem*), Paris 1970, pp. 285–308.

21: "Participation of the Laity in Church Leadership and in Church Elections" in L. and A. Swidler (edd.), *Bishops and People*, Philadelphia 1970, pp. 87–112.

22: "What is the Essence of Apostolic Succession?" in E. J. Dirkswager Jr (ed.), *Readings in the Theology of the Church*, Englewood Cliffs, New Jersey 1970, pp. 125–32.

23: "The Petrine Office" in E. J. Dirkswager Jr (ed.), *Readings in the Theology of the Church*, Englewood Cliffs, New Jersey 1970, pp. 142–67.

24: *"Portrait d'un pape"* in J. de Broucker, *Le Dossier Suenens*, Paris 1970, pp. 273–82.

German version: *"Der Petrusdienst in der Kirche"* in J. de Broucker, *Das Dossier Suenens*, Graz 1970, pp. 311–20.
(Partial) English version: "Portrait of a Pope" in J. de Broucker, *The Suenens Dossier: The Case for Collegiality*, Notre Dame and Dublin 1970, pp. 197–201.

25: *"Bist Du abergläubisch?"* in C. Hüppi and W. Brüschweiler (edd.), *Wort und Bild: Ein Sachlesebuch für das 8. und 9. Schuljahr*, Zürich 1970, pp. 319–20; also in *Wort und Bild: Ein Sachlesebuch für die Sekundarstufe*, Frankfurt 1974, pp. 307–9.

26: *"Die Kirche des Evangeliums"* in H. Häring and J. Nolte (edd.), *Diskussion um Hans Küng "Die Kirche"*, Freiburg, Basle and Vienna 1971, pp. 175–221.

27: *"Interkommunion und Ökumene (Zur Pariser Pfingsteucharistie)"* in op. cit., pp. 293–7.

28: Letter to Yves Congar in op. cit., pp. 301–5.

29: *"Schlusswort"* in op. cit., pp. 307–10.

30: *"Warum bleibe ich in der Kirche?"* in W. Dirks and E. Stammler (edd.), *Warum bleibe ich in der Kirche? Zeitgenössische Antworten*, Munich 1971, pp. 117–24.

31: *"Was ist die christliche Botschaft?"* in *Die Zukunft der*

Kirche: Berichtband des Concilium-Kongresses Brüssel 12.–17.9.1970, Einsiedeln, Zürich and Mainz 1971, pp. 78–85; also in V. Hochgrebe and N. Kutschki (edd.), *Das Unverzichtbare am Christentum*, Mainz and Munich 1971, pp. 28–35.

English translation: "What is the Christian Message?" in G. H. Anderson and T. F. Stransky (edd.), *Mission Trends No. 1: Crucial Issues in Mission Today*, New York, Paramus, Toronto, and Grand Rapids 1974, pp. 101–10.
Dutch translation: *"Wat is de christelijke boodschap?"* in *De Toekomst van de Kerk: Verslag van het wereldcongres "Concilium" te Brussel 12.–17.9.1970*, Amersfoort and Bussum 1970, pp. 75–82.
French translation: *"Qu'est-ce que le message chrétien?"* in *L'Avenir de l'Église: Congrès de Bruxelles 12.–17.9.1970*, Paris 1970, pp. 81–8.
Italian translation: *"Qual è il messaggio cristiano?"* in *L'avvenire della Chiesa: Bruxelles 1970, il libro del Congresso*, Brescia 1970, pp. 117–25.
Polish translation: *"Co to jest chrześcijańskie posłannictwo"* in *Concilium: Materiały Kongresu "Przyszłość Kościoła" Bruksela 12.–17.9.1970*, Poznań and Warsaw 1971, pp. 59–64.
Korean translation in *Chonkyoran muoshinka* ("What is Religion?"), Waekwan 1975, pp. 105–22.

32: *"Wesen und Gestalt des kirchlichen Amtes"* in *Reform und Anerkennung kirchlicher Ämter: ein Memorandum der Arbeitsgemeinschaft ökumenischer Universitätsinstitute*, Munich and Mainz 1973, pp. 163–88.

33: *"La préhistoire de 'Infaillible? Une interpellation'"* in *Église infaillible ou intemporelle?*, Paris 1973, pp. 13–31.

34: *"Les chances d'un Magistère faillible"* in *Mélanges Congar*, Paris 1974, pp. 177–90.

35: *"Oppimiskyvyttömyyttä? Roma locuta, causa aperta"* in

R. Cantell, E. Huovinen and S. S. Salo, *Kirkon ykseys ja reformi: Hans Küngin herättämä ekumeeninen keskustelu*, Helsinki 1974, pp. 70–4.

36: *"Le religioni come interrogativo alla teologia della croce"* in *Sulla teologia della croce*, Brescia 1974, pp. 111–48.

37: *"Het vormsel als voltooing van de doop"* in *Leven uit de geest: Festschrift E. Schillebeeckx*, Hilversum 1974, pp. 105–31.

38: *"Das Besondere des Christentums"* in K. Piper (ed.), *Piper-Almanach zum 70. Jahr 1904–1974*, Munich 1974, p. 479.

39: *"Anmerkungen zu Walter Kasper, 'Christologie von unten?'"* in L. Scheffczyk (ed.), *Grundfragen der Christologie heute*, Freiburg, Basle and Vienna 1975, pp. 170–9.

40: *"15 Thesen: I, Wer ist der Christus? II, Wer ist Gott? III, Wer ist Christ?"* in *Deutscher Evangelischer Kirchentag Frankfurt 1975: Dokumente*, Stuttgart and Berlin 1975, pp. 506, 508–9, 511.

41: *"Heutiges Gottesverständnis"* in W. Trutwin (ed.), *Reden von Gott*, Düsseldorf 1975, pp. 35–7.

42: *"Trinität"* in op. cit. pp. 99–101.

43: "Freedom of the Church" (in Korean) in *Chaiyueul Somyong* ("Summons to Freedom"), Waekwan 1976, pp. 114–53.

44: "Freedom in the World" (in Korean) in op. cit. pp. 213–52.

45: *"Der gesellschaftliche Kontext der Botschaft Jesu"* in J. Schwarte (ed.), *Grundfragen menschlichen Zusammenlebens in christlicher Sicht*, Paderborn 1976, pp. 87–96.

46: Sermon on Rom. 12:1–2 given on 30 November 1975, in *Paulinische Predigt. Gottes Gerechtigkeit: der Menschen Freiheit. 14 Predigten in der Stiftskirche Tübingen*, edited by the Protestant student parish at Tübingen, Stuttgart 1976, pp. 57–71.

47: *"Thesen zum Atheismus"* in D. Papenfuss and J. Söring (edd.), *Transzendenz und Immanenz: Philosophie und Theologie in der veränderten Welt*, Stuttgart 1977, pp. 233–7.

48: *"Wissenschaft und Gottesfrage"* in *500 Jahre Eberhard-Karls-Universität Tübingen 1477–1977: Reden zum Jubiläum*, Tübingen 1977, pp. 97–114.

49: "Vatican III: Problems and Opportunities for the Future" in D. Tracy with H. Küng and J. B. Metz (edd.), *Towards Vatican III: The Work That Needs To Be Done*, New York 1978, pp. 67–90.

V: Contributions to newspapers and periodicals

1: *"Ist Friede Kapitulation? Zum neuesten Werke Friedrich Heers"* in *Civitas* 11 (1965), pp. 1–6.

2: *"Musik christlich?"* (under the pseudonym Wolfgang Rexer) in *Musik und Altar* 8 (1956), pp. 226–9.

3: *"Ist in der Rechtfertigungslehre eine Einigung möglich?"* in *Una Sancta* 12 (1957), pp. 116–1.

4: *"Unsere Mädchen in Paris"* in *Werkblatt der katholischen Mädchenschutzvereine* 45 (1957), pp. 170–3.

5: *"Rechtfertigung in katholischer Besinnung: eine Antwort"* (in reply to H. Stirnimann) in *Schweizerische Kirchenzeitung* 125 (1957), pp. 619–21 and 637–9.

6: *"Es war immer so! War es immer so??"* in *Pfarrblatt St*

Leodegar, Lucerne, 15 February 1958.

7: *"Für oder gegen das Missale?"* in *Pfarrblatt St Leodegar*, Lucerne, 15 May 1958.

8: *"Brief eines Vorbeters"* in *Pfarrblatt St Leodegar*, Lucerne, 1 June 1958.

9: *"Dialog mit Karl Barth"* (review of H. Bouillard, *Karl Barth*) in *Dokumente* 14 (1958), pp. 236–7.

10: *"Zum katholischen Dialog mit Karl Barth"* (reply to H. de Lubac) in *Dokumente* 15 (1959), p. 31.

11: *"Priestermangel in der Schweiz?"* (signed ***) in *Civitas* 14 (1958), pp. 10–16.

12: *"Priestermangel in der Schweiz? Abschliessende Replik"* (signed ***) in *Civitas* 14 (1959), pp. 261–77.

13: *"Die Problematik des Lateins als Kultsprache: Antwort eines Seelsorgers an einen Laien"* (signed -tr) in *Schweizerische Kirchenzeitung* 127 (1959), pp. 70–2, 82–3.

14: *"Die Problematik des Lateins als Kultsprache: abschliessende Bemerkungen eines Seelsorgers zum Plädoyer -ons"* (signed -tr) in *Schweizerische Kirchenzeitung* 127 (1959), pp. 187–9.

15: *"Wie stehen wir zur Religion? Zu Arnold J. Toynbees 70. Geburtstag"* in *Luzerner Neueste Nachrichten*, 20 June 1959.

16: *"Kritik an der Kirche?"* in *Luzerner Neueste Nachrichten*, 21 November 1959.

17: *"Theologie und Wiedervereinigung"* in *Schweizerische Kirchenzeitung* 127 (1959), pp. 729–31.

18: *"Die ökumenische Aufgabe des Konzils"* in *Militär-*

seelsorge 2 (1960), pp. 197–206, also in *Civitas* 15 (1960) no. 6, pp. 1–6.

19: *"Was können wir für die Erneuerung der Kirche tun?"* in *Der christliche Sonntag* 12 (1960), pp. 61–2.

20: *"Theologische Neuorientierungen in der Weltmission"* in *Schweizerische Kirchenzeitung* 128 (1960), pp. 157–9, 170–3, 187–9, 202–3, also in *Priester und Mission* (1960), pp. 111–30.

21: *"Das Collegium Germanicum et Hungaricum und die Einheit der Christenheit"* in *Korrespondenzblatt für die Alumnen des Collegium Germanicum et Hungaricum* 67 (1960), pp. 73–88.

22: *"Konzil und Episkopat: zur Theologie des ökumenischen Konzils"* in *Anima* 15 (1960), pp. 294–300.

English translation: "The Pope with the Bishops" in *Prism* 6 (1962), pp. 7–14.
Dutch translation: *"Naar een Theologie van het Oekumenisch Concilie"* in *De Maand* 5 (1962), pp. 67–72.

23: *"Überlegungen zur Gemeinschaftsmesse"* in *Civitas* 15 (1960) no. 5, pp. 1–6, also in *St Michaelsglocken*, Zug, 5 March 1960.

24: *"Sprichst Du mit Evangelischen?"* in *Voran* (boys' monthly of the Federation of German Catholic Youth), January 1961, pp. 10–11, also in *Morgen* (girls' monthly of the Federation of German Catholic Youth), January 1961, pp. 10–11, in *Materialmappen des Burckhardthauses für die evangelische Jugendarbeit* no. 15/16, Berlin 1961, pp. 3–5, in *Die Führung* 24 (1961), pp. 129–32, in *Jungmannschaft* 51 (1962), pp. 182–3, and in *Kirchenzeitung für das Bistum Aachen*, 13 January 1963.

Bengali translation ("Do you talk to Protestants?") in *Jivan*, March 1964.

206 Bibliography

25: *"Eine kurze Antwort an K.M."* in *Vaterland*, 18 March 1961.

26: *"Zur Erneuerung der Messe"* in *Vaterland*, 1 April 1961, also in *Jungmannschaft* 50 (1961), pp. 154–5, 178.

27: *"Das theologische Verständnis des ökumenischen Konzils"* (inaugural lecture at Tübingen university, 24 November 1960) in *Theologische Quartalschrift* 141 (1961), pp. 50–77.

English translation: "The Ecumenical Council in Theological Perspective" in *Dialog* 1 (1962), pp. 40–9, also in *Theology Digest* 11 (1963), pp. 135–9.

28: *"Wer sind die andern?"* in *Vaterland*, 13 May 1961.

29: *"Het Concilie"* (letter to the editor) in *De Tijd*, 22 July 1961.

30: *"Muss der Katholik alles verteidigen?"* in *Morgen*, September 1961, pp. 14–15, also in *Voran*, September 1961, pp. 14–15, and in *Jungmannschaft* 51 (1962), p. 202.

English translation: "Does a Catholic Have to Defend Everything?" in *The Sign*, February 1963, pp. 11–12. Bengali translation in *Jivan*, April 1964.

31: Book reviews in *Theologische Quartalschrift* 141 (1961), pp. 251–3.

32: *"Vernieuwing en Hereniging"* in *De Maand* 4 (1961), pp. 445–7.

33: *"Kann das Konzil auch scheitern? Bedingungen für den inneren Erfolg des Zweiten Vatikanischen Konzils"* in *Rheinischer Merkur*, 27 October 1961.

English translation: "Can the Council Fail?" in *The Furrow* 13 (1962), pp. 53–5, also in *Cross Currents* 12 (1962), pp. 269–76.

Dutch translation: *"Kan het concilie mislukken?"* in *De Linie,* 24 November 1961, also in *Te elfder ure* 9 (1962), pp. 120–7.

French translation: *"Le concile pourrait-il échouer? Les conditions d'une véritable réussite du Second Concile du Vatican"* in *La Revue Nouvelle* 18 (1962), pp. 65–73.

34: *"Für ein 'Reformkonzil praktischer Art': Replik und Schlusswort zu 'Kann das Konzil auch scheitern?'"* in *Rheinischer Merkur,* 1 December 1961.

35: *"Konzil und Ökumene"* in *Initiative* nos. 1 and 2, November and December 1961.

36: *"Genügt das Kritisieren?"* in *Morgen,* November 1961, pp. 18–19, also in *Voran,* November 1961, pp. 18–19.

English translation: "Is Criticism Enough?" in *The Sign,* February 1963, pp. 12–13.

37: "Venerating Mary: Difficulties in the Way of Reunion" in *Pax Romana Journal* 6 (1961), pp. 13–14.

38: *"Christen – getrennt für immer?"* in *Morgen,* January 1962, pp. 22–3, also in *Voran,* January 1962, pp. 22–3, in *Jungmannschaft* 51 (1962), pp. 220–1, and in *Neue Bildpost,* 16 September 1962.

39: *"Concile et retour à l'unité"* in *Lettre de Ligugé* no. 91 (1962), pp. 13–17.

40: *"Ausserhalb der Kirche kein Heil?"* in *Morgen,* March 1962, pp. 14–15, also in *Voran,* March 1962, pp. 14–15.

41: Book reviews in *Theologische Quartalschrift* 142 (1962), pp. 99–102.

42: "Pope John as a Good Shepherd" in *The Catholic World* 195 (1962), pp. 7–13.

43: *"Was erwarten die Christen vom Konzil? Eine Antwort auf den Bericht im Pfarrblatt des Dekanats Basel-Stadt vom 16. März 1962"* in *Basler Volksblatt*, 14 April 1962.

44: *"Positive Antwort auf negative Bemerkungen zur Konzilsvorbereitung"* in *Neue Zürcher Zeitung*, 19 April 1962.

Dutch translation: *"Positief antwoord op negatieve beschouwingen (over voorbereiding Concilie)"* in *Het Centrum*, 5–6 June 1962.

45: *"Zwischen den Zeiten"* (Easter article) in *Luzerner Neueste Nachrichten*, 21 April 1962.

46: *"Bist Du abergläubisch?"* in *Morgen*, May 1962, pp. 26–7, and in *Voran*, May 1962, pp. 26–7.

47: *"Was ist ein ökumenisches Konzil?"* in *Civitas* 17 (1962), pp. 432–47.

48: *"Gott alles in allem"* (article on the appointment of Professor Hermann Volk as Bishop of Mainz) in *Kirche und Leben* (Münster diocesan weekly), 3 June 1962.

49: *"Hast Du Glaubenszweifel?"* in *Morgen*, June 1962, pp. 18–19 and in *Voran*, June 1962, pp. 18–19.

50: *"Konzil und Wiedervereinigung"* in *Luzerner Neueste Nachrichten*, 15 September 1962.

51: *"Kommt das Konzil zu früh?"* in *Die Weltwoche*, 5 October 1962.

Dutch translation: *"Komt het concilie te vroeg?"* in *Elseviers Weekblad*, 15 September 1962.
French translation: *"Le Concile vient-il trop tôt?"* in *Informations Catholiques Internationales*, 15 October 1962.

52: "Objections to the Council" in *Jubilee* 9, April 1962, pp. 16–19.

53: *"Die Liturgiereform des Konzils und die Wiedervereinigung"* in *Neue Zürcher Zeitung*, 17 November 1962, also in *Initiative* no. 4/5, February 1963, and in *Musik und Altar* 15 (1963), pp. 56–63.

English translation: "Ecumenical Orientations" in *Worship* 37, December 1962, pp. 83–94.
Dutch translation: *"Liturgiehervorming en oecumene"* in *Elseviers Weekblad*, 5 January 1963.

54: *"Warum sind dogmatische Konzilsentscheide heute schwierig?"* in *Kirchenzeitung für das Bistum Aachen*, 16 December 1962, also in *Una Sancta* 18 (1963), pp. 129–31.

55: *"Der Frühkatholizismus im Neuen Testament als kontroverstheologisches Problem"* in *Theologische Quartalschrift* 142 (1962), pp. 385–424.

56: *"Zur Problematik kirchlicher Unfehlbarkeit"* in *Vaterland*, 6 October 1962.

57: "One Flock, One Shepherd" in *Catholic Digest*, November 1962, pp. 31–5.

58: *"Das Vatikanum II nach der ersten Session"* in *Civitas* 18 (1963), pp. 349–58, also in *Attempto* no. 11, April 1963, pp. 15–21.

French translation: *"Vatican II après la première session"* in *La Documentation Catholique* 45 (1963), pp. 821–30.

59: *"Veröffentlichungen zum Konzil: ein Überblick"* in *Theologische Quartalschrift* 143 (1963), pp. 56–82.

60: *"Das Eucharistiegebet: Konzil und Erneuerung der römischen Messliturgie"* in *Wort und Wahrheit* 18 (1963), pp. 102–7.

61: "The Free Church" (letter to the editor) in *The Sunday*

Times, 26 May 1963.

62: "Reflections on the Council" (letter to Father Van Ackeren) in *Theology Digest* 11 (1963), p. 65.

63: "A Word of Thanks" (following his first American lecture tour) in *America* 108 (1963), pp. 826–9.

German translation: *"Ökumenischer Frühling in Amerika: Eindrücke von einer Vortragsreise"* in *Rheinischer Merkur*, 21 June 1963.
Dutch translation: *"Oecumenische lente in Amerika"* in *Sursum Corda* (Amsterdam), 19 and 26 July and 2 August 1963.

64: *"Warum dieser Papst gross war"* in *Die Weltwoche*, 7 June 1963, in *Der Oberthurgauer*, 12 June 1963, and in *Luzerner Landbote*, 14 June 1963.

English translation: "Servus Servorum Dei: Why Pope John was Great" in *The Tablet* 217 (1963), pp. 630–2 and 645–6, and in *Our Sunday Visitor*, 30 June 1963.
Dutch translation: *"Joannes XXIII, groot in het dienen"* in *De Tijd*, 15 June 1963.

65: "The Missions in the Ecumenical Age" in *African Ecclesiastical Review* 5 (1963), pp. 97–108.

66: "Reunion and the Jews: An Answer to Rabbi Arnold Jacob Wolf" in *The Christian Century* 80 (1963), p. 829.

67: *"Sobór, Odnowa i Zjednoczenie"* (extract from *The Council and Reunion*) in *Znak* 15 (1963), pp. 530–60.

68: "The Mass of the Future" in *The Sign* 42 (1963), pp. 18–21.

69: "What Christians Expect of Vatican II" in *Christianity and Crisis* 23 (1963), pp. 156–60.

70: "Latin: The Church's Mother Tongue?" in *Harper's Magazine* 227 (1963), pp. 60–4.

71: "The Council So Far" in *The Catholic Layman* 77 (1963), pp. 6–13.

72: "The Church and Freedom" in *Commonweal* 78 (1963), pp. 343–53.

Spanish translation: *"Iglesia y libertad"* in *Mensaje* 12 (1963), pp. 697–706.
Polish translation: *"Kóściól i Wolność"* in *Tygodnik Powszechny*, 22 September 1963.

73: *"Stückwerk ist unser Erkennen: die historische Kontingenz von Konzilsdekreten"* in *Frankfurter Allgemeine Zeitung*, 26 November 1963.

French translation: *"Que valent les décrets conciliaires?"* in *Informations Catholiques Internationales*, 1 February 1964.

74: *"Zur Diskussion um die Rechtfertigung"* in *Theologische Quartalschrift* 143 (1963), pp. 129–35, and in *Theologie der Gegenwart* 6 (1963), pp. 203–6.

75: *"Program Soboru Powszechnego"* in *Życie i Myśl* 14 (1964), pp. 184–202.

76: *"Geist und Kirche"* (sermon preached at Sursee for the Swiss Students' Association) in *Civitas* 20 (1964), pp. 7–12.

77: *"Das Konzil – Ende oder Anfang? Eine Bilanz am Ende der dritten Sitzungsperiode des Zweiten Vatikanums"* in *Frankfurter Allgemeine Zeitung*, 18–19 November 1964; revised and expanded version in *Tübinger Forschungen* no. 19, December 1964, in *Civitas* 21 (1965), pp. 188–99, and in *KNA Sonderdienst zum Zweiten Vatikanischen Konzil*, 18 February 1965.

English translation: "The Council – End or Beginning?" in

Commonweal 81 (1965), pp. 631–7.
Dutch translation: *"Het Concilie: Einde of Begin?"* in *Elseviers Weekblad*, 6 February 1965.
Polish translation: *"Początek czy koniec Soboru"* in *Życie i Myśl* 15 (1965), pp. 104–13.

78: *"Institut für ökumenische Forschung der Universität Tübingen"* in *Ökumenische Rundschau* 14 (1965), pp. 74–5.

79: *"Eine gemeinsame Bibel für die Konfessionen? Die Zürcher Bibel der Reformierten Kirche jetzt für Katholiken"* in *Frankfurter Allgemeine Zeitung*, 8 March 1965, in *Vaterland*, 2 April 1965, and in *Neue Zürcher Nachrichten*, 10 April 1965.

80: *"Die charismatische Struktur der Kirche"* in *Concilium* (German edition) 1 (1965), pp. 282–9.

English translation: "The Charismatic Structure of the Church" in *Concilium* 1 (1965) vol. 4, pp. 23–33.
Dutch translation: *"De charismatische structuur van de kerk"* in *Concilium* 1 (1965) vol. 4, pp. 40–58.
French translation: *"La structure charismatique de l'Église"* in *Concilium* 1 (1965) vol. 4, pp. 43–60.
Italian translation: *"La struttura carismatica della Chiesa"* in *Concilium* 1 (1965) vol. 2, pp. 7–37.
Spanish translation: *"La estructura carismática de la Iglesia"* in *Concilium* 1 (1965) vol. 4, pp. 44–65.
Portuguese translation: *"Estrutura carismática da Igreja"* in *Concilium* 1 (1965) vol. 4, pp. 31–45.
Polish translation: *"Charysmatyczna strukura Kościoła"* in *Concilium* (1968), pp. 281–93.
Japanese translation in *Concilium* vol. 2 (1968), pp. 144–75.
The English translation also appeared in *The Catholic World* 201 (1965), pp. 302–6.

81: *"Und nach dem Konzil?"* in *Frankfurter Allgemeine Zeitung*, 28 August 1965, and in *Vaterland*, 4 September 1965.

English translation: "And after the Council?" in *Commonweal* 82 (1965), pp. 619–23.
Dutch translation: *"Wat gebeurt er na het Concilie?"* in *De Tijd*, 28 August 1965.

82: *"Dogma, Verdad y Error"* in *El Ciervo* 14, February 1965, p. 9.

83: "The World Religions in God's Plan of Salvation" in *Indian Ecclesiastical Studies* 4 (1965), pp. 182–222.

84: "The Reform of the Roman Church: Reform towards other Christian Churches, Reform towards other Religions, and Reform towards the World" in *The Sunday Times*, 12 December 1965.

85: *"Was hat das Konzil erreicht?"* in *Vaterland*, 17 and 18 December 1965, in *Tübinger Forschungen* no. 27, January 1966, in *Universitas* 21 (1966), pp. 171–86, in *Der katholische Erzieher* 19 (1966), pp. 137–43, in *Deutsche Tagespost*, 8–9 April 1966, and (in a shortened version) in *Jungmannschaft* 55 (1966), pp. 7–8.

English translation: "What has the Council done?" in *Commonweal* 83 (1966), pp. 461–8.
Italian translation: *"Bilancio del Concilio: l'avveramento di una grande speranza"* in *Dialogo* 13 (1966), pp. 20–35.
Polish translation: *"Co Sobór osiągnął?"* in *Kultura* (Paris), 1966, no. 4, pp. 69–82.

86: *"Die 16 neuen Pfeiler von Sankt Peter"* in *Epoca* no. 1, January 1966, pp. 12–19, in *Neue Bildpost*, 16 January 1966, and in *Karmel Stimmen* 33 (1966), pp. 33–46.

Spanish translation: *"El nuevo Espiritu en la Iglesia"* in *Mensajero de San José del Avila* (Caracas) 51, June 1966, pp. 5–14.
Polish translation: *"Sobór Jest Początkiem"* in *Tygodnik Powszechny*, 13 February 1966.

87: *"La liberté dans l'Église"* in *Cahiers universitaires catholiques* 10 (1966), pp. 571–92.

88: *"Freiheit des Christen"* in *Rothenfelser Werkblatt* 16 (1966), pp. 29–31.

89: *"Orientation pastorale et caractère scientifique de la théologie"* in *Convergences* 2 (1967), pp. 1–10.

90: *"Die Zukunft der Kirche"* in *Christ in der Gegenwart* 19 (1967), pp. 61–2.

91: *"Forderungen an die Kirche"* in *Civitas* 22 (1967), pp. 368–74.

92: *"Bedrohte Freiheit der Basler Bischofswahl?"* (under the pseudonym Helveticus) in *Civitas* 22 (1967), pp. 537–41, and in *Luzerner Neueste Nachrichten*, 11 March 1967.

93: *"Unbeantwortete Fragen zur Basler Bischofswahl"* (under the pseudonym Helveticus) in *Vaterland*, 17 March 1967.

94: *"Katholische Schweiz"* in *Civitas* 22 (1967), pp. 579–88.

95: *'Eine Stellungnahme zur Wahrhaftigkeit in der Kirche: Antwort an JBB"* in *Freiburger Nachrichten*, 25 February 1967.

96: *"Eine Herausforderung an die Kirche"* (comment on Charles Davis's decision to leave the Church) in *Orientierung* 31 (1967), pp. 123–6.

English translation: "A Question to the Church" in *The Month* 224 (1967), pp. 259–61.
Dutch translation: *"Stap van Engelse theoloog uitdaging aan de kerk"* in *De Volkskrant*, 27 May 1967.
French translation: *"Analyse d'une 'Affaire': Requête à l'Église"* in *Informations Catholiques Internationales*, 1 July 1967.

97: *"Kirche unter dem Geiste"* (article for Whitsun) in *Luzerner Neueste Nachrichten*, 13 May 1967.

98: *"Zwei entgegengesetzte Stimmen zur Enzyklika über den Zölibat?"* (reply to A.F.) in *Schweizerische Kirchenzeitung*, 24 August 1967.

99: *"Katholiek Nederland op de goede weg"* in *De Volkskrant*, 2 November 1967. in *De Gelderlander Pers*, 2 November 1967, and in *Katholieke Gemeenschap Maassluis* (1967, no. 3), pp. 2–4.

German version: *"Holland auf dem guten Weg"* in *Vaterland*, 10 November 1967.
English translation: "Holland Shows the Way" in *The Tablet* 221 (1967), p. 1250.

100: *"Questions à l'Église"* in *Informations Catholiques Internationales*, 15 November 1967.

101: Reply to a letter to the editor from Father Niing on Hans Küng's lecture on Luther's doctrine of justification, in *Deutsche Tagespost*, 26–27 January 1968, and in *Passauer Bistumsblatt*, 4 February 1968.

102: *"Die Verantwortung des Theologen"* (reply to an article by Mgr Erich Klausener) in *Petrusblatt*, 1968, no. 8.

103: *"El futuro de la Iglesia"* in *Folia Humanistica* 6 (1968), pp. 97–108.

104: *"Thesen zum Wesen der apostolischen Sukzession"* in *Concilium* 4 (1968), pp. 248–51.

English translation: "What is the Essence of Apostolic Succession?" in *Concilium* 4 (1968), vol. 4, pp. 16–19.
Dutch translation: *"Stellingen over het wezen van de apostolische opvolging"* in *Concilium* 4 (1968) vol. 4, pp. 28–34.
French translation: *"Thèses concernant la nature de la*

succession apostolique" in *Concilium* (1968), vol. 34, pp. 29–36.

Italian translation: *"Tesi sulla natura della successione apostolica"* in *Concilium* 4 (1968) vol. 4, pp. 39–47.

Spanish translation: *"Algunas tesis sobre la naturaleza de la sucesión apostólica"* in *Concilium* 4 (1968) vol. 34, pp. 31–9.

Portuguese translation: *"Teses sobre a Essência da Sucessão Apostólica"* in *Concilium* (1968) vol. 4, pp. 26–32.

Polish translation: *"Tezy o istocie sukcesji apostolskiej"* in *Concilium* (1969), pp. 172–6.

105: "With Windows Open to the Street" in *Union Seminary Quarterly Review* 23 (1968), pp. 147–57.

106: *"Ein helfendes Wort"* (on the encyclical *Humanae vitae*) in *Weltwoche*, 9 August 1968.

107: *"Verwirklichung nach dem Geist, der lebendig macht: Vorschläge zur Kirchenreform"* in *Frankfurter Allgemeine Zeitung*, 3 September 1968, in *Luzerner Neueste Nachrichten*, 7 September 1968, and in *Neue Zürcher Nachrichten*, 21 September 1968.

108: *"Manipulation der Wahrheit?"* in *Weltwoche*, 20 September 1968.

109: *"Die nachkonziliare Aufgabe des katholischen Theologen"* in *Luzerner Landbote*, 11 October 1968.

110: "Intercommunion" in *Journal of Ecumenical Studies* 5 (1968), pp. 576–8.

French translation: *"Intercommunion"* in *Christianisme Social* 76 (1968), pp. 553–6.

111: *"Ist das Konzil an allem schuld? Zum zehnten Jahrestag der Wahl Johannes' XXIII"* in *Publik*, 1 November 1968, in *Luzerner Landbote*, 29 November 1968, in *Vaterland*, 4 January 1969, and in *Kleine Zeitung* (Graz), 18 January 1969.

English translation: "Blame everything on the Council" in *The Critic* 27 (1969), pp. 38–41.
Spanish translation: "*¿Tiene el Concilio la culpa de todo?*" in *Folia Humanistica* 7 (1969), pp. 237–42.

112: "*Unfehlbares Lehramt?*" in *Attempto* (1968), no. 29–30, pp. 34–45.

113: "*Karl Barth – einer der geistigen Väter der katholischen Erneuerung*" (address at Karl Barth's funeral) in *Luzerner Landbote*, 17 December 1968, in *Neue Zürcher Zeitung*, 2 March 1969, and in *Ökumenische Rundschau* 18 (1969), pp. 249–51.

English translation: "Tribute to Karl Barth" in *Journal of Ecumenical Studies* 6 (1969), pp. 233–6.

114: "*Zur Volkswahl der Geistlichen*" (reply to Father C. S. and to Father Max Syfrig) in *Vaterland*, 8 February 1969, with a continuation (under the title "*Weder Alleinherrschaft des Einen noch Alleinherrschaft der Vielen*") in *Vaterland*, 15 February 1969.

115: Open letter to Cardinal Suenens in *Publik*, 18 July 1969.

116: "*Wybiła godzina prawdy*" in *Życie i Myśl* 19 (1969), pp. 20–7.

117: "*Portrait d'un pape*" (in the aftermath of Cardinal Suenens' interview) in *Le Monde*, 12 August 1969.

German version: "*Der Petrusdienst in der Kirche: ein Bild des Papstes nach Suenens' Interview*" in *Publik*, 15 August 1969, and in *Neue Zürcher Nachrichten*, 16 August 1969.
Dutch translation: "*Hoe de paus zou kúnnen zijn*" in *De Volkskrant*, 9 August 1969.
Italian translation: "*Come dovrebbe essere il Papa*" in *L'Europeo*, 4 September 1969.

118: *"Ritratto di un Papa"* (reply to Jean Guitton and others) in *Avvenire*, 14 October 1969.

119: "Dissent May Be A Duty" in *The Voice* (Washington) 1 (1969), no. 11, p. 3.

120: Open letter to A. Kolping (in reply to his open letter to Hans Küng on the latter's article, no. 117 above) in *Neue Zürcher Nachrichten*, 30 August 1969.

121: *"Mitentscheidung der Laien in der Kirchenleitung und bei kirchlichen Wahlen"* in *Theologische Quartalschrift* 149 (1969), pp. 147–65.

English translation: "Participation of the Laity in Church Leadership and in Church Elections" in *Journal of Ecumenical Studies* 6 (1969), pp. 511–33.

122: *"Aufforderung zur Selbsthilfe: zum Dekret des Papstes über Mischehen"* in *Frankfurter Allgemeine Zeitung*, 9 May 1970, and in *Neue Zürcher Nachrichten*, 16 May 1970.

English translation: "Mixed Marriages: What is to be Done?" in *The Tablet* 224 (1970), pp. 518–20.
French translation: *"Que faire à propos des mariages mixtes?"* in *Le Monde*, 7–8 June 1970.
Italian translation: *"E adesso che fare? (a proposito dei matrimoni misti)"* in *Idoc*, 1 June 1970, and in *L'Europeo*, 6 August 1970.

123: *"Konvergenz der Fragen und Antworten zum Thema 'Postökumenisches Zeitalter?'"* (together with W. Kasper and J. Remmers) in *Concilium* 6 (1970), pp. 271–2.

English translation: "The Extent of Convergence" in *Concilium* 6 (1970) vol. 4, pp. 54–7.
Dutch translation: *"De overeenstemming in verwachtingen en klachten"* in *Concilium* 6 (1970) vol. 4, pp. 49–52.
French translation: *"Convergence des questions et des*

réponses" in *Concilium* (1970) vol. 54, pp. 49–52.
Italian translation: *"Convergenza delle domande e delle risposte"* in *Concilium* 6 (1970) vol. 4, pp. 72–6.
Spanish translation: *"Que nos separa todavia de la Iglesia católica? Convergencia en las esperanzas y en las quejas"* in *Concilium* 6 (1970) vol. 54, pp. 51–4.
Portuguese translation: *"Convergência das perguntas e respostas"* in *Concilium* (1970) vol. 54, pp. 468–71.
Polish translation: *"Zbieżnoćż w nadziejach i skargach"* in *Concilium* (1970), pp. 261–3.

124: *"Die Gewissensnot bleibt: Antwort an die Deutsche Bischofskonferenz"* (on the papal *motu proprio* on mixed marriages) in *Schwäbisches Tagblatt*, 30 May 1970, in *Publik*, 5 June 1970, and in *Luzerner Landbote*, 5 June 1970.

125: *"Will nur von der Hauptsorge ablenken"* (in reply to readers' letters on the *motu proprio* on mixed marriages) in *Frankfurter Allgemeine Zeitung*, 19 June 1970, and in an abbreviated version in *Rheinischer Merkur*, 17 July 1970.

126: Open letter to Yves Congar (in reply to him on the *motu proprio* on mixed marriages) in *La Croix*, 7 August 1970.

German version: *"Antwort an Yves Congar"* in *Deutsche Tagespost*, 22 July 1970, and in *Münchener Katholische Kirchenzeitung*, 9–16 August 1970 with a correction in the issue of 23 August 1970.
English translation: "Mixed Marriages: A Rejoinder" in *The Tablet* 224 (1970), pp. 782–3.

127: *"Der versprochene Dank"* (thanking the German bishops' conference for their interpretation and application of the *motu proprio* on mixed marriages) in *Publik*, 27 November 1970, and in *Neue Zürcher Nachrichten*, 5 December 1970.

English translation: "Breakthrough on Mixed Marriages"

in *The Tablet* 224 (1970), pp. 1136–8.
French translation: *"Un tournant décisif"* in *Témoignage Chrétien*, 31 December 1970.

128: *"Au service de l'unité"* in *Journal de la vie*, 11 October 1970.

129: *"Unfehlbares Lehramt?"* in *Weltwoche*, 17 July 1970.

130: Response to Magnus Löhrer's review of *Infallible? An Enquiry* in *Schweizerische Kirchenzeitung*, 5 November 1970, and in *Diakonia/Der Seelsorger* 2 (1971), pp. 68–9.

English translation: "Towards a Discussion of Infallibility" in *Worship* 45 (1971), pp. 287–9.

131: *"Unfehlbarkeit? Antwort an Karl Lehmann"* in *Die Welt*, 12 November 1970.

132: *"Nicht unfehlbar?"* – open letter in reply to Dr Teobaldi, in *Katholisches Pfarrblatt für Stadt und Kanton Zürich*, 22 November 1970.

133: *"Was ist die christliche Botschaft?"* in *Publik*, 2 October 1970, in *Luzerner Landbote*, 23 October 1970, in *Neue Zürcher Nachrichten*, 7 November 1970, in *Vaterland*, 24 December 1970, in *Münchener Katholische Kirchenzeitung*, 28 February 1971, in *Welt des Kindes* 49 (1971), pp. 246–52, and in *Kirchenblatt für die reformierte Schweiz*, 3 June 1971.

English translation: "Statement (What is the Christian Message?)" in *Japan Missionary Bulletin*, December 1970, and in (Australian) *Catholic Worker*, November 1975, pp. 9–12.

134: Correction (to A. Guillet's article *"Hans Küng als Grossinquisitor"*) in *Urner Wochenblatt*, 12 December 1970.

135: *"Im Dienst an der christlichen Botschaft"* in *Neue*

Bildpost, 3 January 1971.

136: *"Unfehlbare Sätze – wer hat die Beweislast?"* (reply to Karl Lehmann's article *"Hans Küng auf Kollisionskurs?"*) in *Publik*, 29 January 1971.

137: *"Karl Rahner nicht katholisch?"* (on the controversy between Rahner and Cardinal Höffner on the statement "Jesus is God") in *Neue Zürcher Nachrichten*, 30 January 1971, and in *Deutsche Tagespost*, 26 January 1971; in an abbreviated form in *Münster Presse*, 4 February 1971, and in *Kirchenblatt für die reformierte Schweiz*, 6 May 1971.

138: *"Im Interesse der Sache: Antwort an Karl Rahner"* (on the debate on infallibility) in *Stimmen der Zeit* 96 (1971), pp. 43–64 and 105–22.

English translation: "To get to the heart of the matter: answer to Karl Rahner" in *Homiletic and Pastoral Review* 71 (1971), pp. 9–29, 17–32, and 49–50.

139: "Who Shall Choose the Bishops?" in *The New York Times*, 28 January 1971.

140: *"Warum ich in der Kirche bleibe"* in *Neue Zürcher Nachrichten*, 27 February 1971, in *Vaterland*, 27 February 1971, in *Publik*, 5 March 1971, in *Kirchenblatt für die reformierte Schweiz*, 11 November 1971, and in *Mitteilungen der Vereinigung Christlicher Unternehmer der Schweiz* 24 (1972), pp. 61–4 and 78–80.

English translation: "Why I am Staying in the Church" in *America* 124 (1971), pp. 281–3, in *The Tablet* 225 (1971), pp. 433–5; in (Australian) *Catholic Worker*, June 1971, pp. 4–6, and in *Catholic Herald*, 17 August 1973.
French translation: *"Pourquoi je reste dans l'Église"* in *La Documentation Catholique* 53 (1971), pp. 337–40.
Italian translation: *"Perché non esco dalla Chiesa"* in *L'Europeo*, 8 April 1971.

Spanish translation: *"Por qué permanezco en la Iglesia"* in *El Ciervo* no. 206 (April 1971), pp. 10–11, and in *Christus* (Mexico) 36 (1971), pp. 14–17.
Polish translation: *"Dlaczego pozostaję w kościele?"* in *Za i Przeciw*, 25 April 1971.

141: *"L'Église selon l'Évangile: réponse à Yves Congar"* (on infallibility) in *Revue des Sciences philosophiques et théologiques* 55 (1971), pp. 193–230.

142: "Why Infallibility?" in *The New York Times*, 3 June 1971.

143: "What is the Criterion for a Critical Theology? Reply to Gregory Baum" in *Commonweal* 94 (1971), pp. 326–30.

144: *"Die Zeit der Standessymbole ist abgelaufen"* (on *Why Priests?*) in *Der Spiegel*, 18 October 1971.

145: Letter to the Vatican dated 30 May 1968, in *Kirchenblatt für die reformierte Schweiz*, 9 December 1971.

146: *"Der kirchliche Leitungsdienst: Konstanten und Varianten"* in *Zur Debatte* (*Themen der Katholischen Akademie in Bayern*) 1 (1971 no. 8–9), pp. 1–3.

147: *"Die Kirche für die Weltreligionen"* in *Evangelisches Missions-Magazin* (Basle) 116 (1972), pp. 75–82.

148: "Response" (to A. Dulles' article "The Theology of Hans Küng: A Comment") in *Union Seminary Quarterly Review* 27 (1972), pp. 143–7.

149: *"La sincérité, exigence du message de Jésus"* in *Lettre* no. 167–8 (1972), pp. 40–4.

150: *"Apakah pewartaan kristiani itu?"* in *Orientasi* (Jogjakarta) 4 (1972), pp. 85–106.

151: Letter to the Vatican dated 24 January 1972, in *Origins*

(NC Documentary Service), 16 March 1972.

152: *"Aufs Ganze gesehen"* (*Wort zum Sonntag* I) in *Publik-Forum*, 29 December 1972.

Italian translation: *"Credere in Dio anche utilizzando la ragione"* in *COM* (Rome), 11 February 1973.

153: *"Wer war Jesus? Eine nüchterne Überlegung zum Weihnachtsfest"* in *Frankfurter Allgemeine Zeitung* colour supplement, 23 December 1972.

154: *"Die Gretchenfrage des christlichen Glaubens? Systematische Überlegungen zum neutestamentlichen Wunder"* in *Theologische Quartalschrift* 152 (1972), pp. 214–23.

Hungarian translation: *"A cyógyító és segítséget nyújtó Jézus"* in *Teológia* 7 (1973), pp. 77–83.

155: *"Was ist eigentlich christlich?"* in *Attempto* (1972–3), no. 45–6, pp. 30–6.

156: *"Was in der Kirche bleiben muss: Impulse für die Gesellschaft"* in *Vaterland*, 20 January 1973, and in *Der Christ in der Welt* (Vienna) 23, March 1973, pp. 7–10.

Hungarian translation: *"Néhány időszerű keresztény észrevétel a társadalom számára"* in *Vigilia* 38 (1973), no. 1, pp. 8–11 (German original reprinted pp. 70–2).

157: *"Was in der Kirche bleiben muss* (*Das unterscheidend Christliche*)" in *Christ in der Gegenwart*, 18 February 1973, in *Cursillo Information* (Rottenburg) 4 (1973), no. 2, pp. 3–5, in *Luzerner Tagblatt*, 25 March 1973, and in *Zur Debatte* (*Themen der Katholischen Akademie in Bayern*) (1975 no. 4–5,) p. 16.

158: *"Ein Sanktum Officium in Deutschland?"* in *Publik-Forum*, 23 February 1973, and in *Deutsche Zeitung/Christ und Welt*, 23 February 1973.

159: *"Kleine Bilanz der Unfehlbarkeitsdebatte"* in *Concilium* 9 (1973), pp. 226–30, and in *Dialogikus* 4, May 1973, pp. 4–5.

English translation: "A Short Balance-Sheet of the Debate on Infallibility" in *Concilium* 9 (New Series) (1973), vol. 3, pp. 129–36.
Dutch translation: *"Kleine balans van het debat over de onfeilbaarheid"* in *Concilium* 9 (1973), vol. 3, pp. 141–8.
French translation: *"Petit bilan de débat sur l'infaillibilité"* in *Concilium* (1973), vol. 83, pp. 137–43.
Italian translation: *"Breve bilancio del dibattito sull' infallibilità"* in *Concilium* 9 (1973), vol. 3, pp. 192–202.
Spanish translation: *"Breve balance del debate sobre la infalibilidad"* in *Concilium* 9 (1973), vol. 83, pp. 451–6.
Portuguese edition: *"Resumo do debate sobre a infalibilidade"* in *Concilium* (1973), vol. 83, pp. 383–9.

160: *"Der fehlende Sinn"* in *Jugend und Gesellschaft* (Lucerne), April 1973, p. 3.

161: *"Worte zum Sonntag"* I–III and letter to the editor of *Petrusblatt* dated 17 January 1973 (documentation on Cardinal Bengsch's New Year's Eve sermon) in *Katechetische Blätter* 98 (1973), pp. 261–8.

162: *"Zur Aufhebung des Jesuiten- und Kloster-verbots: Aufruf zum 20. Mai 1973"* in *Vaterland*, 11 May 1973, in *Luzerner Tagblatt/Zuger Tagblatt* 16 May 1973, in *Luzerner Landbote*, 11 May 1973, and in several other Swiss papers.

163: *"Unfehlbarkeit kann tödlich sein"* (*Die Seite der Herausgeber*) in *Theologische Quartalschrift* 153 (1973), pp. 72–4.

164: *Versöhnliches Schlusswort unter eine Debatte* (open letter to Karl Rahner) in *Publik-Forum*, 1 June 1973, in

Vaterland, 23 June 1973, and in *Basler Volksblatt*, 29 June 1973.

English translation: "Authority in the Church: an exchange between Hans Küng and Karl Rahner" in *The Tablet* 227 (1973), pp. 597–8, and in *America* 129 (1973), pp. 9–11.
Spanish translation: *"Küng a Rahner (Polemica Küng-Rahner sobre la infalibilidad)"* in *Hechos y dichos* no. 443 (August–September 1973), pp. 46–7.

165: "Papal Fallibility: O Felix Error!" in *Journal of Ecumenical Studies* 10 (1973), pp. 361–2.

166: *"Unfähigkeit zu lernen? Roma locuta, causa aperta"* (on the Roman declaration *Mysterium Ecclesiae*) in *Frankfurter Allgemeine Zeitung*, 9 July 1973, in *Vaterland*, 6 July 1973, and in *Deutsche Tagespost*, 11 July 1973.

English translation: "The Case is Open" in *The Tablet* 227 (1973), pp. 670–1, and in *America* 129 (1973), pp. 58–60.
Dutch translation: *"Rome heeft gesproken, de zaak blijft open"* in *De Tijd*, 10 July 1973, and in *Knack*, 18 July 1973.
French translation: *"Incapable d'apprendre?"* in *Le Monde*, 8–9 July 1973.
Italian translation: *"Una ricerca comune sull' infallibilità"* in *Il Giorno*, 8 July 1973.
Spanish translation: *"Roma locuta, causa aperta"* in *El Ciervo* no. 233–4, July–August 1973, pp. 16–17.
Finnish translation: *"Oppimiskyvyttömyyttä? Roma locuta, causa aperta"* in *Teologinen Aikakauskirja* 79 (1974), pp. 62–6.

167: *"Die Religionen als Frage an die Theologie des Kreuzes"* (on J. Moltmann's theology of the cross) in *Evangelische Theologie* 33 (1973), pp. 401–23.

168: *"Parteien in der Kirche? Zusammenfassende Thesen zur Diskussion"* in *Concilium* 9 (1973), pp. 594–601, in *Publik-Forum*, 26 July 1974, and in *Deutsches Allgemeines Sonn-*

H.K.   H *tagsblatt*, 1 June 1975.

English translation: "Parties in the Church? A Summary of the Discussion" in *Concilium* 9 (1973) vol. 8, pp. 133–46.
Dutch translation: *"Partijen in de kerk? Samenvattende stellingen ter discussie"* in *Concilium* 9 (1973) vol. 8, pp. 133–45.
French translation: *"Des partis dans l'Église? Conclusions"* in *Concilium* (1973), vol. 88, pp. 135–47.
Italian translation: *"Partiti nella chiesa? Tesi riassuntive per la discussione"* in *Concilium* 9 (1973) vol. 8, pp. 185–203.
Spanish translation: *"Partidos en la Iglesia? Algunas tesis a titulo de sintesis"* in *Concilium* (1973) vol. 88, pp. 290–301.
Portuguese translation: *"Partidos na Igreja? Teses resumidas para discussão"* in *Concilium* (1973) vol. 88, pp. 1025–38.

169: *"Ein menschenfreundlicher Pfarrer"* (on the retirement of Father F. X. Kaufmann, parish priest of Sursee) in *Vaterland*, 8 December 1973, and in *Luzerner Landbote*, 7 December 1973.

170: *"Wozu schon eine zentralschweizerische Universität? Ein offener Brief"* in *Luzerner Landbote*, 18 January 1974, *Luzerner Neueste Nachrichten*, 19 January 1974, in *Luzerner Tagblatt*, 19 January 1974, in *Vaterland*, 19 January 1974, and in *Schweizer Schule* 62 (1975), pp. 244–8.

171: *"Die Firmung als Vollendung der Taufe: Edward Schillebeeckx zum 60. Geburtstag"* in *Theologische Quartalschrift* 154 (1974), pp. 26–47.

English translation: "Confirmation as the Completion of Baptism" in *Colloquium* (Australia and NZ) 8 (1975) no. 1, pp. 33–40, and 8 (1976) no. 2, pp. 5–13, and (in a shortened version) in *US Catholic* 40, July 1975, pp. 19–22.

172: *"Verlust an Glaubwürdigkeit (Sechs Jahre nach Humanae vitae)"* in *Weltwoche*, 6 March 1974.

173: *"Was meint Auferweckung?"* in *Pfarrblatt* (Basle), 14

April 1974, and in *Gemeindebrief der katholischen Kirche in Tübingen*, Easter 1974, p. 5.

174: *"Warum? Zum gewaltsamen Ende Jesu von Nazarets"* in *Frankfurter Allgemeine Zeitung* Colour Supplement, 6 April 1974.

175: *"Zur Entstehung des Auferstehungsglaubens: Versuch einer systematischen Klärung"* in *Theologische Quartalschrift* 154 (1974), pp. 103–17.

English translation: "The Origin of Resurrection Belief" in *Theology Digest* 23 (1975), pp. 136–42.

176: *"Der Streit um die Unfehlbarkeit (Zu einem römischen Glaubensprozess)"* in *Frankfurter Allgemeine Zeitung*, 25 June 1974, in *Schwäbisches Tagblatt*, 29 June 1974, in *Tages-Anzeiger* (Zürich), 25 June 1974, in *Vaterland*, 25 June 1974, in *Luzerner Neueste Nachrichten*, 25 June 1974, in *Luzerner Landbote*, 25 June 1974, in *National-Zeitung Basel*, 25 June 1974, and in *Basler Nachrichten*, 25 June 1974.

English translation: "The Infallibility issue" in *The Tablet* 228 (1974), pp. 662–3, and in *National Catholic Reporter*, 19 July 1974.
French translation: *"Un procès romain sur la foi"* in *Le Monde*, 4 July 1974.

177: Statement on the Swiss bishops' visit to Rome, in *Publik-Forum*, 26 July 1974, and in numerous Swiss papers.

178: *"Mein Spiegelbild"* (reply to *Der Spiegel*) in *Frankfurter Allgemeine Zeitung*, 21 September 1974, in *Basler Nachrichten*, 24 September 1974, in *Luzerner Neueste Nachrichten*, 24 September 1974, and in *Luzerner Landbote*, 27 September 1974.

179: *"Leiden an der Kirche"* in *Weltwoche*, 11 September 1974.

180: *"War Jesus ein Revolutionär?"* in *Vaterland*, 14 September 1974.

181: *"Was die Christen wollen".* in *Deutsches Allgemeines Sonntagsblatt*, 1 September 1974.

182: *"Von Erfahrung gedeckt"* in *Deutsches Allgemeines Sonntagsblatt*, 8 September 1974.

183: *"Jesu Sache ist die Sache Gottes"* in *Deutsches Allgemeines Sonntagsblatt*, 22 September 1974.

184: Three extracts from *On Being A Christian* in *Forum* (Schaffhausen), 26 October and 2 and 9 November 1974.

185: *'Jesus der Massgebende"* in *Publik-Forum*, 4 October 1974.

186: *"Vom Antisemitismus zur theologischen Begegnung"* in *Concilium* 10 (1974), pp. 542–6.

English translation: "From Anti-Semitism to Theological Dialogue" in *Concilium* 10 (1974), vol. 7–8, pp. 103–10.
Dutch translation: *"Van antisemitisme naar theologische ontmoeting"* in *Concilium* (1974) vol. 8, pp. 7–16.
French translation: *"De l'antisémitisme à la rencontre théologique"* in *Concilium* (1974), vol. 98, pp. 11–19.
Italian translation: *"Dall' antisemitismo all' incontro teologico"* in *Concilium* (1974) vol. 8, pp. 25–36.
Spanish translation: *"Del antisemitismo al encuentro teológico"* in *Concilium* (1974) vol. 98, pp. 159–69.
Portuguese translation: *"Do anti-semitismo ao encontro téologico"* in *Concilium* (1974) vol. 98, pp. 963–71.

187: *"Zwanzig Jahre Theologie investiert"* (statement issued at press conference on 10 October 1974 to mark the publication of the German edition of *On being a Christian*) in *Deutsche Tagespost*, 29 October 1974, in *Oberösterreichische Nachrichten*, 5 November 1974, and in *Katholisches Sonn-*

tagsblatt (Bozen-Brixen), 9 February 1975.

English translation: "Being a Christian" in *The Tablet* 228 (1974), pp. 1012–22.
Dutch translation: *"De moed om christen te zijn"* in *De Tijd*, 14 May 1976.
French translation: *"Le sens et le but de 'Christ sein' "* in *L'Église en Alsace* (1975) no. 5, pp. 24–6, and in *La Documentation Catholique* 57 (1975), pp. 182–3.

188: *"Jesus – ein Politiker?"* in *Kölner Stadtanzeiger*, 24–25 December 1974.

189: *"Öffnung der Kirchen"* in *Bücherkommentare*, December 1974, p. 36.

190: *"C'è un futuro per la religione?"* in *COM-Nuovi Tempi*, 19 January 1975.

191: *"Mehr als ein forscher Aufklärer"* (to mark Herbert Haag's sixtieth birthday on 11 February 1975) in *Vaterland*, 7 February 1975, and in *Schwäbisches Tagblatt*, 10 February 1975.

192: *"Jesus und sein Gott"* in *Theologie der Gegenwart* 18 (1975), pp. 1–10.

193: Letter to Cardinal Šeper dated 4 September 1974, in *Vaterland*, 22 February 1975.

194: *"Die Wahrheit wird sich durchsetzen (Ein Akt der Versöhnung?)"* (on the suspension of the Roman proceedings against *The Church* and *Infallible?*) in *Frankfurter Allgemeine Zeitung*, 21 February 1975, in *Frankfurter Rundschau*, 21 February 1975, in *Neue Zürcher Zeitung*, 21 February 1975, in *Basler Nachrichten*, 21 February 1975, in *Vaterland*, 21 February 1975, in *Luzerner Landbote*, 21 February 1975, in *Deutsche Volkszeitung*, 27 February 1975, in *Dialogikus* 6, March 1975, p. 3, in *Deutsches All-*

gemeines Sonntagsblatt, 2 March 1975, and in *Der Sonntag* (Limburg diocesan weekly), 2 March 1975.

195: *"Ist alles aus mit dem Tod? Die Bedeutung der Auferweckung Jesu für uns Menschen"* in *KNA-Sonderdienst* (Easter), 12 March 1975, in *Schwäbisches Tagblatt*, 27 March 1975, in *Kölnische Rundschau/Bonner Rundschau*, 29 March 1975, in *Maria vom guten Rat* (1976) no. 4, pp. 12–13, and in *Deutsche Zeitung/Christ und Welt*, 16 April 1976.

196: *"Keine Angst!"* (reply to Father Placid Jordan) in *Civitas* 30 (1975), pp. 500–5.

197: *"Was ist Inquisition?"* (reply to Dr W. Paschen) in *Kirchenzeitung Erzbistum Köln*, 4 April 1975.

198: *"Etwas mehr christlicher Humor"* in *Nebelspalter*, 11 June 1975.

199: *"Antwort ohne Polemik"* (reply to Robert Mächler's question: "Is Hans Küng still a Catholic?") in *Nationalzeitung Basel*, 28 June 1975.

200: *"Anonyme Christen – wozu?"* (reply to Heinz Robert Schlette) in *Orientierung* 39 (1975), pp. 214–16.

201: "Statement on Women Priests: Theology no Barrier" in *National Catholic Reporter*, 12 December 1975.

202: *"Gottesdienst heute – warum?"* in *Vaterland*, 13 December 1975, in *Süddeutsche Zeitung*, 24–25–26 December 1975, in *Forum* (Schaffhausen), 7, 14, and 21 February and 6 March 1976, in *Glaube und Leben* (Mainz), 14 March 1976, and in *Katholisches Sonntagsblatt* (Rottenburg), 4 April 1976.

English translation: *"Religious Service Today – Why?"* in *Accent* (Adelaide) 10 (1977) pp. 4–14.
Polish translation: *"Sluzba Bogu w niedzielę?"* in *Nasza Droga* (1977) no. 1, pp. 3–11.

Hungarian translation: *"Van-e ma még értelme az isten-tiszteletnek?"* in *Vigilia* 41 (1976), pp. 231–5.

203: *"Grund zu danken"* in *Christ in der Gegenwart*, 4 January 1976.

204: *"Antwort an meine Kritiker: Theologie für den Menschen?"* in *Frankfurter Allgemeine Zeitung* colour supplement, 22 May 1976, in *Basler Nachrichten*, 26 May 1976, and in *Luzerner Neueste Nachrichten*, 29 May 1976.

205: *"Thesen zur Stellung der Frau in Kirche und Gesellschaft"* in *Theologische Quartalschrift* 156 (1976), pp. 129–132, in *Publik-Forum*, 16 July 1976, in *Katholische Presse-Agentur* (Vienna), 20 July 1976, in *Forum* (Schaffhausen), 14 August 1976, in *Luzerner Neueste Nachrichten*, 31 January 1977, and in *Dialogikus*, 25 February 1977.

English translation: "Feminism: A new Reformation (Sixteen Theses)" in *The New York Times Magazine*, 23 May 1976.
French translation: *"Pour la femme dans l'Église: seize points de vue concernant la femme au sein de l'Église et de la société"* in *Femme et homme dans l'Église* (Brussels), no. 20–21, December 1976/January 1977, pp. 25–7.
Spanish translation: *"Tesis sobre el puesto de la mujer en la Iglesia y en la sociedad"* in *Selecciones de teología* 17 (1978), no. 65, pp. 70–2.

206: "Rome must find a way to cope with the growing conflict within the Church" (on the Lefebvre case) in *The Times*, 28 August 1976.

207: "Christianity: Faith and Hope" in *The Catholic Connection* (Alexandria, Va) 1 (1976) no. 6, pp. 1 and 3.

208: "Christ and Change" in *The Catholic Connection* 1 (1976) no. 7, pp. 3 and 6.

209: "Jews and Gentiles" in *The Catholic Connection* 1 (1976) no. 8, pp. 3 and 6.

210: *"Thesen zum Atheismus"* in *Imprimatur*, 3 November 1976.

211: *"Die Glaubwürdigkeit"* (in response to an enquiry on *Die Fundamente unserer Gesellschaft: haben sich unsere Wertvorstellungen verändert?*) in *Frankfurter Allgemeine Zeitung* colour supplement 24 December 1976.

212: "On Being A Christian" (statement issued at press conferences to launch the American and English editions of *On Being A Christian*) in *America* 136 (1977), pp. 1–2, and in *The Tablet* 231 (1977), pp. 79–80.

213: *"Katholisch – Evangelisch: eine ökumenische Bestandsaufnahme"* in *Lutherische Beiträge* 8 (1977), pp. 2–5.

214: "Hans Küng's Answer to Bishop B. C. Butler" in *Catholic Herald*, 25 February 1977.

215: Statement in reply to the declaration by the German bishops' conference of 3 March 1977, in *Vaterland*, 4 March 1977, and in other German and Swiss papers.

French translation: in *La Documentation Catholique*, 1 May 1977.

216: *"Keine Ordination der Frau?"* (*Die Seite der Herausgeber*) (with G. Lohfink) in *Theologische Quartalschrift* 157 (1977), pp. 144–6.

217: *"Die Problematik der Katechismusfrage 'Wozu sind wir auf Erden?'"* in *Concilium* 13 (1977), pp. 493–6.

Dutch translation: *"Waartoe zijn wij op aarde? Fundamentele vragen"* in *Concilium* (1977) vol. 8, pp. 3–8.
French translation: *"Problématique de la question du caté-*

chisme: Pourquoi sommes-nous sur terre?" in *Concilium* (1977), vol. 128, pp. 9–15.
Italian translation: *"La problematica della domanda del catechismo: Per qual fine Dio ha creati?"* in *Concilium* 13 (1977), vol. 8, pp. 13–21.
Spanish translation: *"¿Para qué estamos en la tierra? Problematica de la pregunta del catecismo"* in *Concilium* (1977), vol. 128, pp. 149–56.
Portuguese translation: *"A problemática da pergunta do catecismo: Para que estamos na terra?"* in *Concilium* (1977), vol. 128, pp. 3–9.

218: *"Gott – neu zur Entscheidung gestellt: Wissenschaft und Gottesfrage"* (lecture to mark the five hundredth anniversary of Tübingen university), in *Frankfurter Allgemeine Zeitung*, 10 October 1977, in *Schwäbisches Tagblatt*, 10 October 1977, in *Vaterland*, 22 October 1977, and in *Basler Volksblatt*, 26 October 1977.

219: "What must remain in the Church" in *New Citizen* (New Zealand), 6 and 20 October and 3 and 17 November 1977 (continued in 1978).

VI: Interviews, etc.

(Only those interviews and conversations that have appeared in print are included, and the list does not therefore include any interviews broadcast on radio or television.)

1: *"Ante el proximo Concilio ecumenico"*: interview with J. I. Tellechea (Madrid, 1959) which appeared in about fifty Spanish papers.

2: *"Was erwarten Sie vom Konzil?"* (an enquiry among German, Swiss and Austrian Catholics) in *Wort und Wahrheit* 10 (1961), pp. 626–8.

3: Interview with J. B. Sheerin, in *The Catholic World* 197

(1963), pp. 159–63.

4: *"Les propositions de Hans Küng pour une réforme de l'Église":* interview with T. de Quénétain, in *Réalités*, September 1963, pp. 23–8.

English translation: "A Brotherly Approach from Both Sides" in J. A. O'Brien (ed.), *Steps to Christian Unity*, New York, 1964, pp. 74–85.

5: Interview with D. O'Grady, in *Way* 20 (1964), pp. 11–13.

6: "Conversation at the Council" (with J. C. Murray, G. Weigel, G. Diekman and V. A. Yzermans) in *The American Benedictine Review* 15 (1964), pp. 341–51.

7: Interview (on liturgical reform), in *Feuerreiter*, 6 March 1965.

Irish translation in *An Sagart*, Summer 1965, pp. 12–13.

8: "The Church and the Council": interview with D. Fisher in *Catholic Herald*, 18 June 1965, and in *St Louis Review*, 25 June 1965.

9: "The Spirit of Change in the Church": interview with P. Granfield, in *The Homiletic and Pastoral Review* 66, October 1965, pp. 17–21.

10: *"Die neue Freiheit ist nicht mehr auszulöschen"*: interview with W. Harenberg, in *Der Spiegel*, 24 January 1966, and in *Luzerner Landbote*, 29 April 1966.

English translation in *Listening – Current Studies in Dialog* 1 (1966), pp. 172–82.

11: "The Roman Curia Must be Reformed": interview with J. Horgan, in *The Irish Times*, 18 November 1967, in *St Louis Review*, 8 December 1967, and in *The Advocate*

(Melbourne), 25 January 1968.

12: Discussion with J. van de Walle, in *De Maand* 11, January 1968, pp. 27–32.

13: Interview with G. Puchinger, in G. Puchinger, *Christen en secularisatie*, Delft 1968, pp. 401–13.

14: Discussion with M. van der Plas, in *Elseviers Weekblad*, 2 November 1968.

15: *"Immer noch die Methoden der Inquisition!"*: telephone interview, in *Weltbild* (Augsburg), 15 November 1968, and in *Sonntag* (Olten), 8 December 1968.

16: *"Kein Zurück zur vorkonziliaren Kirche"*: in *Evangelische Kommentare* 1 (1968), pp. 676–9.

17: Interview with R. G. Mateo, in *El Ciervo*, February 1969, pp. 8–9.

18: Interview by post, in *Mitarbeiterhilfe* 24, 1969 no. 3, pp. 40–1.

19: *"Ein Laiensenat sollte den Papst mitwählen"*: in *Tages-Anzeiger* (Zürich), 7 June 1969.

20: Interview (on *Truthfulness*), in *Opération vérité*, supplement to *La Vie Protestante* (Geneva), 31 October 1969.

21: *"Hans Küng et l'intercommunion"*: interview with C. Biber, in *La Vie Protestante*, 7 November 1969.

22: *"Rom steuert auf Kollisionskurs"*: interview with F. Weigend, in *Stuttgarter Zeitung*, 14 February 1970.

23: *"Zölibat sollte freiwillig sein"*: interview with H. Fleig, in *Zürcher Woche Sonntags-Journal*, 21–22 February 1970.

24: *"Zölibat – süsses Joch oder alter Zopf?"*: in *Die Welt-woche*, 27 February 1970.

25: *"Forderungen an die Synode"* (views of well-known writers): in *top* (Nuremberg), 10 October 1970.

26: *"Conversación en los pasillos del Congreso de Teología de Bruselas"*: in *Hechos y Dichos*, November 1970, pp. 34–5.

27: *"Une infaillibilité à visage humain"*: interview with C. F. Jullien, in *Le Nouvel Observateur*, 1–7 March 1971.

Italian translation: *"Le tentazioni che non ho mai avuto"* in *Sette Giorni*, 7 March 1971.

28: *"Disputen rond roerige Hans Küng"*: interview with M. van der Plas, in *Elseviers Magazine*, 6 March 1971, pp. 111–118, and 13 March 1971, pp. 59–67.

29: *"Aufbruch oder Schisma?"*: interview with H. Kühner, in *Junge Kirche* 32 (1971), pp. 109–15.

30: *"L'Église est soutenue dans la vérité à travers toutes ses erreurs"*: interview with J. P. Manigne, in *Informations Catholiques Internationales*, 1 April 1971.

31: *"Oude wereld vergaat"*: interview with H. Kolks, in *De Gelderlander Pers*, 20 April 1971.

32: Interview with A. MacLeod, in *The New Zealand Listener*, 18 October 1971.

33: "Infallibility Questioned": discussion with R. Murray, in *The Month* 232, October 1971, pp. 117–21.

Italian translation in *IDOC internazionale*, 15 December 1971.

34: *"Wie aktuell ist die christliche Botschaft?"*: in *Sonntag* (Olten), 29 March 1972.

35: Interview with J. O'Connor, in *Intellectual Digest* (New York) 2, March 1972, pp. 19–22.

36: *"O teólogo rebelde"*: interview with C. Struwe, in *Veja* (São Paulo), 24 May 1972.

37: *"Ich bin nicht gegen das Papsttum"*: interview with P. Jaeggi, in *Tele* (Zofingen), 25 May 1972.

38: *"Unbequeme Eidgenossen: Hans Küng, der kirchentreue Reformator"*: discussion with A. W. Scheiwiller, in *Woche* (Olten/Zürich), 14 June 1972.

39: *"Im Streit mit der Kurie auf seiten der Kirche"*: discussion with C. Zodel, in *Schwäbische Zeitung*, 14 July 1972.

40: *"Ausserhalb der Kirche erreicht man weniger"*: interview with F. P. Schaller, in *Weltbild* (Augsburg), 12 July 1972.

41: *"Uusi Luther?"*: interview with R. Cantell, in *Suomen Kuvalehti*, 24 November 1972.

42: *"Ainostaan jumala on erehtymätön"*: interview with R. Cantell, in *Suomen Kuvalehti*, 1 December 1972.

43: "I Refuse a Totalitarian Papacy": interview with R. Koch, in *Newsweek*, 27 August 1973.

44: *"Irrtümer über die Kirche?"*: in *Herder-Korrespondenz* 27 (1973), pp. 422–7, and in a shortened version in *Vaterland*, 1 September 1973.

English translation: "Mysterium Ecclesiae" in *The Tablet* 227 (1973), pp. 835–9.

45: *"Ich springe nicht aus dem Boot der Kirche"*: interview with F. Weigend, in *Stuttgarter Zeitung*, 21 September 1974, in *Luzerner Tagblatt/Zuger Tagblatt*, 24 September 1974, and in *Basler Volksblatt*, 28 September 1974.

46: *"Christ sein – hier und heute"*: interview with A. A. Häsler, in *Die Tat*, 28 September 1974, and in A. A. Häsler (ed.), *Gott ohne Kirche?*, Olten and Freiburg-im-Breisgau 1975, pp. 25–52.

Spanish translation: *"A la intemperie"*, in *Incunable*, 12 February 1976, pp. 16–20.

47: *"Ein ständiger Aufruf zur Reform"*: in *Imprimatur*, 16 December 1974.

48: *"Mi sono formato sotto Pio XII"*: in L. Furno (ed.), *Viaggio attraverso la teologia scomoda*, Rome 1975, pp. 103–12.

49: *"Geduldig seinen Platz behaupten"*: discussion with S. von Kortzfleisch, in *Lutherische Monatshefte* 14 (1975), pp. 194–9.

50: *"Die Bergpredigt und die Gesellschaft"*: interview with A. A. Häsler, in *Ex Libris* no. 4, April 1975, pp. 11–19.

51: Interview with John Wilkins, in *The Tablet* 229 (1975), pp. 381–2, correction p. 414.

52: *"Drohbotschaft – Frohbotschaft"*: discussion with Hans Küng, in *ru* (*Zeitschrift für die Praxis des Religionsunterrichts*) 5 (1975), pp. 113–15.

53: *"Misst Rom mit ungleichem Mass?"* (on the withdrawal of recognition from Archbishop Lefebvre's seminary at Ecône): in *Neue Zürcher Zeitung*, 3 October 1975.

54: *"Papa di chi"*: interview with M. Leone, in *Panorama*, 4 December 1975.

55: *"Gottesdienst heute, warum?"*: discussion with P. Brenni, in *Ehe – Familie* (Einsiedeln), September 1976, pp. 268–9.

56: *"Cristo com face humana"*: interview with C. Struwe, in *Veja* (São Paulo), 19 January 1977.

57: *"Der Kern der Krise ist eine Autoritätskrise"*: interview on the Lefebvre case with J. C. Weiss, in *Academia* 1977, no. 1, pp. 4–8.

58: "A Catholic Maverick": interview with W. F. Willoughby, in *Washington Star*, 28 February 1972.

59: *"Wenn es nach Jesus ginge . . ."* (on the ordination of women): in *Annabelle*, 31 March 1977.

60: *"Mirando a Dios desde 'abajo' "*: interview with R. Plaza, in *Yelda* (Madrid), April 1977, pp. 22–5.

61: "We can't go backward": interview with A. M. Kerr, in *The Catholic Connection* (Alexandria, Va), June–July 1977.

62: *"Verständlich machen, was Gott und Christus für den Menschen bedeuten"*: interview with Q. Scheble, in *Katholisches Sonntagsblatt* (Rottenburg), 27 November 1977.

VII: Forewords and introductions

1: Introduction to V. A. Yzermans, *A New Pentecost: Vatican Council II, Session 1*, Westminster, Md, 1963, pp. xix–xx.

2: Foreword to L. Swidler, *The Ecumenical Vanguard: The History of the Una Sancta Movement*, Pittsburgh, Pa, 1966, pp. ix–xi.

3: Preface to J. Möller, H. Haag and G. Hasenhüttl, *The Unknown God?*, New York 1966, pp. 7–9.

4: Preface to K. Rahner, *Belief Today*, New York 1967, pp. 5–6.

5: Introduction to the German translation of G. Baum, *Glaubwürdigkeit: zum Selbstverständnis der Kirche*, Freiburg, Basle and Vienna 1969, pp. 5–14.

6: Introductory remarks to J. Nolte, *Dogma in Geschichte*, Freiburg, Basle and Vienna 1971, pp. 5–7.

7: Foreword to H. Krömler (ed.), *Horizonte des Lebens: zur Frage nach dem Sinn des Lebens*, Zürich, Einsiedeln, Cologne and Göttingen 1976, pp. 8–10.

8: Foreword to R. Modras, *Paul Tillich's Theology of the Church. A Catholic Appraisal*, Detroit 1976, pp. 11–13.

VIII: Gramophone records

1: *Was ist die christliche Botschaft? Warum ich in der Kirche bleibe.* Christophorus-Verlag, Freiburg-im-Breisgau, 1971, SCLX 75 998.

2: *Die neue Frage nach Gott* (lecture to mark the 500th anniversary of Tübingen University). Attempto-Verlag, Tübingen, 1977.

IX: Tapes and cassettes

1: "The Infallibility of the Church": lecture and discussion at Glasgow University (tape). Peter Okell Sound Features, Salford, 1970.

2: Five lectures and two discussions at Melbourne University, 1971 (two tapes). Klarion Enterprises Pty Ltd, South Melbourne, 1971.

3: "Jesus – Challenge to the Church": lecture in Chicago, 1971 (two cassettes). The Thomas More Association, Chicago, 1971.

4: "The Ministry – What Must Remain": lecture in Chicago, 1971 (two cassettes). The Thomas More Association, Chicago, 1971.

5: *"Was in der Kirche bleiben muss"*: lecture in St Peter's church, Basle, 1973 (two cassettes). Audiothek ex libris, Zürich 1974, CWO 7025A & B.

Appendix: The Institute for Ecumenical Research

The Institute for Ecumenical Research

Since its establishment during the winter semester 1963–4, the Institute for Ecumenical Research has been directed by Professor Hans Küng. Its primary concern is the elaboration of controversial questions in the ecumenical field. Research is concentrated on the three important problem areas of the Church and its constitution, grace and justification, and the sacraments. Alongside its teaching work within the framework of Catholic theology the Institute is specially concerned with the ecumenical education of theologians who have completed their basic studies and are working for a doctorate. In the field of theology the ecumenical aspect is more than ever something that cannot be forgone.

A: Library and archives

The Institute has at its disposal a library that concentrates on the three problem areas mentioned above. Special consideration is given to works on the theology of the Reformation and the relevant works by theologians writing in English. In addition there is the following archive material which is of great value for research in the relevant fields:

(1) Original documents of Vatican II (thirty dossiers of material supplied only to the Council fathers and to official periti along with supplementary material).

(2) The debate on infallibility (eighteen dossiers, containing: statements and reviews on Hans Küng's writings on the subject; studies carrying the argument a stage further; statements by the Church authorities; reactions to

Mysterium Ecclesiae; supplementary material).

(3) *Concilium* (the only complete set of this international theological journal in the ten languages in which it has been published, apart from that at Nijmegen).

(4) International reactions to Hans Küng's writings (twenty-four dossiers to date).

B: International theological documentation catalogue

This catalogue offers documentation, on an international, interdenominational, systematic, and as far as possible comprehensive basis, of the books and articles that have appeared since 1945. It is arranged according to the accepted sub-divisions of the fields of study concerned and classified according to subject matter, defined as precisely and rigorously as possible. The catalogue enables one to see at a glance what the current position is in the literature on any subject and its data are easily available in card-index form. Books and articles are listed by their titles and where necessary are entered under all the relevant headings. From 1974 on all the university library's recent acquisitions in the theological field have been included.

It is an undertaking in the field of theology that so far is without parallel either in Germany or abroad. It far exceeds the needs of the Institute itself: it is of interest for the entire theological world and is a valuable aid for all kinds of research and also for studies for seminars and degree and entrance examinations. At the moment the catalogue includes about 168,000 cards, with new cards being added at the rate of some 12,000 a year.

C: Series of publications

I. ECUMENICAL STUDIES
Founded by H. Küng and J. Ratzinger, now edited by H. Küng and J. Moltmann with the co-operation of E. Jüngel

and W. Kasper (Herder, Freiburg, Basle and Vienna, 1967 on).

1: ECCLESIOLOGICAL SECTION

H. Küng, *Die Kirche*, 1967 (D:I:11, p. 189 above).

V. Dias, *Vielfalt der Kirche in der Vielfalt der Jünger, Zeugen und Diener*, 1968.

A. Ganoczy, *Ecclesia Ministrans: Dienende Kirche und kirchlicher Dienst bei Calvin*, 1968.

G. Hasenhüttl, *Charisma: Ordnungsprinzip der Kirche*, 1969.

H. Häring, *Kirche und Kerygma: Das Kirchenbild in der Bultmannschule*, 1972.

H. Scholl, *Calvinus Catholicus: Die katholische Calvinforschung im 20. Jahrhundert*, 1974.

B. Greco, *Evangelium und Kirche: Das Kirchenbild Ernesto Buonaiutis*, 1978.

2: SOTERIOLOGICAL SECTION

H. Küng, *Menschwerdung Gottes: Eine Einführung in Hegels theologisches Denken als Prolegomena zu einer künftigen Christologie*, 1970 (D:I:13, p. 190 above).

U. Baumann, *Erbsünde? Ihr traditionelles Verständnis in der Krise heutiger Theologie*, 1970.

J. Nolte, *Dogma in Geschichte: Versuch einer Kritik des Dogmatismus in der Glaubensdarstellung*, 1971.

G. Mueller-Fahrenholz, *Heilsgeschichte zwischen Ideologie und Prophetie: Profile und Kritik heilsgeschichtlicher Theorien in der ökumenischen Bewegung zwischen 1948 und 1968*, 1974.

K. Fischer, *Der Mensch als Geheimnis: Die Anthropologie Karl Rahners*, 1974.

G. Kraus, *Vorherbestimmung: Traditionelle Prädestinationslehre im Licht gegenwärtiger Theologie*, 1977.

K.-J. Kuschel, *Jesus in der deutschsprachigen Gegenwartsliteratur*, 1978.

3: SACRAMENTOLOGICAL SECTION

J. Amougou-Atangana, *Ein Sakrament des Geistempfangs? Zum Verhältnis von Taufe und Firmung*, 1974.

4: SUPPLEMENTARY SECTION: MINOR ECUMENICAL
WRITINGS

H. Küng, *Wahrhaftigkeit: Zur Zukunft der Kirche*, 1968
(D:I:12, pp. 189f above).

G. Baum, *Glaubwürdigkeit: Zum Selbstverständnis der
Kirche*, 1969.

P. Lengsfeld, *Das Problem Mischehe: Einer Lösung ent-
gegen*, 1970.

J. Gründel and H. van Oyen, *Ethik ohne Normen? Zu den
Weisungen des Evangeliums*, 1970.

H. Häring and J. Nolte (edd.), *Diskussion um Hans Küng
"Die Kirche"*, 1971.

E. Jüngel and K. Rahner, *Was ist ein Sakrament? Vor-
stösse zur Verständigung*, 1971.

N. Schiffers and H.-W. Schütte, *Zur Theorie der Religion*,
1973.

W. Kasper and G. Sauter, *Kirche – Ort des Geistes*, 1976.

P. Lapide, F. Mussner, and U. Wilckens, *Was Juden und
Christen voneinander denken: Bausteine zum Brücken-
schlag*, 1978.

II: OTHER MONOGRAPHS PREPARED AT THE INSTITUTE
BUT PUBLISHED OUTSIDE THE SERIES "ECUMENICAL
STUDIES"

H. Küng, *Unfehlbar? Eine Anfrage*, Zürich/Einsiedeln/
Cologne 1970 (D:I:14, pp. 190–1 above).

H. Küng (ed.), *Fehlbar? Eine Bilanz*, Zürich/Einsiedeln/
Cologne 1973 (D:I:19, pp. 192–3 above).

J. C. Dwyer, *Paul Tillich's Theology of the Cross* (Tübingen
dissertation 1973, not yet published).

H. Küng, *Christ sein*, Munich 1974 (D:I:20, p. 193 above).

R. Modras, *Paul Tillich's Theology of the Church*, Detroit
1976.

C. Hempel, *Rechtfertigung als Wirklichkeit: Ein katholisches Gespräch: Karl Barth – Hans Küng – Rudolf
Bultmann und seine Schule*, Bern/Frankfurt 1976.

H.-J. Schmitz, *Frühkatholizismus bein Adolf von Harnack,
Rudolf Sohm und Ernst Käsemann*, Düsseldorf 1978.

H. Küng, *Existiert Gott? Antwort auf die Gottesfrage der*

Neuzeit, Munich 1978 (D:I:26, p. 149 above).

III: THE FOLLOWING PROJECTS ARE IN PREPARATION:
The Young Luther's Image of the Church (H.-J. Schmitz).
Friedrich Schleiermacher's Image of the Church (A. Weirich).
The Understanding of Ministry in Lutheran Confessional Writings and at the Council of Trent (R. Collins).
The Understanding of Justification in R. Niebuhr (T. Walsh).
Natural Theology as an Ecumenical Task (G. Kraus).
The Sacraments (H. Küng).
The Sacramentality of Marriage (U. Baumann).

D: Co-operation in the work of the Association of University Ecumenical Institutes

This association is formed by the six university ecumenical institutes of Bochum, Heidelberg, Munich (Catholic and Protestant), Münster and Tübingen. Its first publication, on the recognition of ministries, the fruit of several years' work, has gained considerable attention in theological and Church circles: *Reform und Anerkennung kirchlicher Ämter: Ein Memorandum der Arbeitsgemeinschaft ökumenischer Universitätsinstitute* (Munich/Mainz, 1973). The Tübingen Institute was responsible for the preparatory bibliographical work, for the section on the nature and form of ecclesiastical ministry (pp. 163–88), and for seeing the work through the press.

In the Autumn of 1977 an important symposium took place at Heidelberg university on the subject "An Ecumenical Papacy", with well-known scholars from different Churches taking part. Work is going ahead on the publication of the papers given at this meeting and the discussions they gave rise to.

E: Future developments in the field of research

In keeping with the continual progress of theological research and the changes that have taken place in the Christian world the Institute has of recent years increasingly devoted itself to the positive themes of an ecumenical theology of the future as well as the classic questions of controversy.

It was in this context that Hans Küng's book *On Being A Christian* came into being. Like *The Church* before it and *Does God Exist?* after it, it was to a considerable extent used as a textbook for students before publication.

The following projects are in preparation:

The Power of Evil in Contemporary Philosophical and Theological Discussion (H. Häring).

The Pre-existence of Christ: the Examination of a Christological Idea (K.-J. Kuschel).

F: Theological Meditations

The aim of this series, to which numerous authors from outside the Institute have contributed, is to link theology and spirituality. The series, edited by Hans Küng, has been published by Benziger (Einsiedeln/Zürich/Cologne) since 1964. The first nine titles were published in English translation by Sheed and Ward (London) in 1965 and 1967.

1: H. Küng, *Freiheit in der Welt* (*Freedom in the World*), 1964 (D:I:6, pp. 187–8 above).
2: H. Haag, *Am Morgen der Zeit* (*The Dawn of Time*), 1964.
3: H. Küng, *Theologe und Kirche* (*The Theologian and the Church*), 1964 (D:I:7, p. 188 above).
4: K. H. Schelkle, *Ihr alle seid Geistliche* (*A Priestly People*), 1964.
5: K. Rahner, *Alltägliche Dinge* (*Everyday Things*), 1964.
6: H. Küng, *Kirche in Freiheit* (*The Church and Freedom*), 1964 (D:I:8, p. 188 above).

7: M. Pfliegler, *Der Zölibat (Celibacy)*, 1965.

8: G. Hasenhüttl, *Der unbekannte Gott? (Who is God?)*, 1965.

9: K. Rahner, *Im Heute glauben (Faith Today)*, 1966.

10: H. Haag, *Er ward mir zum Heil*, 1965.

11: K. H. Schelkle, *Wort Gottes*, 1965.

12: H. Küng, *Christenheit als Minderheit: Die Kirche unter den Weltreligionen*, 1965 (D:I:9).

13: H. U. von Balthasar, *Zuerst Gottes Reich: Zwei Skizzen zur biblischen Naherwartung*, 1966.

14: J. Möller, *Fragen wir nach Gott?*, 1966.

15: T. Sartory, *Wandel christlicher Spiritualität*, 1967.

16: H. Haag, *Wenn ihr betet . . .*, 1967.

17: A. Sustar, *Gewissensfreiheit*, 1967.

18: H. Küng, *Gott und das Leid*, 1967 (D:I:10).

19: D. Wiederkehr, *In den Dimensionen der Zeit*, 1968.

20: K. H. Schelkle, *Schuld als Erbteil*, 1968.

21: K. Rahner, *Ich glaube an Jesus Christus*, 1968.

22: A. Grabner-Haider, *In Gottes Zukunft*, 1968.

23: H. Haag, *Abschied vom Teufel*, 1969.

24: T. Schneider, *Gewandeltes Eucharistieverständnis?*, 1969.

25: J. Sudbrack, *Abwesenheit Gottes*, 1971.

26: A. Stock, *Kurzformeln des Glaubens: Zur Unterscheidung des Christlichen bei Karl Rahner*, 1971.

27: A. Exeler, *Hilfe zum Glauben: Adventsmeditationen*, 1971.

28: H. Haag, *Gott und Mensch in den Psalmen*, 1972.

29: H. Waldenfels, *Unfähigkeit und Bedürfnis zu glauben: Versuch einer Diagnose unserer Zeit*, 1972.

30: H. Küng, *Was in der Kirche bleiben muss*, 1973 (D:I:18).

31: N. Greinacher, *Christliche Rechtfertigung – gesellschaftliche Gerechtigkeit*, 1973.

32: W. Kasper and J. Moltmann, *Jesus ja – Kirche nein?*, 1973.

33: H. Leroy, *Nicht Knechte, sondern Freunde*, 1973.

34: O. H. Pesch, *Busse konkret – heute*, 1974.

35: H. Häring, *Anerkennen wir die Ämter!*, 1974.

36: J. Moltmann, *Wer ist der "Mensch"?*, 1975.

37: H. Waldenfels, *Meditation – Ost und West*, 1975.
38: A. Auer, *Utopie: Technologie: Lebensqualität*, 1976.
39: E. Jüngel, *Gott – für den ganzen Menschen*, 1976.
40: H. Küng, *Was ist Firmung?*, 1976 (D:I:22).
41: K. Rahner, *Glaube als Mut*, 1976.
42: P. Lapide, *Juden und Christen*, 1976.
43: H. Küng, *Gottesdienst – warum?*, 1976 (D:I:24).
44: E. V. Barabanow, *Das Schicksal der christlichen Kultur*, 1977.
45: J. Imbach, *Im Angst leben?*, 1977.
46: R. Schaeffler, *Fähigkeit zum Glück*, 1977.
47: K. P. Fischer, *Zufall oder Fügung?*, 1977.
48: T. R. Peters, *Der Tod wird nicht mehr sein*, 1978.

The staff of the Institute for Ecumenical Research:

Director	Professor Hans Küng
Akademischer Rat	Dr Hermann Häring
Wissenschaftlicher Angestellter	Dr Karl-Josef Kuschel
Wissenschaftlicher Assistent	Dr Urs Baumann
General secretary	Dr Margret Gentner
Secretary	Frau Annegret Dinkel